"I welcome this text for educators and practitioners. It fills a gap in writing about urbanisation and planning focused on the Commonwealth, and particularly the historical realities of the Commonwealth. This book offers a wide range of materials by authors from varying Commonwealth countries and backgrounds that truly reflect the past, present, and future of Commonwealth urbanisation."

Dr Carol Archer, *Professor of Urban Planning and Public Policy, University of Technology, Kingston, Jamaica*

"The book eloquently traces the development of sustainable urbanisation and lays out a futuristic vision from a transnational planning perspective. Its unique narrative style draws on an eclectic selection of papers ranging from environment, governance and representation. Tracing key milestones, the book stands out in its diverse spatio-temporal perspective and the pragmatic institutional approach towards sustainable urbanisation and planning."

Professor Debolina Kundu, *National Institute for Urban Affairs, Delhi, India*

"This unique book records first-hand accounts by activist planners of the progress of modern planning within the context of urban change over the last fifty years. It offers a holistic perspective on the future role of the planning profession for delivering sustainable urbanisation and development across the Commonwealth and beyond."

Dr Shilpi Roy, *Associate Professor of Urban and Rural Planning, Khulna University, Khulna, Bangladesh*

"Reflecting on 50 years of the Commonwealth Association of Planners, this book, written by past presidents and key activists, provides a rare insight into an international planning institution, its initiatives to assert how planning reinvented can contribute to sustainable urbanisation, and why it matters. It offers a rich, illuminating account of planning pasts and possible futures."

Professor Alison Todes, *School of Architecture and Planning, University of the Witwatersrand, Johannesburg, South Africa*

PLANNING, SUSTAINABLE URBANISATION AND THE COMMONWEALTH

By 2050, an additional 2.5 billion people will be living in the world's towns and cities, almost 50% of them in the 56 Commonwealth countries. To a significant extent, the future of the planet hangs on how cities and human settlements are managed. It is in our cities that the emissions creating climate catastrophe are stoked and where change can – and must – make a difference at scale. Food security, water, basic services, migration, shelter, jobs, environment: sustainable urbanisation is about changing direction to strive for a fairer and less environmentally damaging future.

This well-illustrated book by authors from around the Commonwealth tells how the Commonwealth Association of Planners across five decades has campaigned to make a difference. It also looks ahead, scoping the urgent, practical action that is now required.

Cliff Hague, OBE, has been President of CAP (2000–2006) and of the Royal Town Planning Institute (1996). He is Emeritus Professor in Planning and Spatial Development at Heriot-Watt University in Edinburgh. He has been Secretary General of CAP and Chair of Built Environment Forum Scotland.

Clive Harridge was President of the Royal Town Planning Institute in 2006. He served as the Secretary-General of CAP between 2010 and 2021 and is currently a Trustee and Honorary vice president. He is a former Director and Head of Planning, Transport and Design at the international consultancy Wood.

Bryce Julyan is a Fellow of the New Zealand Planning Institute and an Honorary Fellow of the Planning Institute of Australia. He leads the Planning and Engagement Practice at Beca, a New Zealand headquartered consultancy covering the Asia-Pacific region. Bryce has served on the CAP Executive Committee since 2014.

Ruiz Nik is a Council Member of the Malaysian Institute of Planners and is the Principal Director of Rekarancang, a Malaysian planning consultancy established since 1977. He has served as Malaysia's representative on CAP since 2018.

Ian Tant is a planning practitioner and a former Senior Partner of UK-based consultancy Barton Willmore (subsequently part of Stantec). He was President of the Royal Town Planning Institute in 2019 and has been the UK's vice president of CAP since 2020.

 Commonwealth Association of Planners

PLANNING, SUSTAINABLE URBANISATION AND THE COMMONWEALTH

The Commonwealth Association of Planners, Past, Present and Future

Edited by Cliff Hague, Clive Harridge, Bryce Julyan, Ruiz Nik and Ian Tant

NEW YORK AND LONDON

First published 2023
by Routledge
605 Third Avenue, New York, NY 10158

and by Routledge
4 Park Square, Milton Park, Abingdon, Oxon, OX14 4RN

Routledge is an imprint of the Taylor & Francis Group, an informa business

© 2023 selection and editorial matter, Commonwealth Association of Planners; individual chapters, the contributors

The right of Commonwealth Association of Planners to be identified as the author of the editorial material, and of the authors for their individual chapters, has been asserted in accordance with sections 77 and 78 of the Copyright, Designs and Patents Act 1988.

All rights reserved. No part of this book may be reprinted or reproduced or utilised in any form or by any electronic, mechanical, or other means, now known or hereafter invented, including photocopying and recording, or in any information storage or retrieval system, without permission in writing from the publishers.

Trademark notice: Product or corporate names may be trademarks or registered trademarks, and are used only for identification and explanation without intent to infringe.

Library of Congress Cataloging-in-Publication Data
Names: Hague, Cliff, editor. | Harridge, Clive, editor. | Julyan, Bryce,
    editor. | Nik, Ruiz, editor. | Tant, Ian, editor.
Title: Planning, sustainable urbanisation, and the commonwealth : the
    commonwealth association of planners, past, present and future / edited
    by Cliff Hague, Clive Harridge, Bryce Julyan, Ruiz Nik and Ian Tant.
Description: New York, NY : Routledge, 2023. | Includes bibliographical
    references and index.
Identifiers: LCCN 2022060777 (print) | LCCN 2022060778 (ebook) |
    ISBN 9781032414010 (hardback) | ISBN 9781032414027 (paperback) |
    ISBN 9781003357933 (ebook)
Subjects: LCSH: City planning. | Sustainable development—Planning. |
    Community development, Urban. | City planning—Forecasting.
Classification: LCC HT166 .P5425 2023 (print) | LCC HT166 (ebook) |
    DDC 307.1/216—dc23/eng/20230109
LC record available at https://lccn.loc.gov/2022060777
LC ebook record available at https://lccn.loc.gov/2022060778

ISBN: 978-1-032-41401-0 (hbk)
ISBN: 978-1-032-41402-7 (pbk)
ISBN: 978-1-003-35793-3 (ebk)

DOI: 10.4324/9781003357933

Typeset in Bembo
by Apex CoVantage, LLC

Cover image: The first image of the front cover was taken in 2001 in part of Kibera, Nairobi, which has been described as the biggest slum in Africa. It has grown since then. The photo captures one moment in time in one place, but in other ways it tells an important story about urbanisation in the Commonwealth. In the background it shows rudimentary houses in the course of construction in fields: this is the process by which cities have been built in much of the Commonwealth since 2001, rapidly and informally by poor people seeking shelter and access to urban opportunities. In the foreground is an ebullient group of young people, desperate to have their photographs taken.

At the time of writing this book there are 2.5 billion people in the Commonwealth and 60% of them are aged 29 or under. They are its future. The challenge for our planners and policy makers is to make a decisive shift towards sustainable urbanisation and create a future for this and later generations, by making our cities and human settlements 'safe, inclusive, resilient and sustainable' (UN Sustainable Development Goal 11).

The second image is of Singapore which for over 100 years was a colony and served as an entrepôt. As the photo shows, in the decades that followed and in particular after its independence in 1965 this small island state became a global financial centre, while also focusing on the quality of the living environment and green infrastructure through planning. Singapore has a 40–50 year strategic plan for land use and transport, which is then translated into more detailed 10 to 15 year plans for implementation.

Dedication

We dedicate this book to the memory of Her late Majesty, Queen Elizabeth II (1926–2022) through whose leadership, service and devotion the modern Commonwealth has grown into a family of 56 independent and equal nations, united by the values and principles set out in the Commonwealth Charter.

This book is also dedicated to the many planners in the Commonwealth who over 50 years have contributed on a voluntary basis to help CAP become one of the world's leading international planning organisations, aiming to achieve a more sustainable future for everyone.

Cliff Hague, Clive Harridge, Bryce Julyan, Ruiz Nik and Ian Tant

CONTENTS

List of photographs	xii
List of tables	xv
Acknowledgements	xvi
Abbreviations used in the book	xviii
Commonwealth Association of Planners member organisations 2022	xx

PART 1
Messages and introduction 1

Message from the Rt Hon Patricia Scotland KC, Secretary-General, Commonwealth of Nations 1
Message from Dr Anne T. Gallagher AO, Director-General, Commonwealth Foundation 3
Message from Maimunah Mohd Sharif, Under-Secretary-General and Executive Director United Nations Human Settlements Programme (UN-Habitat) 5
Messages From Our Sponsors 9

1 Planning, sustainable urbanisation and the work of CAP 11
   Clive Harridge

PART 2
The first 50 years 21

Introduction 21

2 Pointing a path to sustainable urbanisation: CAP in a changing Commonwealth 1971–2021 25
   Cliff Hague

3 1970–1988: laying the foundations for a Commonwealth-wide Profession 50
   Clive Harridge (with Peter Pun)

4 1988–2000: new technologies and an existential crisis 67
   Bill Robertson

5 2000–2006: re-inventing planning for sustainable urbanisation 77
   Cliff Hague

6 2006–2014: towards the Sustainable Development Goals and the New Urban Agenda 88
   Christine Platt

7 2014–2020: building global partnerships for sustainable urbanisation 104
   Dyan Currie

8 2020–2022: the road to the Kigali Declaration on sustainable urbanisation and beyond 116
   Eleanor Mohammed and Kelley Moore

9 Gender and sustainable urbanisation – the work of the CAP Women in Planning Network 126
   Jua Cilliers and Kristin Agnello

PART 3
The next 50 years 137

Introduction 137

10 Planning for sustainable urbanisation: issues and challenges 139
   Cliff Hague and Christine Platt

11 Planners will not be the man in the horned rimmed glasses:
    the future is civil not civic   159
    Vijay Krishnarayan

12 Young people driving sustainable urbanisation   168
    Olafiyin Taiwo

13 Education for planning a sustainable future   177
    Barbara Norman

14 Endpiece: perspectives on the past and future of planning
    in the Commonwealth   187
    *Cliff Hague, Clive Harridge, Bryce Julyan, Ruiz Nik and
    Ian Tant*

Appendix 1   Chronology of key events in CAP's 50-year history   211
Appendix 2   Biographies of editors, authors and contributors   217
Appendix 3   Sponsor details   226
Appendix 4   Glossary   228

Index   *233*

PHOTOGRAPHS

0.1	Patricia Scotland with Clive Harridge (when CAP Secretary-General), Marlborough House, London. March 2018	2
0.2	Dr Anne T. Gallagher AO	4
0.3	Maimunah Mohd Sharif	6
0.4	Maimunah Mohd Sharif with the former Prince of Wales reviewing children's model of their dream city. Malaysia, 2017	7
1.1	Meeting Her late Majesty Queen Elizabeth II and the former Prince of Wales	17
2.1	Informal settlement, Kibera, Nairobi, Kenya	29
2.2	Informal urbanisation, Kibera, Nairobi, Kenya	30
2.3	Informal hotel: Kibera, Nairobi, Kenya	30
2.4	Informal business district, Dhobi Ghat, Mumbai, India	31
2.5	Density contrasts, Calgary, Canada	38
2.6	Early New Town Housing: East Kilbride, Scotland	40
2.7	Waterfront regeneration, Vancouver, Canada	41
2.8	Regeneration of former docks, Salford Quays, England	41
2.9	Media City, Salford Quays, England	42
2.10	Strategic Planning to drive development: Putrajaya, Malaysia	45
2.11	Long-term planning for a Global City, Singapore	46
2.12	Singapore Housing and Development Board, The Pinnacle@Duxton, Singapore	47
3.1	Delegates at CAPs Inaugural Conference, New Delhi, India, 1973	61
3.2	Delegates at CAP Americas Regional Conference, Barbados, 1974	62
3.3	Hong Kong: Transition from British Colony to Global Hub	65
4.1	Delegates at the CAP Business Meeting, Hong Kong, 1988	69
4.2	Bill Robertson and Jacqueline daCosta	72

5.1	On site in the Faisalabad Area Upgrading Project, 1993	79
5.2	Increasing the presence and visibility of CAP, Kuala Lumpur, 2004	84
5.3	CAP's work recognised: Cliff Hague OBE	86
6.1	Meeting the Minister for Housing and Lands, Barbados 2007	91
6.2	West Africa Workshop – CAP in Action, 2009	93
6.3	Outside the Health and the City Conference, London, 2011	95
6.4	Congratulating Christine Platt on her SAPI Award	101
7.1	CAP Executive Committee Business Meeting, Sonaisali, Fiji 2016	106
7.2	Delegates at the Sustainable Development Conference, Sonaisali, Fiji, Nov. 2016	108
7.3	CAP Executive Committee at the Business Meeting in Cape Town, South Africa, 2018	109
7.4	CAP Awards 2019	110
7.5	Hurricane damaged school, Road Town, Tortola, British Virgin Islands, 2018	112
7.6	CAP partner representatives at WUF9, Kuala Lumpur, Malaysia, 2018	113
7.7	The five presidents at CIP Centenary celebrations, Ottawa, Canada, July 2019	114
8.1	The Rapid Planning Toolkit in action	118
8.2	At the side-event, CHOGM, Kigali, Rwanda 2022	120
9.1	The Commonwealth Women in Planning Network Manifesto was adopted in 2018 at the CAP Business Meeting, SAPI Conference, Cape Town, South Africa	130
9.2	Women in Planning event in South Africa, 2020	132
9.3	Promoting a Women in Planning Open Event in Australia, 2021	133
10.1	Natural disasters – hurricane damage in Tortola, British Virgin Islands, 2018	140
10.2	Natural disasters – Tsunami threat, Fiji at venue of CAP business meeting.	140
10.3	Car-oriented growth, Gaborone, Botswana	141
10.4	Emerging urban clusters blur urban-rural differences, Ncepheni, Kwa-Zulu Natal, South Africa	142
10.5	Informal densification in a Slum Relocation Colony, Mandanpur Khadar Colony, Delhi, India	150
10.6	Women preparing to have the crop weighed: Orange Flesh Sweet Potato project, Ghana	153
10.7	Future Street, a scale demonstration embedding green and smart infrastructure and technology, Sydney, New South Wales, Australia	154
11.1	Vijay Krishnarayan and Clive Harridge	160
11.2	Climate change protest in Trafalgar Square, London	162
11.3	Community-based watershed management study visit, Trinidad and Tobago	164

11.4	Public Protest, New Delhi, India	165
12.1	Olafiyin Taiwo at CHOGM, Kigali, Rwanda 2022	169
12.2	Testing the Rapid Planning Toolkit, Bo, Sierra Leone	170
12.3	Young planner speaking up	171
12.4	Youth Forum at CHOGM, Kigali, Rwanda 2022	175
13.1	The vulnerability of coastal settlements and livelihoods, Sri Lanka	179
13.2	Devastation caused by the 2004 tsunami in Sri Lanka	181
13.3	Wildfire damage, New South Wales, Australia	183
14.1	Lutyens and Baker's New Delhi	189
14.2	A Colonial Garden City, Taiping, Perak, Malaysia	190
14.3	The vibrancy of the street, Lagos, Nigeria	192
14.4	Mobile shop, Galle, Sri Lanka	192
14.5	Street trading, Dodanduwa, Sri Lanka	193
14.6	Farmers' Market, Fredericton, New Brunswick, Canada	194
14.7	Development and Management of Sacred Landscapes, Maungawhau (Mt Eden), Tāmaki Makaurau (Auckland), Aotearoa-New Zealand	196

TABLES

2.1 Urban households living in slums, 1990–2018 in selected Commonwealth countries. 32
3.1 Select results from CAPs 1973 Survey of Planning in Commonwealth Countries 59

ACKNOWLEDGEMENTS

The editorial team wishes to begin by thanking Bill Robertson, Christine Platt, Dyan Currie, Eleanor Mohammed, Kelley Moore, Kristin Agnello, Jua Cilliers, Vijay Krishnarayan, Olafiyin Taiwo and Barbara Norman – the authors who contributed such wonderful chapters to the book.

The texts by the past presidents in Part 2 of the book demonstrate their massive contribution to CAP during their time in office (as well as before and afterwards), whilst those authors who look forward in Part 3 provide profound and thoughtful insights into what the future may hold. It is a privilege to have a contribution to Chapter 3 of the book from the earliest living CAP President Dr K. S. Peter Pun of the Hong Kong Institute of Planners who was CAP President in 1984–1988.

Thanks are due to the many who provided photographs for the book, particularly Christine Platt who has supplied numerous excellent photographs as will be seen. We are also very grateful to Jua Cilliers for her early support to the editing process.

The team is hugely appreciative of the encouragement and support for the book given by Eleanor Mohammed as CAP President, Kelley Moore as Secretary-General and by all on the CAP Executive who fully backed the book from the outset.

We are proud to have Beca, Turley and Atkins as sponsors of the book and their support for the book's theme of sustainable urbanisation.

Annette O'Donnell, CAP's Administrator, proved indispensable throughout the preparation of the book in answering the Editorial Team's many queries drawing on her incredible knowledge of CAP events over the 20 plus years she has been involved in CAP.

CAP has always had excellent relationships with the Commonwealth Secretariat and the Commonwealth Foundation and so it gives the team great pleasure to thank the Right Honourable Patricia Scotland KC and Dr Anne T. Gallagher AO respectively for their lovely messages congratulating CAP on reaching the 50th anniversary milestone.

Over the last 20–25 years CAP's relationships with United Nations' agencies have grown from strength to strength, most noticeably with UN Habitat. Thank you to Maimunah Mohd Sharif, Executive Director of UN Habitat, for writing such a special message for the book and for all the support given to CAP.

The Prince's Foundation has given great support to CAP over a number of years: our collaboration on the Commonwealth Sustainable Cities Initiative and the Rapid Planning Toolkit is recounted in Chapters 6 to 8 of this book. Our thanks go to Jeremy Cross, Ben Bolgar and Alice Preston-Jones from the Foundation for their help in many ways in producing the book.

Thanks are due to Vincent Nadin, Professor Emeritus of Spatial Planning, TU Delft, for making possible the link with Routledge and to Kate Schell and Megha Patel of Routledge in the USA and Spandana PB of Apex CoVantage, India, for their encouragement and help. As the editorial team's knowledge of USA and New York publishing laws was limited to say the least, we were hugely grateful for the pro bono legal advice given to us by Neil Jacobs of N. I. Jacobs and Associates of New York arranged through the wonderful organisation Advocates for International Development (a4id) which has provided valuable support to CAP over recent years in other projects as well.

The book draws on the tremendous work of CAP member organisations since the founding of CAP over 50 years ago. The editorial team has been truly inspired by the enormous dedication and excellent professional skills of CAP members over the years – virtually all of this work conducted with great enthusiasm on a volunteer basis. Our thanks go out to all CAP member organisations – without them there would be no CAP. We hope the book provides a suitable testament to their contributions to CAP and for the massive achievements that through their work has placed CAP at the forefront of planning internationally.

Finally, the editorial team acknowledge the tremendous support given to each of us by our families who showed great tolerance in putting up with our spending hours working on the book and holding meetings at unsocial times when we would have otherwise been with you: your extreme patience and forbearance are peerless!

The Editorial Team
Cliff Hague, Clive Harridge, Bryce Julyan, Ruiz Nik, Ian Tant

ABBREVIATIONS USED IN THE BOOK

AUSAID	Australian Agency for International Development
APA	African Planning Association (also used for American Planning Association)
BEPIC	Built Environment Professionals in the Commonwealth
CAA	Commonwealth Association of Architects
CAP	Commonwealth Association of Planners
CASLE	Commonwealth Association of Surveying and Land Economy
CEM 2021	City Expo Malaysia 2021
CEC	Commonwealth Engineers Council
CF	Commonwealth Foundation
CHEC	Commonwealth Human Ecology Council
CHOGM	Commonwealth Heads of Government Meeting
CIDA	Canadian International Development Agency
CIP	Canadian Institute of Planners
COP26	26th United Nations Climate Change Conference of the Parties
CPF	Commonwealth Peoples Forum
CSCI	Commonwealth Sustainable Cities Initiative
CSCN	Commonwealth Sustainable Cities Network
CWIP	Commonwealth Women in Planning Network
GIS	Geographical Information System
GPN	Global Planners Network
HCP	Habitat Conservation Plan
HKIP	Hong Kong Institute of Planners
HPF	Habitat Professionals Forum
IDP	Integrated Development Plan
IGUTP	International Guidelines on Urban and Territorial Planning
IPCC	Inter-Governmental Panel on Climate Change

LIT	Land Information Technology
MDGs	United Nations Millennium Development Goals
NUA	New Urban Agenda
NGO	Non-Governmental Organisation
NZ	New Zealand
ODA	Overseas Development Administration
P4CA	Planners for Climate Action
PIA	Planning Institute of Australia (see also RAPI)
PIPA	Pacific Island Planning Association
PITP	Pula Institute of Town Planners, Botswana
RAPI	Royal Australian Planning Institute (now the Planning Institute of Australia, PIA)
RIBA	Royal Institute of British Architects
RTPI	Royal Town Planning Institute (see also TPI)
SAPI	South African Planning Institute
SDGs	Sustainable Development Goals
SIDS	Small Island Developing States
SWPR	South West Pacific Region
TPI	Town Planning Institute (now the Royal Town Planning Institute, RTPI)
UEF	Urban Economy Forum
UK	United Kingdom
UN	United Nations
UNCHS	United Nations Commission on Human Settlements
UNCRD	United Nations Centre for Rural Development
UNDRIP	United Nations Declaration on the Rights of Indigenous Peoples
WUC	World Urban Campaign
WUF	World Urban Forum

COMMONWEALTH ASSOCIATION OF PLANNERS MEMBER ORGANISATIONS 2022

BAP	Belize Association of Planners
BIP	Bangladesh Institute of Planners
BTPS	Barbados Town And Country Planning Society
CATP	Cyprus Association of Town Planners
CIP	Canadian Institute of Planners
FiPA	Fiji Planners Association
GIP	Ghana Institute of Town Planners
ITPI	Institute of Town Planners India
ITPSL	Institute of Town Planners Sri Lanka
JIP	Jamaican Institute of Planners
KIP	Kenya Institute of Planners
MIP	Malaysian Institute of Planners
MCP	Malta Chamber of Planners
NITP	Nigerian Institute of Town Planners
NITRP	Namibia Institute of Town and Regional Planners
NZPI	New Zealand Planning Institute
PAD	Planners Association of Dominica
PIA	Planning Institute of Australia
PITP	Pula Institute of Town Planners (Botswana)
RTPI	Royal Town Planning Institute
RUPI	Rwanda Urban Planning Institute
SAPI	South African Planning Institute
SIP	Singapore Institute of Planners

SLILUP	Saint Lucia Institute of Land-Use Planners
TITP	Tanzania Institute of Town Planners
TCTP	Town & Country Planning Brunei Darussalam
TTSP	Trinidad & Tobago Society of Planners
UIPP	Uganda Institute of Physical Planners
ZIP	Zambia Institute of Planners

PART 1
Messages and introduction

Message from the Rt Hon Patricia Scotland KC, Secretary-General, Commonwealth of Nations

Our Commonwealth – home to 2.5 billion people in 56 countries, stretching across 5 continents and 6 basins of our one shared ocean – is a place where people come together. We analyse the challenges of our time together; we craft and implement solutions together.

For 50 years, the Commonwealth Association of Planners (CAP) has exemplified that spirit. CAP brings together more than 40,000 planners across 29 countries, committed to sharpening the tools we need to meet the challenges of urbanisation and sustainable development.

From Australia and Dominica to Ghana, Malta and Malaysia, CAP members have helped to ensure that people across the Commonwealth have safer, healthier, more vibrant and more resilient places to live.

CAP has a record to be proud of. That record is rightly celebrated in this book.

However, given the unique blend of demographic, economic and environmental challenges we have before us, it is clear that CAP's most important work lies ahead.

Rapid urbanisation is a challenge facing many Commonwealth countries. Ensuring the Commonwealth's towns and cities are sustainable and resilient, with equitable provision of municipal services, will be critical in tackling climate change and in creating the conditions in which people everywhere can flourish.

At the 2022 Commonwealth Heads of Government Meeting in Kigali, leaders agreed a Declaration on Sustainable Urbanisation which reflects this ambition.

The Declaration is historic. It is built on more than 20 years of CAP's advocacy, experience and expertise.

It recognises that 'the long-term trajectory of urbanisation across Commonwealth members will have important consequences for national economies and that by 2050, an additional 2.5 billion people will be living in the world's towns and cities, almost 50% of them in the Commonwealth.'

DOI: 10.4324/9781003357933-1

In doing so, it gives us the mandate to create integrated strategies for safe and sustainable urban development that enhance community well-being and security. It offers support to local governments to develop comprehensive, scalable programmes to address key challenges of sustainable urbanisation. And it encourages cities to create enabling environments which support local economic development and job creation and attract investment.

Delivering these goals will require the kind of acuity and determination which CAP has long demonstrated. It will also require the cross-Commonwealth dialogue and skills development in which CAP excels.

I encourage everyone who reads this book to absorb its lessons and look with admiration on CAP's contribution over the last half-century. Above all, however, I ask you to reflect on how you can help the whole Commonwealth family work together to meet the challenges of urbanisation in the age of climate change and make the world safe for future generations.

The breakthrough decision of Heads of Government in Kigali is an endorsement of – and a mandate for – the work of the Commonwealth Association of Planners. I congratulate CAP on 50 years of success, and I am confident that, 50 years from now, CAP members will be able to reflect on their most decisive contribution of all.

PHOTO 0.1 Patricia Scotland with Clive Harridge (when CAP Secretary-General), Marlborough House, London. March 2018.

Source: Clive Harridge

Message from Dr Anne T. Gallagher AO, Director-General, Commonwealth Foundation

I am delighted to play my own very small role in celebrating the 50th anniversary of the Commonwealth Association of Planners (CAP). The organisation I lead – the Commonwealth Foundation – was created by Heads of Government to advance the aspirations and needs of the 2.5 billion citizens of the Commonwealth. The Association exemplifies what Commonwealth leaders understood: civil society is critical to functioning democracies and to thriving communities. Connecting civil society across national borders is a proven strategy for overcoming common obstacles and moving us all ahead to greater freedom and prosperity.

It is through CAP that I have come to understand the critical and often hidden role that those involved in imagining and creating our communities and our cities play. Planners are in many ways the visionaries – understanding and bringing together the elements required for healthy, sustainable and safe living environments.

The achievements of CAP over the past 50 years stand as a testament to the value of our Commonwealth, most especially its capacity to bring people together under the umbrella of shared values. I am especially struck by how the Association has transcended national borders, bringing Commonwealth citizens together to consider and address some of the most critical issues of our time, asking the questions that really matter: how do we use planning to advance economic and social goals? How do we plan for food security and healthy societies? How do we ensure that planning legislation is fit for purpose and that it reflects contemporary needs rather than externally imposed values?

The role of planners and of planning in our Commonwealth is central and will continue to be so. Around half of the projected increase in the world's urban population is forecast to take place within the Commonwealth in the decades to 2050. The Association's own reports detail that much of the Commonwealth's urban population resides in slums. The threat of climate change, the increasing frequency and intensity of natural disasters and unmanaged internal and international migration are compounding the challenges that come with rapid urbanisation. We cannot rest while so many of our fellow Commonwealth citizens are living in unacceptable and highly precarious conditions. This is the message CAP and its partners brought to the 2022 Commonwealth Heads of Government Meeting in Rwanda in the form of an urgent Call to Action. CAP's tireless work contributed to the historic Declaration of Sustainable Urbanisation subsequently made by Commonwealth leaders, an achievement of which its members and partners can feel immensely proud.

This book documents the strong track record of CAP in so many areas of critical importance to human well-being and growth. The next chapter is yet to be written but I am convinced that, with the support it deserves, the Association will continue its vital work of sharing ideas, knowledge and skills within and between countries in ways that will help ensure greater prosperity across our Commonwealth and help deliver sustainable urbanisation. My congratulations to all involved for a job well done. I look forward to working alongside you in the coming years.

PHOTO 0.2 Dr Anne T. Gallagher AO.

Source: Commonwealth Foundation

Message from Maimunah Mohd Sharif, Under-Secretary-General and Executive Director United Nations Human Settlements Programme (UN-Habitat)

In this Decade of Action to achieve the Sustainable Development Goals (SDGs), collaborative efforts are needed to address emerging issues for a more prosperous, inclusive and sustainable urban future. Recovery from the COVID-19 pandemic, urban resilience and climate action are critical priorities, even as the 2030 Agenda for Sustainable Development provides the broader roadmap for global action. To meet the 17 SDGs and the New Urban Agenda, we need integrated, actionable and localised initiatives to spur sustainable urban development.

The Commonwealth Association of Planners (CAP) has been exercising an important leadership role in the global debate on sustainable urban development and the role of urban planning. Its leadership helped advance the 'Call for Action' on Sustainable Urbanisation across the Commonwealth, adopted by the Commonwealth Heads of Government in Kigali in June 2022. CAP effectively combines this global stewardship and partnership building with pilot activities and capacity building, supported by strong evidence and innovative approaches. In the Commonwealth, CAP has been supporting capacity development of professionals and updating of curricula and strengthening of the national associations of planners and has led a continuous dialogue with governments and decision makers. The numerous initiatives, the normative and research documents and partnerships attest to that. But even beyond the Commonwealth, CAP has advocated for the planning profession globally to come together and speak with one voice and take a more deliberate role in global discourse and advocacy. Its leadership in this has been exemplary and continues to this day, in collaboration with like-minded associations of planners.

CAP has built a strong and long-lasting relationship with UN-Habitat over the past two decades. It has been instrumental in moving planning – literally – to the centre of the discussion on sustainable development and sustainable urbanisation, the work of UN-Habitat and, eventually, the New Urban Agenda. Its reflections

PHOTO 0.3 Maimunah Mohd Sharif.
Source: UN-Habitat

on making planning 'fit for purpose' led to the Vancouver 2006 Declaration on Reinventing Planning which was endorsed by major planning associations around the globe. That greatly influenced both individual and collective professional perspectives on planning, as well as UN-Habitat's future orientations in this area. UN-Habitat's 2009 Global Report on Human Settlements which focused on Planning for Sustainable Cities was its first ever major report that focused on planning. Subsequently, CAP and UN-Habitat joined hands to strengthen national associations of planners in countries across Africa and in the Caribbean. CAP also played a leading role in the development and implementation of the International Guidelines on Urban and Territorial Planning, adopted by the UN-Habitat Governing Council in 2015, which provide a 'blueprint' for improved planning practice and planning systems around the world. The contribution of CAP to the Habitat III process and the development of the New Urban Agenda is equally well recognised.

PHOTO 0.4 Maimunah Mohd Sharif with the former Prince of Wales reviewing children's model of their dream city. Malaysia, 2017. Mr Mohammad Mentek, Secretary-General Malaysia Ministry of Housing and Local Government (L). Ruiz Nik, Malaysian Institute of Planners representing CAP (R). At the time of the photo Maimunah Mohd Sharif was Mayor of Seberang Perai, Malaysia.

Source: BERNAMA, Malaysian News Agency

We are delighted to have been able to count on this partnership and deeply appreciate CAP's commitment to reinforcing the role of planning in sustainable urban development. Six years after Quito, I call upon CAP to continue its visionary work and expand its reach, in order to advance on the achievement of the SDGs and the implementation of the New Urban Agenda, across the Commonwealth and beyond.

Messages From Our Sponsors

Beca

Our purpose at Beca is to make every day better. Better for people, better for the planet and better for prosperity. This is something we aim to bring to our projects and to achieve through all our interactions with the people and communities we work with.

We are proud to support the Commonwealth Association of Planners – the collaboration between planners across the Commonwealth helps make a better future for both our cities and the natural environment. Beca celebrated its centenary in 2020 and are delighted to congratulate the Commonwealth Association of Planners on its Golden Jubilee.

Turley

Whilst Turley's professional practice is within the UK and Ireland, our perspective is much broader. Through our Charitable Trust we have been delighted to support programmes of sustainable urbanisation around the world. These have included helping to build capacity by upskilling local built environment professionals along with financial and 'sweat equity' support for projects providing new schools and healthcare facilities.

It is an honour to be able to support the work of CAP in using this significant anniversary to celebrate and share leading thinking and practice in achieving rapid urbanisation in truly sustainable ways.

Atkins

Atkins, a member of the SNC Lavalin Group, is proud to mark its ongoing relationship with CAP through sponsorship of this book. Through its employees' involvement in CAP over the years, including that of our Associate Director and Practice Manager Viral Desai who led the CAP Young Planners Network for six years, Atkins has helped develop understanding of the issues that are posed by rapid urbanisation across the Commonwealth.

Addressing the social, economic and environmental factors that impact different parts of the world is key to creating a more sustainable future for all. Town planners should be recognised as the key professionals who can lead the built environment in a cohesive and integrated way, whilst allowing the natural environment to flourish in a sustainable manner.

1

PLANNING, SUSTAINABLE URBANISATION AND THE WORK OF CAP

Clive Harridge

This book traces the development of planning and sustainable urbanisation in the Commonwealth through the work of the Commonwealth Association of Planners from when it was established in 1971 through to the 2022 Commonwealth Heads of Government Meeting (CHOGM) in Kigali, Rwanda and beyond. It records key events and CAP's many activities over the past 50 years whilst highlighting the challenges of sustainable urbanisation and looking ahead to what might lie in store in the next 50 years.

What is CAP?

CAP is an umbrella organisation. Its members are the professional planning institutes in Commonwealth countries, who pay annual subscriptions based on the number of their own members. Many small Commonwealth countries simply do not have a sufficient critical mass of planners to form and sustain a separate professional planning body. However, as the list of members shows, CAP still has a substantial reach, stretching across five continents. As later chapters show, CAP has sought to reach out to and support planners in smaller states, especially island states where the challenges of interaction with other professional planners are considerable.

Some countries have legislation that regulates the use of the title 'town planner' or similar, with registration overseen by an agency that stands apart from an independent body representing planners. This is the case, for example, in South Africa, where the South African Council for Planners (SACPLAN) is the statutory body, and the South African Planning Institute (SAPI) is the independent body. Nigeria has a Town Planners Registration Council defined by an Act of Parliament and set up in the late 1980s, while the Nigerian Institute of Town Planners was set up in 1966.

Where there is no registration body, anybody can call themselves a 'town planner.' That is the case in the UK, for example, where the Royal Town Planning Institute

DOI: 10.4324/9781003357933-2

(RTPI) is both independent of government but also determines through its membership rules who can call themselves a 'chartered town planner.'

The significance of these distinctions is that, other things being equal, professionalism can be constructed in two ways. It can be a means to claim exclusivity in access to jobs (through registration), and/or it can be an expression of expertise serving the public, independent of government and so more able – but not necessarily willing – to 'speak truth to power.' It is generally these more independent institutes and associations, rather than the statutory registration bodies, that are members of CAP.

CAP is managed by an executive that is elected at business meetings by representatives of the member organisations. While accountable to the rest of the executive and through them to the member organisations, the presidents of CAP have been allowed discretion to use their professional judgements on how to respond to events and to take CAP forward, since for most of CAP's first 50 years, communications technology did not allow speedy consultation across the membership. Throughout, CAP has relied on the unpaid work of those serving in executive posts or other capacities: from 2000 onwards a one-day-a-week equivalent administrator, based in the RTPI office in Edinburgh but paid for by CAP, has supported their efforts. This fragile infrastructure is fundamental to understanding the history and future of CAP.

What is sustainable urbanisation?

As the book shows, the notion of sustainable urbanisation came to dominate CAP's activities in the 21st century. Chapter 9 of the landmark (Brundtland, 1987) Report on sustainable development highlighted 'The Urban Challenge.' The chapter focused on what it called 'Third World Cities.' observing:

> Few city governments in the developing world have the power, resources, and trained staff to provide their rapidly growing populations with the land, services, and facilities needed for an adequate human life: clean water, sanitation, schools, and transport. The result is mushrooming illegal settlements with primitive facilities, increased overcrowding, and rampant disease linked to an unhealthy environment.
>
> *(para.9)*

It explained how 'uncontrolled' and 'haphazard development' made provision of housing, infrastructure and public services unnecessarily expensive, destroyed agricultural land and consumed landscapes and public open spaces (para.13). It lamented the low priority given to urban problems.

The Brundtland Commission recognised that what it called 'Industrial World Cities' were responsible for a large share of environmental pollution, resource use and energy consumption (para.15). They also had a range of other problems, but crucially they had the resources to tackle the issues. However, the deindustrialisation, consumerism and decades of neo-liberalism that followed came to weaken the capacity of many local governments to tackle these problems.

Brundtland identified many issues that rather than being resolved would still resonate 35 years later. Though the report gave pointers for action, such as national urban policies or government action to provide cheap plots for housing close to employment centres, it did not crystallise 'sustainable urbanisation' as a concept. The 1996 Habitat II conference committed to 'sustainable human settlements.' a valuable but slightly static notion. 'Sustainable urbanisation' is a more dynamic concept, recognising the process of urban development, while also suggesting questions about how and by whom that process is planned and managed.

Fundamentally, there are two propositions at the core that go back to Brundtland, which begins 'The Earth is one but the world is not.' First, growing demands on scarce resources, together with the pollution created by their use and discarding, risks transgressing thresholds that endanger the capacity of systems to regenerate and so sustain life on earth. This is the inter-generational dimension, which is now widely acknowledged, albeit too often overridden in practice. Second, poverty and inequality, both between and within countries, are central to the crises, a connection that gets glossed over. This is the intra-generational dimension.

Just as urbanisation varies between cultures and places, so sustainable urbanisation can take different forms across the diverse Commonwealth. However it is possible to point to some essential common themes. Conservation of finite resources and working towards a circular economy is an urgent priority, particularly in the rich countries where consumption is highest. This implies use of planning systems to deliver refurbishment and reuse of buildings and protection of forests, rivers and landscapes. Similarly, consumption of non-renewable energy and associated air pollution needs to be curbed by planning for active travel and use of public transport. Instead of car-dependent suburbs spreading across agricultural or forested land, planners should work for compact cities and transit-oriented development with higher densities around hubs and interchanges. Housing needs to be affordable and accessible to jobs and essential services. Public open space, green and blue corridors are important for sustainable urbanisation. Food security also requires fresh thinking about urban agriculture and peri-urban land use.

Sustainable urbanisation implies a more holistic view of the scope of planning than is the case at present. The connections between place and health, a driver for the introduction of formal planning systems at the start of the 20th century, needs to be reclaimed. Planning needs to connect the environmental, economic and social components of urban change.

Tackling poverty and other forms of exclusion is also critical at all scales of planning from local to the global. Planning for sustainable urbanisation means that the needs of poor and marginalised groups such as youth, women, ethnic minorities and refugees are prioritised. It means a form of planning rooted in universal human rights.

All this matters because the world will continue to urbanise for at least a generation, and cities are both the engines of unsustainable development and inequality and also the best means of delivering sustainable development at scale. The UN Sustainable Development Goals 2016–2030 (SDGs) made clear the meaning of sustainable development for our time. Goal 11 called for cities and human settlements to be made safe, inclusive, resilient and sustainable. Planning for sustainable urbanisation is integral to delivery on that and related goals.

The content and structure of the book

The book opens in the early 1970s and shows how over subsequent decades challenges for communities in the Commonwealth were changing as populations grew and urban centres experienced increasingly rapid growth. Through this period and against a background of global initiatives such as Habitat I, II and III; the SDGs; the Millennium Development Goals and the New Urban Agenda and growing awareness of climate change, it became widely recognised that the need for sustainable forms of urban development was urgent. Over this period the concept of sustainable urbanisation evolved and began to be championed by CAP and others at successive international forums such as the World Urban Forum and Commonwealth Heads of Government Meetings.

For any voluntary organisation to have operated continuously and so successfully for over 50 years is a huge achievement in itself and testament to the hard work and dedication of the many individuals who have given their time and efforts freely to the organisation and to planning in the Commonwealth. Through its member organisations, CAP now represents over 40,000 individual planners across the Commonwealth.

The context for the book is the Commonwealth which is made up of independent countries that work together to pursue common goals and promote development, democracy and peace. The Commonwealth with 2.5 billion citizens across 56 nations, large and small, rich and poor, is critical to the future of the world. It includes India with a population of 1.4 billion and Nauru with its 11,000 people. The Commonwealth offers unique institutional channels for the delivery of messages from civil society to government leaders influencing the agenda for Commonwealth Heads of Government meetings (CHOGM). Acknowledgement of critical issues by CHOGM then become key 'hooks' for advocacy work by CAP and others.

Like many organisations run by volunteers, CAP had not been good at recording its own history or managing its archives. CAP's Golden Jubilee in 2021 prompted action to recall events and activities over its 50 years of existence. Planning History is a long-established field and includes some classic texts such as Hall (1988) and Freestone (2000). Understandably, the focus has been on the 20th century, stopping short of depicting shifts in planning in the new millennium, not least in the rapidly urbanising world and through the channels of the United Nations (UN), with which CAP has been closely and directly involved over many years.

Similarly, planning histories have often been rooted in a single country or shaped by world views from North America and Europe. Until now, there has not been a modern history of planning focused on the Commonwealth and constructed by persons directly involved in the events. Recording first-hand accounts of planning and events over the late 20th and early 21st centuries seemed a worthwhile model for celebrating CAP's 50th anniversary. From this germ of an idea the book as now published has emerged with contributions from CAP presidents as well as from Richard Gill in Barbados who was present at a meeting in London in 1970 where it was originally agreed to establish an association for planners in the Commonwealth.

Such autobiographical writing has not been common in planning, especially where it is mainly the voices of practitioners, as is the case here. Haselsberger (2017) edited a volume of autobiographical essays by spatial planning academics. Krumholz and Forester (1990) produced a landmark account of Krumholz's city level practice experiences in Cleveland, Ohio. However, decades later Sager (2019, p. 35) noted that 'There are still types of activist planners whose stories have not been told.' This is certainly true of those practitioners who have voluntarily given their time to get deeply involved over a period of years in international organisations representing the planning profession.

> The Planning Institute of Australia (PIA) looks to CAP to draw our vision to the global scale and join up our thinking with other planning bodies right around the Commonwealth.
>
> David Williams, Chief Executive Officer, PIA

The contributors to this book come from across the Commonwealth. It sets the actions of planners in an international organisation in relation to key partners and stakeholders. Thus the differing backgrounds and nationalities of the contributors are a key and deliberate feature of the book. Necessarily this means that, while not all countries can be represented by authors, there is variety in styles of writing, giving authenticity and richness to the text. The editors decided that the diverse, unique and personal insights were key building blocks for the book, rather than seeking the consistency of style and argument of a conventional academic text or professional report. It should be noted that the comments provided by the authors are not necessarily the views of the editors – or of CAP.

CAP's story stretches from the age of airmail letters to webinars, through a number of financial crises, engagement with the UN and other international organisations and in the early 2020s through a global pandemic. It tells how Commonwealth planners addressed the dramatic changes that followed decolonisation and urban transitions and how CAP became a highly respected international voice, developing the idea of sustainable urbanisation and so reshaping concepts of the scope and nature of planning. Many contributed to CAP's work over a long period: there were discontinuities, and aspirations varied. That reality is reflected in the variety of contributions.

Part of the story is about institution building and the difference that institutions can make internationally. Over those 50 years CAP's standing grew to become one of the world's leading and most influential international planning organisations. It contributed effectively to thought leadership in the planning profession globally as well as providing a valuable vehicle for planners at a grassroots level to share experiences and learn from one another. What sets CAP apart as a professional planning organisation are the institutionalised conduits which the Commonwealth provides, as well as links to an active network of Commonwealth intergovernmental, civil society, cultural and professional organisations sharing common goals and values. The Commonwealth as an institution – and CAP's status as a Commonwealth organisation – permeate the book.

> CAP provides an opportunity for Canadian planning professionals to connect with planners across the globe, exchange knowledge and ideas and contribute to shared project priorities.
>
> Beth McMahon, Chief Executive Officer,
> Canadian Institute of Planners

The respect and reputation that CAP has achieved is recognised at the highest levels in the Commonwealth and beyond, as reflected in the congratulatory messages included in Part 1 of the book. Members of CAP have also been privileged to meet with Her late Majesty Queen Elizabeth II on several occasions in her capacity as Head of the Commonwealth as well as with the former Prince of Wales (Photo 1.1) who has supported CAP over many years.

Part 2 opens with an overview by Emeritus Professor Cliff Hague of changes in the Commonwealth and in planning over the past 50 years and how these have impacted upon CAP. This is followed by a review of the early years of CAP, then chapters written by former presidents of CAP and the president and the convenor of the Women in Planning Network at the time of writing. A short chronology of key activities is included in Appendix 1.

CAP has not kept a systematic record of its activities, particularly in the early years, so tracing its history was difficult. However, thanks to the Indian Town Planning Institute we have a copy of the proceedings of CAP's inaugural conference held in 1973 in New Delhi. This provides an excellent record of the first few years of CAP, along with the results of a survey of the state of the profession in the Commonwealth at the time, which informed the writing of Chapter 3, 'Laying the Foundations for a Commonwealth-wide Profession: 1970–1988.'

The planners in Hong Kong played a key role in the first two decades of CAP's existence and so the contribution made to this book by Dr Peter Pun from the Hong Kong Institute of Planners who was CAP's President in 1984–1988 is most welcome. Subsequent CAP presidents have written their reflections on their time as president. Each brought their own leadership approach and style to the organisation.

PHOTO 1.1 Meeting Her late Majesty Queen Elizabeth II and the former Prince of Wales. Clive Harridge (front) and Cliff Hague at a reception for civil society organisations held in advance of CHOGM at Clarence House, London, October 2015.
Source: British Ceremonial Arts

As well as maintaining the ongoing functioning of CAP, each took the organisation forward in different ways.

> The objects of CAP are to promote dynamic inclusive and integrated town and country planning practice, education and research. The Institute of Town Planners India (ITPI) is committed to achieve these objectives with a strength of more than 5,000 active members.
>
> Pradeep Kapoor, Secretary General, ITPI

The Presidents' contributions illustrate CAP's increasing influence in major Commonwealth activities such as CHOGM and CAP's proactive engagement with UN Habitat and other UN agencies in contributing to the formulation of the SDGs and the New Urban Agenda (NUA), as well as addressing the many challenges associated with rapid urbanisation and climate change. Specific activities referred to by the Presidents include the Land Information Technology (LIT) programme developed in Hong Kong in the 1980s, the establishment of networks for young planners and women in planning, a rapid urbanisation toolkit and research focussed on many issues including disaster recovery, food security, the planning profession, sustainable cities, health and planning legislation.

> CAP membership has provided Te Kokoriniga – New Zealand Planning Institute (NZPI) with the opportunity to strengthen relationships between planning organisations within Oceania and other parts of the world. . ... NZPI values the equal opportunity CAP extends to all members to contribute to and help shape global planning policy (e.g. SDGs New Urban Agenda and Sustainable Cities).
>
> David Curtis, Chief Executive and Bryce Julian
> CAP vice president, NZPI

For the first 30 years CAP operated without the benefits of the internet. Most communication was through hard copy correspondence and newsletters and one-to-one telephone calls. Despite this, CAP's influence grew.

The Presidents' contributions identify ways national organisations of planners have benefitted over the years by being a member of CAP, such as through sharing ideas and policy approaches, contributing to global initiatives, being part of special interest groups and networks, receiving support for in-country initiatives, sourcing technical practical planning guidance and providing help at times of emergency. In addition, Part 2 traces the growth of gender as an issue through the work of CAP's Women in Planning Network which has sought to address gender inequalities which remain widespread across the Commonwealth.

> The work by CAP in placing planning at the forefront of any development process was vital for the Chamber to press the authorities for better planning and recognition of the profession.
>
> Anthony Ellul, General Secretary,
> Malta Chamber of Planners

As will be seen in Part 2, over the 50 years of CAP's existence the challenges faced by planners across the Commonwealth have changed in many ways. In the early years CAP, like the planning profession, was evolving and finding its feet – this was well before the concept of sustainable urbanisation was developed. In the early 1970s planning was an emergent profession in many countries. During the later 20th century the rate of urban growth began to increase rapidly and has continued to put enormous pressure on urban areas in accommodating massive urban sprawl and population growth. Against this background at the start of the new millennium

CAP took a leading role in promoting the need for sustainable urbanisation – a campaign that has continued ever since, increasingly making the connections to climate change and extreme weather events.

As will be seen in reading Part 2 and the Chronology, CAP is a very active campaigning organisation and has taken part in numerous initiatives over the years, working alone or more often in collaboration with Commonwealth and other international organisations. Initiatives undertaken in more recent times include the following:

- Active participation in the successful global campaign for an urban based SDG.
- Key member of the World Urban Campaign targeted at achieving the urban dimension of the SDGs by 2030 and implementing the NUA.
- Launched the UN Planners for Climate Action initiative with partners at COP23 in Bonn.
- Launched CAP's Women in Planning Manifesto which inter alia seeks partnerships with UN Women, Women in Cities International, Women Transforming Cities and other international organisations to advance the SDGs in particular Goal 5: Gender Equality.
- Prepared and issued with partners a Call to Action for Commonwealth nations to give greater recognition to sustainable urbanisation to address the challenges of urban growth and development.

A major breakthrough came with the 2022 CHOGM in Kigali, Rwanda agreeing on the Declaration on Sustainable Urbanisation (The Commonwealth, 2022) which reflects 20 years of advocacy by CAP and others.

More information about all of these and many more are to be found in the book.

> CAP is an invaluable link and partner with the RTPI, providing connection to Commonwealth nations, UN Habitat and a host of partner organisations with a shared aim of promoting the art and science of Planning.
>
> Timothy David Crawshaw, RTPI President, 2022

What of the future? Climate and biodiversity emergencies, widening inequalities, food security and natural disasters all require urgent action and all are intertwined with the way human settlements are developed. Part 3 of the book explores the next 50 years from different perspectives beginning with an overview of the issues and challenges to be faced by planners in the Commonwealth written by Cliff Hague and Christine Platt. Diverse contributors then ponder how the context for planning might develop and how planning itself as a profession – and CAP as an organisation – might evolve against a background of a changing Commonwealth. The increasing significance of civil society is explored by Vijay Krishnarayan, and the importance of a youth focus and effective planning education are expounded by Olafiyin Taiwo and Professor Barbara Norman respectively. Whilst there are many challenges and huge uncertainties, not least concerning the Commonwealth itself, one aspect that comes through all of the future gazing is positivity about the future of the planning profession and the role of CAP.

The book's Endpiece presents concluding thoughts reflecting on all the previous chapters and challenges for the future, whilst acknowledging the colonial background and its impact on the design and layout of urban areas today. It highlights the value of internationalism amongst professional planners and the benefits of embedding Commonwealth values in their work. It also stresses the critical importance of sustainable urbanisation in the design of urban areas and buildings to help achieve a more sustainable future for the Commonwealth and beyond.

The book set out to present perspectives on the past and future of planning and sustainable urbanisation in the Commonwealth. It is a time capsule garnering, while it can, the first hand experiences of planners over 50 years – but also challenging practitioners and students from all across the Commonwealth and beyond to think creatively about our shared future.

References

Brundtland, G. (1987), *Report of the World Commission on Environment and Development: Our Common Future*, New York: United Nations General Assembly document A/42/427.
Freestone, R. (ed.), (2000), *Urban Planning in a Changing World: The Twentieth Century Experience*, Abingdon and New York: Routledge.
Hall, P. (1988), *Cities of Tomorrow: An Intellectual History of Urban Planning and Design in the Twentieth Century*, Oxford and Malden, Massachusetts: Blackwell.
Haselsberger, B. (ed), (2017), *Encounters in Planning Thought: 16 Autobiographical Essays From Key Thinkers in Spatial Planning*, New York and London: Routledge.
Krumholz, N. and Forester, J. (1990), *Making Equity Planning Work: Leadership in the Public Sector*, Philadelphia: Temple University Press.
Sager, T. (2019), 'Activism by Lay and Professional Planners: Types, Research Issues, and Ongoing Analysis', *PlaNext –Next Generation Planning*, 8, pp. 32–39, https://doi.org/10.24306/plnxt/44.
The Commonwealth. (2022), *Declaration on Sustainable Urbanisation*. Available at https://thecommonwealth.org/news/chogm-2022-communique-leaders-statement-and-declarations-delivering-common (Accessed 7 March 2023).

PART 2
The first 50 years

Introduction

As Clive Harridge explains in the preceding chapter, this book commenced as a commemoration of the first 50 years of the Commonwealth Association of Planners and set out to tell its story from its inception in the early 1970s to the present day, drawing on archive material acquired and accrued by Clive during his decade as Secretary-General (from 2010 to 2021).

Plentiful though that material is, by its nature it is sporadic (much was produced, transmitted and stored in paper form, before the days of desktop computers, email and the internet) and the story therefore relies on the recollections of the past presidents of the Association and of the leaders of the Commonwealth Women in Planning Network. Part 2 of the book therefore sets out the story of CAP in the words of those who have played leading roles in the organisation.

These are not academic assessments of the history – rather, they are akin to oral histories – and each needs to be understood in its broad context of world and Commonwealth events. Part 2 therefore commences with an explanation by Cliff Hague of the history of the Commonwealth since CAP's founding in 1971 and of the changing role of planning globally and within the Commonwealth. The chapter highlights the emergence of concerns over the growing pace of urbanisation across the globe, of climate change, and the increasing need for sustainability in tackling poverty, poor housing, environmental change and urban growth.

In Chapter 3, Clive Harridge tells the story of the early years of CAP from the initial plenary meeting (inevitably, in London) in 1970 that led to the formal creation of the Association from 1971 to 1988. The chapter draws largely on archive material but includes recollections of the earliest surviving president – Dr Peter Pun of Hong Kong – and highlights the overriding concern of the period to promote

DOI: 10.4324/9781003357933-3

planning (or physical planning) as a profession throughout the Commonwealth. Whilst CAP may have been a campaigning organisation from its outset, its campaign throughout the 1970s and 1980s was for the acceptance of planning itself. But the early presidents and members of CAP forged an organisation capable of broadening its concerns into wider issues than the profession itself, as subsequent chapters show.

In Chapter 4, Bill Robertson from New Zealand relates the events of his two periods as president from 1988 to 1991 and 1996 to 2000. His account reflects the growing focus of CAP on enhancing planning practice across the Commonwealth, primarily through the use of new technologies, particularly Geographical Information Systems (GIS), but he also relates the serious financial difficulties that almost brought an end to the organisation in 1995. Bill's return to the presidency in 1996 helped to stabilise CAP and proved the foundation for a reinvigorated organisation.

Cliff Hague from the UK describes his term as president from 2000 to 2006 in Chapter 5. The era marks the turning point in CAP's history from an organisation that sought not just to promote planning as a profession to one that had a clear vision of what planning was *for* – seeking to tackle real-world issues of poverty, poor housing and environmental degradation. CAP increasingly connected itself to the Istanbul Declaration and Habitat Agenda agreed at the UN Conference on Human Settlements (Habitat II) in 1996, with central themes of 'adequate shelter for all' and 'sustainable human settlements.' In turn, this was the basis on which CAP would drive a focus on sustainable cities at the World Urban Forum in Vancouver in 2006 and subsequently make its contribution to creating the Sustainable Development Goals of 2015 and New Urban Agenda of 2016.

Christine Platt's description of her presidency from 2008 to 2014 in Chapter 6 reflects the accelerating role and influence of CAP in advocating the role of planning in sustainable urbanisation. Christine, from South Africa, describes CAP's work as a facilitator in forging connections and building grassroots partnerships in order to respond to the challenges and opportunities, including across the Pacific, Africa and the Caribbean. Notably, CAP's partnerships were not only amongst planners and its members but more widely with bodies such as UN Habitat and The Prince's Foundation.

UN Habitat III in Quito in 2016 cemented planning's place in delivering sustainable development but also CAP's place in setting agendas and delivering change. In Chapter 7, Dyan Currie from Australia relates her role on behalf of CAP in the preparation of the Sustainable Development Goals and the New Urban Agenda. Developing from these, the CAP Conference and Business Meeting of 2016 was held in Fiji and led to an important partnership with the Princes Foundation to develop the Rapid Urbanisation Toolkit and, in turn, to create the Commonwealth Sustainable Cities Initiative, working with The Prince's Foundation, Commonwealth Association of Architects (CAA), Commonwealth Local Government Forum (CLGF), Association of Commonwealth Universities (ACU) and others.

These partnerships and the important campaigns to promote planning, sustainable urbanisation and deliverance of the Rapid Urbanisation Toolkit – as well as continuing involvement with UN Habitat, including through the Habitat Professionals Forum – remain core activities for CAP into 2023 under the current president, Eleanor Mohammed of Canada. In Chapter 8, Eleanor draws together the threads of the various workstreams that have occupied CAP and its partners in recent years and which focus on the role of planning in advocating for and delivering sustainable settlements. The success of this advocacy is marked by the Kigali Declaration – the joint statement of all the Commonwealth Heads of Government in June 2022 that they should give greater focus to sustainable urbanisation – and by the commitments of the Leaders of the Group of 7 (G7) the following week to accelerate efforts to achieve the Sustainable Development Goals.

With input from Kelley Moore, the current Secretary-General, Eleanor also reflects on the importance in planning of working to apply equity, diversity and inclusivity, including efforts to address the impacts of historic colonisation on indigenous peoples – an ongoing task for the years ahead.

The history of CAP is completed in Chapter 9 by a review of the origins and work of CAP's Women in Planning Network and the importance of gender-equality and social justice in delivering sustainable urbanisation. The Chapter is written by Kristin Agnello of Canada and Jua Cilliers of South Africa (but based in Australia).

These chapters paint a picture of an organisation with London origins that enabled the gathering-together of planning bodies across the Commonwealth to support and help develop planning as a profession. From early – and sometimes troubled – years building a campaigning capability and accruing respect with other Commonwealth bodies, CAP transformed itself into a connected, socially and environmentally conscious group with a powerful reach in advocating the role of planning in delivering sustainable urbanisation. In its partnership work with UN Habitat, The Prince's Foundation and fellow Commonwealth organisations, CAP stands at the outset of its next 50 years with a strong mission in helping to address poverty, poor housing, climate change and the pressures of achieving sustainable development.

And yet, there are points to address in relation to the capabilities of a volunteer-led and run organisation and to the role of planning and planners in a Commonwealth perspective. Whilst celebrating the achievements of the Association in surviving for 50 years and for its increasingly effective advocacy of the role of planning in sustainable urbanisation over the past 20 years, it is in the nature of planning that we ask, what next? How do we learn from the experience of the past to do things differently/better in the future? In Part 3 of this book we consider the future for CAP, planning and planners from a number of perspectives before concluding with a reconsideration of the history and of the future expectations in the Endpiece.

2
POINTING A PATH TO SUSTAINABLE URBANISATION

CAP in a changing Commonwealth 1971–2021

Cliff Hague

This chapter begins by outlining the development of the Commonwealth in the period from the foundation of Commonwealth Association of Planners (CAP) in 1971 to the Association's 50th Anniversary. This forms the backdrop to a discussion of how urban and rural development and planning changed during those years. Thus the chapter sets a framework for those that follow, by sketching the context in which CAP's history was set and in which its future will be shaped.

The Commonwealth 1971–2021

The Commonwealth was formed in 1926, during the high noon of British imperialism. The fifth Imperial Conference, hosted by King-Emperor George V and held in London, brought together the Prime Ministers of the United Kingdom (UK), Australia, Canada, New Zealand (NZ), Newfoundland and South Africa (SA), as well as the Earl of Birkenhead representing India and a group of officials in what was then the recently created Irish Free State. With the exception of India, these were the Dominions, i.e. self-governing states. All were to be equal members of The British Commonwealth of Nations, a community within the British Empire, owing allegiance to the British monarch but not ruled over by the UK.

The 'Modern Commonwealth' came years later in 1949, after India had become a republic. The Declaration from that 1949 London meeting of Prime Ministers allowed republics and other countries to be members of the Commonwealth. In 1961 SA withdrew from the Commonwealth over apartheid, which divided the Commonwealth Heads of Government Meeting (CHOGM) that year. Coinciding with moves to establish CAP, in 1971 the Singapore CHOGM Declaration (Commonwealth Secretariat, 2004) marked a further transition. It defined core beliefs of the Commonwealth – equal rights for all, democratic self-determination, anti-racism,

DOI: 10.4324/9781003357933-4

world peace and an end to gross inequality – and committed to work together to achieve them. Recognising the Cold War and the independence of several former colonies, the 1971 Declaration affirmed that members could be 'non-aligned' or members of other communities or alliances. At that time there were thirty-two member countries, and the fundamental geography and diversity of the Commonwealth was recognised in the Declaration: six continents, five oceans, rich and poor, different races, languages and cultures.

Thus CAP was formed at a time when the Commonwealth was adjusting to the emergence of independent states from colonial status: a further 14 countries, mostly small island states, would join in the next decade. As 1971 closed, India triumphed in a war with its Commonwealth neighbour Pakistan, leading to the formation of Bangladesh.

The Commonwealth Secretariat (CS) had been set up in 1965. A year later the Commonwealth Foundation (CF) had been established, as a Charitable Trust, to bring together people outside of governments. The Foundation's early focus was rather narrowly on the role of professional associations within the Commonwealth. This was broadened in 1982, reflecting the growth of Non-Government Organisations (NGOs) during the previous decade, and more emphasis was given to culture and to gender issues.

Queen Elizabeth remained the Head of the Commonwealth, and the CS and the CF remained London-based. However, on a number of occasions there were tensions amongst Commonwealth members. A Commonwealth Fund for Technical Cooperation had been established in 1971 to provide development assistance to poorer countries. While many of the newly independent countries had pressed for this, 'old Commonwealth members' were less enthusiastic (Commonwealth Secretariat, 2016).

Then in the 1980s, apartheid divided Commonwealth members once more. The 1985 CHOGM called for an end to white minority rule in SA, and the following year an Eminent Persons' Group set up by the Commonwealth Secretary General called for sanctions, a measure the UK government refused to support. A widespread boycott of the 1986 Commonwealth Games in Edinburgh followed as a consequence. Notwithstanding the UK's position, the Commonwealth played an important role in mobilising support for sanctions amongst other countries.

By 1991 there were 50 Commonwealth members, and the Harare Declaration set out a commitment to democratic values and human rights, reaffirming support for gender equality, access to education for all and environmental protection. As the end of the Cold War ushered in a new era of optimism, the Declaration sought to chart a way forward for the Commonwealth. There were signs of progress in SA too, sufficient for the CHOGM to agree to phase out sanctions. SA re-joined the Commonwealth in 1994. Thus the early 1990s saw a reinvigoration of the Commonwealth and a more united and ambitious future.

A Commonwealth Group of Experts (1989), predominantly drawn from 'developing countries', had already produced a report for the Secretary General on the dangers of climate change. This came after catastrophic flooding in Bangladesh and inundation in the Maldives that had followed high storm surges. Jamaica had been badly hit by Hurricane Gilbert in 1988, while there had been droughts in African countries, India and Canada. The report followed the establishment of the Intergovernmental Panel on Climate Change (IPCC) in 1988 and highlighted the particular situation in the Commonwealth: 'since the Commonwealth includes a disproportionate number of small, low-income states, any change which increases their vulnerability and aggravates problems of poverty is to be regarded with the greatest concern' (p. 2).

As the new millennium approached and the UN adopted the Millennium Development Goals (MDGs), issues surrounding globalisation and debt cancellation came to the fore. The Fancourt Declaration, agreed at the 1999 CHOGM in Durban, identified the need for poverty reduction and people-centred development: 'above all, we recognise the responsibilities of national governments to promote pro-poor policies and human development. If the poor and the vulnerable are to be at the centre of development, the process must be participatory' (Commonwealth Secretariat, 1999). However, there remained a blind spot about urbanisation and local level action. The Declaration stated, for example, 'Good governance requires inclusive and participatory processes at both national and international levels.' However, the 1997 Edinburgh CHOGM had included the first Commonwealth Youth Forum and a Commonwealth Centre for NGO presentations, which became the model for the Commonwealth People's Forum.

Twenty years after the 1989 report from the Group of Experts, the Commonwealth again produced a major statement on climate change (Commonwealth Secretariat, 2009). It noted that 'Science, and our own experience, tells us that we only have a few short years to address this threat.' Crafted ahead of Conference of Partners (COP) 15 in Copenhagen, it argued that the global reach of the Commonwealth could 'help forge the inclusive global solutions needed to combat climate change.' However, COP15 was a failure: 'everyone talked; but no one really listened' (BBC, 2009).

In some other respects, the Commonwealth changed greatly in the 50 years after 1971. India's population increased from around 568 million in 1971 to 1.39 billion in 2021, making it by far the most populous Commonwealth country and dominating any data aggregated at Commonwealth level. After bitter struggles, white minority governments were displaced in southern Africa; though while SA re-joined the Commonwealth, Zimbabwe withdrew in 2003. Mozambique and Rwanda, neither of them former UK colonies, joined. By 2021, there were 54 member states, 22 more than in 1971 (Togo and Gabon also joined in 2022). Thirty-two of the world's forty-two small states had become members, many of them facing unprecedented challenges from the climate emergency but also in terms of development and urbanisation (See Box 2.1). While London remains the hub, the direction of change must be towards the other members and their regional groupings and networks.

The murder of George Floyd by a white police officer in Minneapolis in 2020 was followed by a new international level of recognition that 'Black Lives Matter.' The history of slavery and colonialism, which too often had been glossed over, became a live issue. The enduring legacy of inequality and racism became a focus for understanding the relationships between people and between countries. Calls for reparations gained momentum: the abolition of slavery had compensated slave

> **BOX 2.1 THE NEED FOR SUSTAINABLE URBANISATION IN THE COMMONWEALTH: THE SOLOMON ISLANDS.**
>
> The Solomon Islands is an archipelago of almost 997 islands in 9 main island groups. In the 19th century the islands were colonised by the UK and by Germany, though by 1899 all the main island groups were a UK protectorate. Internal self-government was granted in 1976, followed by independence two years later, at which point the Solomon Islands joined the Commonwealth. In 1971 the total urban population at 14,885 was less than 10% of the total population. By 2021 the Solomon Islands were still predominantly rural, but the urban population was 176,900, roughly one in four. The annual growth rate of the urban population has never been less than 4% over those 50 years. The country is very vulnerable to climate change: the majority live less than 1.5km from the coast; it is in the cyclone zone and extreme rainfall is common.
>
> Source: World Bank (2022).

owners, not enslaved people. In the Caribbean and the UK the 'Windrush scandal' in 2017 had also exposed the enduring institutional racism that hundreds of Commonwealth citizens had suffered after migrating to the UK. They had been detained, deported and denied legal rights, as the Home Office required them to prove they had UK residency before 1973. In other 'white' Commonwealth countries, the long campaigns for rights by indigenous and native peoples had started to gain traction from the 1990s onwards, though often slowly and in the face of opposition.

As even this brief history shows, the transition within the Commonwealth since 1971 has seen increasing concerns about economic disparities, human rights, equity and the impacts of climate change. This reflects the increased presence of low income and transition countries and small island states amongst the membership. The role of civil society and professional organisations has been recognised also, but to a significant degree the Commonwealth remains primarily an inter-governmental body, focused on relations between national level governments. Seen from the perspective of civil servants in Foreign Ministries, planning is a purely local level concern; even urbanisation is not seen as having the kind of far reaching significance accorded to trade, health, education, gender equality, democracy or the catch-all concept of 'development'. This lacuna is a significant aspect of the context in which CAP has operated and continues to be so.

Human settlements and planning 1971–2021

In 1971, Mumbai was still Bombay, with a population of about 6.5M, which was less than that of London. By 2021, Mumbai was one of the world's megacities, home to over 20M, the population having doubled since 1991 and now boasting more than twice the population of London. Much of the growth was due to migration from elsewhere in India. The city/metropolitan region had changed from a classic colonial seaport city with textile mills to a financial capital, home to Bollywood and high technology businesses and a leading centre in renewable technologies. Some 9M Mumbai residents live in slums. Around a million of them are in Dharavi, the second largest slum in Asia, behind only Orangi in Karachi, Pakistan, another Commonwealth country (World Population Review, 2023).

Mumbai illustrates a story of Commonwealth urbanisation over half a century. Urbanisation has been rapid and megacities have grown, with much of the growth being slum led rather than planned, while intra-urban inequalities have increased (see Photos 2.1, 2.2, 2.3 and 2.4). Intermediate cities have also grown dramatically across the Commonwealth during this period. To give just one example, according to the World Population Review website, the Malaysian city of Seremban had a population of around 100,000 in 1971 but 5 times that by 2022. Similarly, urban growth has been not only a phenomenon of large countries. World Bank data indicates that only 7,500 people are classed as urban residents in Tuvalu, but they amount to almost two-thirds of the population, whereas in 1971 less than a quarter of this small island state's people were urban.

The Commonwealth's urban transition will continue in the coming decades, as Chapter 10 explains. Table 2.1 reveals a simple but critical point about the form that this transition is taking in relation to sustainable urbanisation. The data used to compile the table is not available for all Commonwealth countries, but Table 2.1 reveals that in all the seven countries selected the proportion of urban households living in slums had reduced quite substantially between 1990 and 2018. This indicates

PHOTO 2.1 Informal settlement, Kibera, Nairobi, Kenya. Kibera is thought to be the largest slum in Africa. The photo shows only a small area. About 60% of Nairobi's population are slum dwellers, occupying some 6% of the city's land.

Source: Cliff Hague

PHOTO 2.2 Informal urbanisation, Kibera, Nairobi, Kenya. Some of the new residents of the informal housing under construction. One reason why the Commonwealth is rapidly urbanising and will continue to do so is because it has a young population – more than 60% of Commonwealth citizens are under 30.

Source: Cliff Hague

PHOTO 2.3 Informal hotel: Kibera, Nairobi, Kenya. Informal settlements typically contain a wide range of small businesses and local services that sustain livelihoods. Demolitions and forced evictions can destroy these.

Source: Cliff Hague

PHOTO 2.4 Informal business district, Dhobi Ghat, Mumbai, India. This traditional open-air laundry district in the south of Mumbai soaks, washes, dries and presses garments from a wide catchment. It employs around 200 families. As Mumbai has grown and globalised, Dhobi Ghat has become a site for international tourism. Modern high buildings are being developed nearby.

Source: Christine Platt

TABLE 2.1 Urban households living in slums, 1990–2018 in selected Commonwealth countries.

Country	% of urban households living in slums 1990	% of urban households living in slums 2018	Urban population living in slums 1990 (Thousands)	Urban population living in slums 2018 (Thousands)
Bangladesh	87.3	47.6	18,366	29,025
Ghana	65.5	25.2	3,490	4,826
Kenya	54.9	46.1	2,151	6,354
India	54.9	34.8	122,141	160,330
Pakistan	51	38	16,792	27,954
South Africa	46.2	26.4	9,030	10,059
Uganda	75	46	1,449	4,838

Source: UN Habitat (2021).

progress towards sustainable urbanisation. However, in each case the actual numbers living in slums, hence the extent of slum areas, has increased. Comparing the proportions and the absolute numbers also suggests that inequalities within the cities have widened. The scale of the challenge facing planners striving for sustainable urbanisation has become greater, not less. This duality – progress and setback at the same time – is due to the dramatic increase in the urban population as a whole in each of the countries. Furthermore, the data begs questions about the comparative performance of countries. On this very limited data, Ghana appears to have done better than any of the other six; India is much larger than Kenya but also seems to have done relatively better in relation to slums (though the absolute numbers in India's slums are overwhelming). If the Commonwealth had taken urbanisation seriously, it would have probed, compared and evaluated the dynamics of slum growth, through comparative analysis that could have built knowledge networks and inform policy and practice. In the 50 years from 1971, this was a significant missed opportunity that the 2022 Kigali Declaration could rectify.

In the early 1970s there was some international awareness, in and beyond the Commonwealth, of a growing environmental crisis. The 1972 UN Conference on the Human Environment was the first significant global event that made the environment its major focus. It was held in Stockholm, following an initiative by the Swedish government which made two fundamental points that bear repeating because of their continuing relevance, not least to the Commonwealth. The Swedes argued that 'changes in the natural surroundings, brought about by man, had become an urgent problem for developed as well as developing countries, and that these problems could only be solved through international co-operation' (UN, 2012).

The world was industrialising, and pollution and resource depletion were the dominant concerns. However, Principle 15 (out of the 26 agreed at the summit) stated that

> Planning must be applied to human settlements and urbanization with a view to avoiding adverse effects on the environment and obtaining maximum social,

economic and environmental benefits for all. In this respect, projects which are designed for colonialist and racist domination must be abandoned.

(UN, 1973)

Thus, the role of planning was recognised internationally and defined, albeit in very general terms, in an integrative and comprehensive manner. It is also important to note that there was recognition that planning could also be used for oppressive purposes, an ugly truth that many professional planners find hard to confront. In the decades that followed 1971, the Commonwealth, like the rest of the world, struggled to find a way to enjoy the benefits of economic growth without putting the global environment at risk.

Stockholm paved the way for Habitat I, the first UN Conference on Human Settlements, held in Vancouver, Canada in 1976. The Declaration highlighted adequate shelter and services as a basic human right (UN, 1976, p. 7). It recognised that the problems of human settlements 'cannot be set apart from existing unjust international economic relations' (p. 2), which is again a message that should resonate amongst Commonwealth planners today. Similarly, it recognised that 'The goals of settlement policies are inseparable from the goals of every sector of social and economic life' (p. 4). The Declaration set 'Guidelines for Action'. These scoped the architecture of a plan-led approach to urban and regional development, including:

- 'Spatial strategy plans and human settlements policies' to guide social and economic development.
- 'Discouragement of excessive consumption' for 'social justice and a fair sharing of resources'.
- 'The increase in the value of land as a result of public decision and investment should be recaptured for the benefit of society as a whole'.
- 'Implementation of conservation and recycling technologies'.
- Public participation.
- Taking account of the impacts of development on women.
- Being 'led by public sector action . . . with priority to the most deprived'.

BOX 2.2   VIEW ON URBAN-RURAL DISPARITIES AT HABITAT I, 1976.

It is of paramount importance that national and international efforts give priority to improving the rural habitat. In this context, efforts should be made towards the reduction of disparities between rural and urban areas, and as needed between regions and within urban areas themselves, for a harmonious development of human settlements.

Vancouver Declaration, 1976

Source: United Nations (1976), pp. 6–7.

Necessarily this is a selective summary, but it is not a distortion of the thrust of the Declaration. Habitat I strongly endorsed a planned, redistributive and environmentally informed approach to planning (see Box 2.2). It also led to the formation of the UN's Centre for Human Settlements in 1978, which became UN-Habitat in 2002 with enhanced status within the UN system. However, with hindsight it is startlingly clear that, with the possible exception of public participation, the bullet points listed earlier were not delivered. Indeed they were inverted. Spatial plans did not guide economic development; excessive consumption was encouraged and tolerated by planning systems; land value increase remained captured by land owners; conservation remained a marginal concern within planning systems focused on facilitating new development; gender was not mainstreamed in planning practice.

Environmental concern increased in the 1980s and 1990s. The World Commission on Environment and Development was given a brief by the UN to come up with environmental strategies that would achieve 'sustainable development by the year 2000 and beyond' (Brundtland, 1987). The landmark report put the idea of sustainable development – if not the practice – on the international agenda. It fed directly into the UN Conference on Environment and Development of 1992 (20 years after Stockholm). This 'Earth Summit' adopted Agenda 21 (United Nations, 1993) as a comprehensive action plan, which importantly recognised the need for action at local level. However, 'urbanisation' was only mentioned five times in Agenda 21. Urban planning was discussed particularly in relation to pre- and post-disaster planning and to better integration with transport planning. Despite calls for integration, much of the text worked around a sector-based planning approach. While paragraph 10.7 called for revisions to 'planning and management systems to facilitate an integrated approach', 10.7(c) urged governments to 'Establish a general framework for land-use and physical planning within which specialized and more detailed sectoral plans (e.g., for protected areas, agriculture, forests, human settlements, rural development) can be developed'.

The 1992 Earth Summit also began to reveal some of the international fault lines that would bedevil attempts to reach agreements over the following decades. Put simply, richer countries were perceived to be urging poorer countries to prioritise environment over development to 'save the planet,' while having themselves been the chief beneficiaries of the economic system that had stoked the crisis. Also, as Brundtland recognised, there had been significant shifts in the ambience and practices of global politics (see Box 2.3). Scientists and professionals were delivering messages that politicians found uncomfortable and which were often unpopular. In addition, the Washington Consensus, driven by the IMF and the World Bank, pressed countries to adopt de-regulation, privatisation and full cost recovery so as to repay their debts.

Almost half of the world's people were living in cities by Habitat II in 1996 in Istanbul. The main themes were adequate shelter for all and sustainable human settlements. There was recognition of the challenges of metropolitan regions and plenty of endorsements for public participation and (again) the need for integration. While the Declaration (UN, 1996) made reference to 'inadequate planning' it

BOX 2.3 A RETREAT FROM SOCIAL CONCERNS IN THE 1980S.

The present decade has been marked by a retreat from social concerns. Scientists bring to our attention urgent but complex problems bearing on our very survival: a warming globe, threats to the Earth's ozone layer, deserts consuming agricultural land. We respond by demanding more details, and by assigning the problems to institutions ill-equipped to cope with them. Environmental degradation, first seen as mainly a problem of the rich nations and a side effect of industrial wealth, has become a survival issue for developing nations. It is part of the downward spiral of linked ecological and economic decline in which many of the poorest nations are trapped.

Chairman's Forward, Brundtland Report

Source: Brundtland (1987).

BOX 2.4 THE FORGING OF THE NEW URBAN AGENDA.

A range of forces led to the NUA: the tip-over to a world where a majority live in cities; the recognition of the economic significance of cities, and the potential of urbanisation to lift people out of poverty; the climate emergency and extreme weather events (e.g. Hurricane Katrina in New Orleans); fear of cities as incubators of political violence. Within the UN, China and the G77 group of less rich countries pushed to connect environmental actions to issues around poverty.

Hague, 2021, p. 680.

never really focused on how planning could engage with the surge of urbanisation. Planning was not mentioned in the section of commitments to adequate shelter for all and only three times in the equivalent section on sustainable human settlements (once in relation to water planning and another in respect to disasters).

Similarly, urbanisation and planning did not feature prominently in the MDGs. Target 7D was to achieve significant improvement in the lives of 100 million slum dwellers by 2020. This was relatively easy to achieve but missed the more fundamental point that the rate of new slum formation meant that the total number of slum dwellers increased significantly over the 15 year lifespan of the goals. The dynamics of urbanisation and the role of planning had not been grasped.

In the new millennium a concerted attempt was made to get the international community to realise the centrality of urban development to sustainable development. As later chapters show, CAP played a key role, though not the only one (see Box 2.4). There was a successful campaign for an 'Urban Goal' in the 2016–2030

Sustainable Development Goals (SDGs) and a strong endorsement in the New Urban Agenda (NUA) for the role of planning. In addition, UN Habitat produced International Guidelines which emphasised that urban and territorial planning 'is more than a technical tool, it is an integrative and participatory decision-making process' (UN-Habitat, 2015, p. 8).

In summary, during the first 50 years of CAP's existence, the priority attached by the global community to planning waxed and waned. The 1970s saw human settlements issues recognised for the first time as a global concern, with strong support for a plan-led approach. This was aided by a new recognition of a growing environmental crisis. That crisis has got steadily worse in the following decades, despite the widespread support in principle for sustainable development. Similarly, the 'middle ages' of CAP's first 50 years saw a dramatic growth of urban areas across the globe alongside a diminution of the role accorded to planning as deregulation drove economic thinking and practice. However, by the second decade of the new millennium it was clear that the development trajectory was bringing the earth towards a climate catastrophe and inequalities on a destabilising scale. Urbanisation was an essential part of the problem and of the solutions. The SDGs and the NUA represented a significant new approach but also a big challenge – re-invent planning.

The Commonwealth as an inter-governmental grouping did not exert a coherent influence on human settlements policy at the UN. As hinted earlier, issues of environment, development and climate often divided richer countries from countries still hampered by the legacies of colonialism and even slavery. Similarly, although the 1990s onwards saw significant urban growth in the 'old' Commonwealth, partly linked to international migration, the really high rates of urbanisation and of absolute urban poverty were in what became known as the 'Global South.' One consequence was that it took time and tragedies for the globally connected nature of our systems of environment and human settlements to be grasped by politicians and policy makers, including planners.

Fifty years of planning in Commonwealth countries

Planning practice is driven by national, provincial and local legislation and procedures. This reflects the diverse situations in different countries, but it also limits horizons and complicates international communications amongst professional planners. This section of the chapter sketches some key features of the development of planning in member countries during CAP's first five decades.

In 1971, planning was still a relatively new profession, with small numbers of qualified practitioners across the Commonwealth. Although the Canadian institute had been founded in 1919, and the Town and Country Planning Institute of Australia was formed in 1934, it was not until 1951 that a country-wide Australian organisation, the Royal Australian Planning Institute, formed, the same year as for the India institute and two years after NZ, while for Nigeria the year was 1966. Indeed, the report of the 1970 meeting to discuss the formation of CAP

(Town Planning Institute, 1970) recorded that planning institutes existed in only eight countries. Furthermore, few countries provided planning education, and typically these were in the 'old' Commonwealth. The RTPI had a significant reach: in several Commonwealth countries an RTPI qualification underpinned the formation of a national body of planners, while elsewhere planners were subsumed within the professional organisations of older construction professions.

For many practitioners, planning was a second qualification after architecture, engineering or surveying. Even the RTPI, formed in 1914, displayed some insecurity as a profession. In 1964–1965 there had been internal acrimony over whether planning should be a separate and distinct profession or open to membership of all persons making a professional contribution to planning. The 'separate profession' won the vote, but by 1971 there was further professional navel gazing, prompted by the rise of community participation, the new environmental awareness and the recognition voiced by that year's president, addressing the annual conference: 'Planning is a process which may be applied to many sets of circumstances, and is characterized by its analytical techniques, its synoptic concern for the total environment, its decision systems and its orientation towards problem-solving actions' Amos (1971, p. 305).

The early 1970s were turbulent years for planning across much of the Commonwealth. In many recently independent countries in particular there was an ambition to connect the colonial planning system to the new priorities of national development planning. Specifically 'physical planning' was sought as a complementary process to economic planning, connecting the background and practices of planners and planning in design and the construction professions to the emerging agendas of governments. However, the problems were elaborated in that CAP preparatory meeting in London (TPI, 1970):

> while economic planning had now been accepted by government authorities, physical planning had not so far been accepted. . . . Planning was not popular, and too often physical planning was related to controls and the suggestion of restrictions while economic planning always promised "results".

Political instability and outmoded legislation presented further obstacles. Acheampong (2018) described the situation in Ghana, which had echoes in other Commonwealth countries. Ghana's National Physical Development Plan (1963–1970) sought to integrate the physical, economic and social aspects of development and to set a framework for regional and local development plans. However, the government was overthrown in 1966 and a series of military governments followed. The planning system became 'virtually dormant' and unable to keep pace with urbanisation (p. 45). Legislation in 1994 created a system of 'Development Planning' mainly concerned with poverty reduction and economic development but weak on spatial aspects. This marginalised 'Land Use Planning' as a limited function concerned with producing layouts and operating development control.

However, in 2016 Ghana's colonial planning legislation dating from 1945 was finally replaced, and the concept of spatial planning was introduced. It was 'a deliberate attempt to institute a new tradition of integrated and multi-scale planning that delivers wider socio-economic and environmental development imperatives with the traditional design and regulatory function of town planning' (Acheampong, 2018, p. 50).

The experience of Ghana can stand as a broad depiction of the ways in which planning was reshaped across the Commonwealth during CAP's first 50 years. Planning legislation, procedures and presumptions were inherited from an earlier era. As the 1970s approached this largely meant that quite detailed land use plans were prepared on the basis of extensive surveys. These 'master plans' sought to direct the location and form of development for a period of 20 or more years. Orderly development and segregated land uses conforming to prescribed standards was the intention.

In the 'settler countries' of the Commonwealth, systems like this managed the spread of suburbs, making houses with gardens widely affordable, albeit with an urban form that was car/cheap oil dependent (see Photo 2.5). However, in other Commonwealth countries the master plans proved inappropriate to the challenges. They took too long to prepare, could not be enforced effectively, and set minimum

PHOTO 2.5 Density contrasts, Calgary, Canada. Planning has regulated the subdivision of land for suburban plots enabling development of low density suburbs and high density commercial and residential uses in the downtown area. This facilitated spacious and relatively affordable housing in suburbs but also car dependency because of the low densities.

Source: Cliff Hague

> **BOX 2.5 SLOW PLANS AND RAPID URBANISATION: THE 1966 LAHORE MASTER PLAN.**
>
> The 1966 Lahore Master Plan had a 25–30 year time horizon. It took two years to prepare but seven years to approve. Part One is a 70 page very detailed Survey and Analysis; Part Two is 66 pages of 'Planning Standards and Proposals.' Groote et al. (1989) laconically observed 'if anything can be called a blow by blow description, it is certainly this plan.' They further noted that 'The accent lies heavily on physical planning. . . . It is a static, pictorial plan. . . . No attention was given to implementation and coordination.' By 1981 around a quarter of Lahore residents were living in informal settlements known as Katchi Abadis.
>
> Source: Groote et al. (1989).

standards that were unaffordable for the poor. Planning systems rooted in legislation and in bureaucracies were ill equipped to cope with the rapid growth of informal urbanisation: see Box 2.5.

CAP was formed at a time when planning was being challenged. The early 1970s were marked by increasing unease about the universalist and modernist ideas that underpinned the theory and practice of planning. There was opposition to planned redevelopment from communities who were affected. New forms of environmental action emerged. Famously in Sydney building workers staged 'green bans.' refusing to work on developments (approved through the planning system) that they felt were environmentally or socially damaging, such as highway schemes that threatened affordable housing. Bedrock professional beliefs were becoming contested. In the deindustrialising UK, for example, the New Towns were criticised in the mid-1970s for having thrived at the expense of the inner cities, by attracting jobs and skilled workers (see Photo 2.6), and the programme was wound down.

The 1980s saw some significant shifts in planning towards a market facilitating, 'entrepreneurial' approach. A de-regulatory spatial initiative, special economic zones, played a key part. Although they take many different forms, broadly speaking these are demarcated spaces in which more liberal tax and regulatory regimes apply. They are usually equipped with infrastructure to support development of an industrial park or mixed use development. Backed by the World Bank, they were also seen as ways to open economies and drive economic reform. By the early 1970s many former colonies were industrialising and saw such zones as a means to attract investment. India had established an export processing zone at Kandla in 1965, and Malaysia, Singapore and Sri Lanka took similar initiatives in the early 1970s. Such ventures had far reaching effects: Malaysia's Penang Island zone recorded annual growth rates of over 13% in the 1970s and created the basis for the country's electronics industry.

In such places a new international division of labour was triggered and with it the rapid growth of cities but also the decline of previous manufacturing centres in Europe

PHOTO 2.6 Early New Town Housing: East Kilbride, Scotland. The New Towns built in the UK in the mid-20th century provided attractive and affordable living environments through public land acquisition and planning. However, an unintended consequence of their success was that they attracted jobs and skilled workers from older cities and so increased problems there. East Kilbride, near Glasgow, was particularly successful.

Source: Cliff Hague

and North America. With this came profound implications for planning in the Commonwealth. Systems that had been predicated on achieving orderly management of relatively slow urban growth were not well adjusted to the new realities. Plans were outdated, irrelevant and sidelined. Furthermore, planning as a form of public sector regulation was in a newly hostile political climate. A tension that had been latent in planning earlier in the twentieth century was now raw, between a redistributive, market-directing view of planning and a more adaptive and facilitating approach that relied on decisions by private investors to implement a plan. 'Regeneration' of older urban areas (see Photos 2.7, 2.8 and 2.9) sought to restore market confidence, for example, through direct and indirect subsidies to developers (e.g. through land assembly and remediation). While exciting designs were often created and young professionals were attracted to higher density city living, regeneration was often accompanied by gentrification and displacement of traditional sources of employment. Planners' employers, skill sets and outlooks changed; projects superseded plans.

The 1980s also were marked by growing critiques of planning in relation to gender and ethnicity. Initially these were more vocal in planning education; a generation

Pointing a path to sustainable urbanisation 41

PHOTO 2.7 Waterfront regeneration, Vancouver, Canada. Vancouver has capitalised on its waterfront assets offering spectacular views through extensive high density regeneration of brownfield sites, with high quality landscaping and good pedestrian routes.

Source: Christine Platt

PHOTO 2.8 Regeneration of former docks, Salford Quays, England. The Manchester Ship Canal was opened in 1894 bringing trans-Atlantic ships into Manchester (one dock was called the Ontario Basin). The docks closed in 1982 as containerisation altered shipping patterns. The Salford part of the docks became the focus for a major mixed-use regeneration project.

Source: Colin Wood

PHOTO 2.9 Media City, Salford Quays, England. The BBC decentralised part of its activity from London to Salford and other media companies have set up in Salford Quays, bringing jobs and opportunities, theatre, cafes and restaurants. Culture has been a driver of regeneration in several de-industrialised British cities.

Source: Colin Wood

of mainly white, male senior practitioners who saw planning as a technical process treating everyone equally struggled to grasp the idea that treating everyone the same, when their needs differed, could be unfair. In the decades that followed, there was also a notable shift in planning in New Zealand, Canada and Australia, for example, to recognise and begin to redress the historic wrongs that had been done to indigenous peoples. Previously, as Johnson et al. (2017) observed, there had been scant interest amongst planners in Indigenous land rights (see Box 2.6).

BOX 2.6 CUSTOMARY LAND TENURE, URBANISATION AND PLANNING: PAPUA NEW GUINEA.

In Papua New Guinea, 97% of the land is held in customary land tenure, the system that existed before colonisers arrived in the early 1800s. Such land is owned by tribes, clans and similar groups, with rights enshrined in local customs and beliefs. Customary land is sacred, not a commodity, rather it connects past, present and future generations. The Physical Planning Act (1989) extended planning over the whole territory. There are conflicts over

> the spread of urban development, with informal settlements accounting for much of the growth. In 2020 only around 13% of the population was urban, but the urban population was increasing at about 2.7% a year, and the rate was on an upwards trajectory and exceeding the national average rate of population increase. Rural to urban migration was a factor. 'Due to the absence of key urban policies such as land use planning and housing, lack of capacity, poor management, and dysfunctional governance structures, all levels of government have become major stumbling blocks to development in Papua New Guinea'.
>
> Source: Pyati (2022).

The deep involvement of 'settler' planning systems with land use continues to bring planners directly into contact, sometimes conflict, with attempts by Indigenous peoples to regain their territorial and political rights (Porter and Barry, 2018). As CAP approached its fiftieth anniversary its Outstanding Practice Awards demonstrated that there was at least some recognition that land justice requires a decolonised form of planning practice, going beyond consultation and according Indigenous people a leading role in determining what development should happen and how.

Cultural understanding and representation of diversity within the profession have come increasingly to the fore in the 21st century. The ending of apartheid saw necessary and dramatic changes in South Africa, demonstrating that change of planning systems does not need to be incremental. Let there be no doubt, town planning was an essential means of delivering apartheid. At every scale, spatial segregation on the basis of race was planned. Dormitory townships for non-whites were separated by green belts, known locally and more accurately as 'buffer zones'. For some planners the narrative of planning as a technical design process obfuscated the ethical issues, but other planners had been active in resistance. Thus when the regime crumbled there was informed professional momentum for a transformation of planning practice.

In 1996 South Africa instituted a system of Integrated Development Plans (IDPs). In rural areas in particular there had been a void in local government, and the IDPs were designed to be a quick, inclusive means to build a vision and align a range of services behind it. Part of the role of an IDP is to provide a land use management system guided by a spatial development framework. In addition South Africa has produced a number of national-scale spatial development frameworks (Oranje and Merrifield, 2010; Republic of South Africa, 2018), which, for example, set out development corridors, most notably the trans-continental Maputo-Pretoria-Gaborone-Walvis Bay Corridor. South Africa also introduced new planning legislation in 2013.

The South African experience has demonstrated some important points for planning across the Commonwealth. Sadly, it shows just how difficult it is to eradicate deep-rooted inequalities – between people and between places. Infrastructure and development last for decades and shape the spatial pattern of future investment. Economically marginalised communities in spatially marginalised locations provide a deep and long-lasting challenge, both for public transport and also for micro-scale business development. In addition, it is clear that spatial integration of sector investments will only happen if there is high-level political support and institutional arrangements.

Rediscovery and change

The Commonwealth changed during CAP's first 50 years. The increase in members meant that although many countries were still predominantly rural, urbanisation was a common theme. However, for much of the period in many countries, policy makers saw urban and rural as opposites and prioritised rural development as the best means to tackle poverty. The connection made at Vancouver in 1976 between the problems of human settlements and 'unjust international economic relations' was not taken forward at CHOGMs. Rather, for 30 years or so, the international implications of the concentration of vast numbers of poor people in urban areas were not addressed. Even when the MDGs put slums on the global agenda, there was still a wide perception that urbanisation was a national/local matter.

Similarly, across most of the Commonwealth, only incremental updates were made to colonial era planning legislation, thereby marginalising the practice. Planning legislation was even used to evict the poor from unauthorised developments, most notoriously in the case of Zimbabwe in 2005 where Operation Murambatsvina/Restore Order resulted in the forced eviction of some 700,000 poor people, in the name of cleaning up 'filth' (Kamete, 2007). While informality – and also street vending – are crucial to the livelihoods of the urban poor, they remain a major conceptual and practical challenge for many planners. However, there are some positive signs, for example the planning programme at the University of Zambia has students working on live projects with slum dwellers through a partnership with Slum/Shack Dwellers International (Siame, 2016).

Over the 50 years, even the countries that were already highly urbanised experienced a spread of urban areas that outstripped the rate of urban demographic growth. East Asian countries that embraced planning as a means of driving development achieved significant economic benefits (see Photos 2.10, 2.11 and 2.12). As climate change finally came to be recognised as an issue, planners worked to increase urban densities and find ways to promote active travel and public transport.

By the early 2020s there were some signs that the climate emergency, the COVID pandemic and international migration were underlining the need for international

PHOTO 2.10 Strategic Planning to drive development: Putrajaya, Malaysia. Putrajaya was planned as Malaysia's Administrative Centre 20 kms south of Kuala Lumpur. The original plan from 1995 has been adapted. Along with its neighbour city Cyberjaya and the Multimedia Super Corridor, it is designed to be a 'green' city that drives innovation. Incorporating the principles of sustainable urbanisation, with extensive open space, water and wetlands, it provides a good environment for its residents and workers.

Source: Perbadanan Putrjaya and Miss Salliza Salleh

cooperation. One consequence was to push planners across the Commonwealth to reconnect their profession with concerns for public health and the shared public realm. The importance of free access to open space and the value of trees was increasingly recognised. Design skills, which in some countries had atrophied, saw a revival. However, urban design now had to be sensitive to women's safety, the needs of children, disabled people and the creation of dementia-friendly environments. 'Place-making' became a new defining task, a distancing from the regulatory 'planning' regimes that still defined much practice. The edges and interfaces of the planning profession became fertile ground for new ideas and practices, encompassing for example digital collaborations or maritime spatial planning or forms of tactical urbanism.

Through the 50 years CAP had been a beacon for planning and the planning profession in the Commonwealth. It reached out to support the many small

PHOTO 2.11 Long-term planning for a Global City, Singapore. Singapore's dynamic growth has entailed long-term planning. The first 'Concept Plan' was produced in 1971. It was reviewed in 1991, where the vision for Singapore evolved from meeting basic needs to creating development corridors and a hierarchy of commercial centres to facilitate high tech growth and bring jobs closer to homes and alleviate congestion in the city centre. The 2001 iteration of the plan sought to transform Singapore into a global financial hub by setting aside land in the city centre to support the growth of financial and services sectors. More recent versions emphasised affordable housing, greenery and a good living environment.

Source: Clive Harridge

Commonwealth countries where there are few planners but great need. In the 21st century CAP played a considerable role in the recovery of the idea that planning matters, for people, places and the planet. 'No sustainable development without sustainable urbanisation, and no sustainable urbanisation without effective planning' became the strapline. However, a hard road still lies ahead, to make Commonwealth human settlements safe, inclusive, equitable and genuinely resilient places.

PHOTO 2.12 Singapore Housing and Development Board, The Pinnacle@Duxton, Singapore. Planning and development of high density housing, including in New Towns, with good public transport connections, has been central to Singapore's post-independence growth. The Pinnacle@Duxton dates from 2009, is a 50 storey residential development in the city centre and includes two 500 metre-long sky gardens.

Source: Christine Platt

References

Acheampong, R.A. (2018), *Spatial Planning in Ghana: Origins, Contemporary Reforms and Practices, and New Perspectives,* New York: Springer.

Amos, F.J.C. (1971), 'The Development of the Planning Process', *Journal of the Royal Town Planning Institute,* 57 (7), pp. 304–308.

BBC. (2009), *Why did Copenhagen Fail To Deliver a Climate Deal?* Available at http://news.bbc.co.uk/1/hi/8426835.stm (Accessed 14 January 2022).

Brundtland, G. (1987), *Report of the World Commission on Environment and Development: Our Common Future,* New York: United Nations General Assembly document A/42/427. Available at www.un-documents.net/wced-ocf.htm (Accessed 22 August 2022).

Commonwealth Group of Experts. (1989), *Climate Change: Meeting the Challenge,* London: Commonwealth Secretariat, Available at https://thecommonwealth.org/sites/default/files/inline/9781848594579_1.pdf (Accessed 11 January 2022).

Commonwealth Secretariat. (1999), *Fancourt Declaration on Globalisation and People-Centred Development*, Available at https://thecommonwealth.org/fancourt-declaration-globalisation-and-people-centred-development (Accessed 14 January 2022).

Commonwealth Secretariat. (2004), *Singapore Declaration of Commonwealth Principles 1971*, London: Commonwealth Secretariat, Available at https://thecommonwealth.org/sites/default/files/history-items/documents/Singapore%20Declaration.pdf (Accessed 6 January 2022).

Commonwealth Secretariat. (2009), *The Commonwealth Climate Change Declaration*, Available at https://thecommonwealth.org/commonwealth-climate-change-declaration (Accessed 14 January 2022).

Commonwealth Secretariat. (2016), *From the Archive: The Birth of the Commonwealth Fund for Technical Co-operation*, Available at https://thecommonwealth.org/media/news/archive-birth-commonwealth-fund-technical-co-operation (Accessed 11 January 2022).

Groote, P., de Jonge, R., Dekker, J.B.R. and de Vries, J. (1989), 'Urban Planning in Lahore: A Confrontation with Real Development', *Onderzoeksverslagen*, 30, https://doi.org/10.13140/2.1.1963.1683

Hague, C. (2021), 'Do Planners Want to Lead the New Urban Agenda or are They Being Led by it?' *Town Planning Review*, 92 (6), pp. 677–685, https://doi.org/10.3828/tpr.2021.30

Johnson, L., Porter, L. and Jackson, S. (2017), 'Reframing and Revising Australia's Planning History and Practice', *Australian Planner*, 54 (5), pp. 225–233, https://doi.org/10.1080/07293682.2018.1477813

Kamete, A.Y. (2007), 'Cold-Hearted, Negligent and Spineless? Planning, Planners and the (R)Ejection of "Filth" in Urban Zimbabwe', *International Planning Studies*, 12 (2), pp. 153–171, https://doi.org/10.1080/13563470701477959

Oranje, M. and Merrifield, A. (2010), 'National Spatial Development Planning in South Africa, 1930–2010: An Introductory Comparative Analysis', *Town and Regional Planning*, 56, pp. 29–45.

Porter, L. and Barry, J. (2018), *Planning for Coexistence? Recognizing Indigenous Rights through Land Use Planning in Canada and Australia*, London: Routledge.

Pyati, V. (2022), *UN Habitat in Papua New Guinea: Country Information*, Available at https://unhabitat.org/papua-new-guinea (Accessed 15 April 2022).

Republic of South Africa. (2018), *Draft National Spatial Development Framework*, Pretoria: Department of Rural Development and Land Reform and Department of Planning, Monitoring and Evaluation, Available at www.gov.za/documents/national-spatial-development-framework-draft-30-apr-2019-0000 (Accessed 14 April 2022).

Siame, G. (2016), 'The Value and Dynamics of Community-Based Studio Projects in Planning Education in the Global South', *Berkeley Planning Journal*, 28 (1), pp. 40–67, https://doi.org/10.5070/BP328133858

Town Planning Institute. (1970), *Report of a Meeting to Discuss the Formation of a Commonwealth Association of Planners held in London from 21st to 24th September 1970*, London: Town Planning Institute.

UN-Habitat. (2015), *International Guidelines on Urban and Territorial Planning*, Nairobi: UN-Habitat.

UN-Habitat. (2021), *Urban Data Site – Proportion of Urban Population Living in Slum Households by Country or Area 1990–2018 (Percent)*, Available at https://data.unhabitat.org/datasets/GUO-UN-Habitat:proportion-of-urban-population-living-in-slum-households-by-country-or-area-1990–2018-percent/explore (Accessed 22 August 2022).

United Nations. (1973), *Report of the United Nations Conference on the Human Environment, Stockholm 5–16 June 1972*, New York: United Nations, Available at https://digitallibrary.un.org/record/523249?ln=en (Accessed 22 August 2022).

United Nations. (1976), *Report of Habitat: United Nations Conference on Human Settlements, Vancouver, 31 May – 7 June 1976,* New York: United Nations, Available at https://digitallibrary.un.org/record/793768?ln=en (Accessed 22 August 2022).

United Nations. (1993), *Agenda 21: Programme of Action for Sustainable Development, Rio Declaration on Environment and Development, Statement of Forest Principles: The Final Text of Agreements Negotiated by Governments at the United Nations Conference on Environment and Development (UNCED), 3–14 June 1992, Rio de Janeiro, Brazil,* New York: United Nations. Available at https://sustainabledevelopment.un.org/outcomedocuments/agenda21 (Accessed 22 August 2022).

United Nations. (1996), *Report of the United Nations Conference on Human Settlements (Habitat II), Istanbul, 3–14 June 1996,* A/CONF.165/14, New York: United Nations, Available at https://digitallibrary.un.org/record/222703?ln=en (Accessed 22 August 2022).

United Nations. (2012), *Declaration of the United Nations Conference on the Human Environment,* United Nations Audiovisual Library of International Law, Available at www.un.org/en/conferences/environment/stockholm1972 (Accessed 18 March 2022).

World Bank. (2022), *Urban Population – Solomon Islands,* Available at https://data.worldbank.org/indicator/SP.URB.TOTL?locations=SB (Accessed 19 August 2022).

World Population Review. (2023), *Mumbai Population 2023.* Available at https://worldpopulationreview.com/world-cities/mumbai-population (Accessed 9 February 2023).

3

1970–1988

Laying the foundations for a Commonwealth-wide Profession

Clive Harridge (with Peter Pun)

This chapter reviews the early years of CAP from its founding through to 1988 when Bill Robertson was elected president. Over this 20-year period, from the germ of an idea in the 1960s, CAP developed to be a major international planning organisation connecting professional planners across the world. This period was well before the term *sustainable urbanisation* was being used and the focus in CAP was on the establishment of international networks of planners and the building of the planning profession across the Commonwealth where in some parts planning was still a nascent activity.

The establishment of CAP

The impetus which led to the establishment of CAP began in the late 1960s against a background of growing international connectedness and an increasing number of Commonwealth countries making progress in achieving political independence; however, there were only four independent planning institutes in those countries (Rathbone, 1970, p. 9).

> When the invitation was received for Barbados to send a professional Town Planner to a meeting in London, there were only two qualified Town Planners in our Planning Department, the newly appointed Chief Town Planner, Luther Bourne, and myself.
>
> Richard Gill on the 1970 meeting to explore setting up CAP

The growing international dimension of the planning profession at the time was reflected in the United Kingdom's Town Planning Institute (TPI) having official branches in Malaysia, Rhodesia, Malawi, Singapore, Hong Kong and Ireland. In

DOI: 10.4324/9781003357933-5

addition, national planning organisations in Australia, India, South Africa and New Zealand were affiliated with the TPI. Most of these branches and organisations helped form the basis of CAP during the early years.

The idea to form an association bringing together planners from across the Commonwealth developed during the late 1960s led by the TPI, with Arthur Ling who was TPI president in 1968/1969 taking a key role. The inaugural meeting was held at the TPI in London in September 1970 and was attended by delegates from 19 Commonwealth countries, although Canada was a notable absentee. A draft Constitution was agreed and it was unanimously resolved that CAP would be formally established a year later in 1971, provided that a majority of the would-be member organisations had ratified the Constitution.

Richard Gill, a young planner at the time, represented Barbados at the 1970 meeting and has been involved in CAP affairs ever since. His recollections of the matters discussed at the meeting include the following which reflect many of the issues tacked by CAP in subsequent years and through to the present day:

> The need for professional and technical staffing, for appropriate legislation, additional educational institutions and improved mapping and information were discussed. Clearly CAP would have a significant role in encouraging the formation of professional organisations in Commonwealth countries and in the exchange of ideas and experience. We could not of course have foreseen the great impact of CAP internationally in more recent years through UN Habitat and otherwise.

This was followed by a meeting held in Accra in 1971 at which CAP was formally established and the Constitution agreed. This meant that for the first time town planners in Commonwealth countries had the means of being in touch with one another in an organised way. The formation of CAP was part of a wider trend in the Commonwealth with several other professional associations being established around this time.

The Constitution covered the objects of the Association, the conditions of membership and a range of administrative procedures. The Constitution provided CAP with a sound foundation giving it professional standing and an excellent basis for subsequent development and growth. In writing the Constitution, CAP showed great foresight, and despite many refinements being made over the years, the fundamental principles remain largely the same today including the objects of the Association which are summarised in Box 3.1.

The geographical spread of CAP members meant that it was not financially possible for members to meet often, and in recognition of this the Constitution provided for a 'Conference of Delegates' (all CAP members) to meet every four years at which the president and an executive committee would be elected. The four-year frequency was subsequently reduced to two years which continues through to the present day. As will be seen in the following chapters the name of the Conference of Delegates changed over the years and was variously known as the CAP Plenary and more recently as the CAP Business Meeting. The Executive

> **BOX 3.1   SUMMARY OF THE OBJECTS OF CAP IN THE FIRST CONSTITUTION (1971).**
>
> - To promote cooperation between members to achieve the most effective contribution of planners to the well-being of society and the creation of a satisfactory environment.
> - To encourage the establishment of professional planning societies in countries where none exist.
> - To maintain contact with planners in countries where their small numbers would not justify a separate association.
> - To encourage the development of planning education, research and standards with the aim of free movement of planners and reciprocity of qualifications.
> - To promote and sustain appropriate standards of professional conduct.
> - To promote the exchange of professional, education, research and technical information.
> - To promote collaboration between planners and other professions.
> - To encourage liaison and collaboration with Commonwealth and international bodies.
>
> Source: CAP Archives.

> **BOX 3.2   FOUNDING MEMBER COUNTRIES OF CAP.**
>
> - Africa Region: Ghana, Kenya, Nigeria, Sierra Leone.
> - Americas Region: Barbados, Bermuda, Jamaica.
> - South East Asia Region: Hong Kong, Malaysia, Singapore.
> - South West Asia Region: India.
> - Europe Region: United Kingdom.
> - South West Pacific: Australia, New Zealand.
>
> Source: CAP Archives.

Committee, which was expected to meet between Conferences of Delegates, was made up of representatives of members in six world regions, namely Africa, the Americas, South East Asia, South West Asia, Europe and the South West Pacific as shown in Box 3.2.

In days well before the internet and the use of telephone conference calls, meetings were only held face to face, which was both costly and time consuming. Looking back from our incredibly well-connected world in 2023 it is remarkable that CAP achieved so much in the years before the internet began to be widely used, which was around the year 2000 during Cliff Hague's Presidency.

CAP's first President was Arthur Ling who had been named as interim President at CAP's inaugural meeting. Ling served for two terms as CAP President (1970–1973 and then 1973–1976). His successor was A. Ligale from Kenya who held office until the next meeting which was in 1980.

Early priorities

Understandably, the meeting in London in 1970 concentrated on procedural matters: should a CAP be established, and if so what would it do and how would it be governed? However, some of these concerns had direct implications for development and equality. Delegates recognised that in many small Commonwealth countries there were very few planners, and 'effective means of professional organisation were lacking' (Rathbone, 1970, p. 7). If the proposed Association could help overcome this then it would reduce inequalities.

Beyond the actual numbers of professional planners there was a more profound challenge to be addressed. The report of the meeting records (p. 8) that economic planning had become widely accepted, but 'physical planning' had not been. However, the reasons underpinning this disregard do not appear to have been probed in any depth. There was recognition that physical planning tended to be seen as regulatory and restrictive, while 'economic planning always promised "results".' However, the remedy was seen as active promotion of physical planning to politicians, civil servants, other professionals and the public.

This acceptance of a shared mission, 'physical planning', was rather contradicted by strong recognition that planning education provided in the UK was 'not oriented to overseas problems' (p. 8), and neither was research. If the nature of urban and regional change was different 'overseas' might a more fundamental rethink about practice, as well as education, be required? Similarly, a high priority was attached to the 'training' of student planners, but there was agreement that study should be 'in depth' – in effect, that meant slow and expensive (and also, therefore, exclusionary). The prime aim was to bolster and grow the profession.

> A great deal of the discussion centred on the need to relate planning education to the needs of the countries concerned, rather than TPI standards which were not necessarily suited to developing countries.
>
> Rathbone (1970, p. 8)

It would be unfair to criticise that 1970 meeting for not engaging with the really fundamental questions of what kind of planning was needed in those 'developing countries,' what kind of planners were needed, and how they might be quickly and cheaply created. These might be matters that could be explored once an association had been formed. That concern about the relevance of the TPI education policy illustrates the transition that was taking place in the wider Commonwealth at the time, with newly independent countries growing in number and in voice.

The professional backgrounds of those participating in the meeting also give us an insight into the way they would have seen the scope and purpose of planning and the nature of professionalism. Of the 23 main delegates, at least 11 had qualifications in architecture. The two UK university planning programmes which were invited to attend, Edinburgh and Nottingham, were both represented by architect-planners. This reflected broadly the profile of the profession and of planning education at the time, although people from a social science background had become more numerous in planning and in planning schools over the previous decade.

CAPs survey of planning in the Commonwealth in the early 1970s

When CAP was formally established in 1971, planning was still considered in many parts of the Commonwealth as a relatively new profession. Whilst most national governments at the time recognised town planning in some form, in reality decisions on the ground in many Commonwealth countries were made on a pragmatic day-to-day basis with little or no reference to town planning as we would recognise it now. Nevertheless, as planning became more established there was growing recognition of the need for, and value of, effective planning and the contribution that national planning associations and international connectedness could make.

It was around the same time as CAP was established that town planning began to be seen as much more than the traditional physical planning of urban and rural areas that prevailed in many locations. Planning was based on three principles – social, economic and environmental, although environmental issues have grown considerably in more recent years especially in response to concerns around climate change.

One of the first activities undertaken by CAP was to undertake a survey of planning in the Commonwealth focussed on 27 countries and territories which responded to a survey questionnaire. The unpublished findings provide a unique and valuable snapshot of the state of the planning profession and the challenges it faced at the time. This was the first such survey of its kind and demonstrated the value of CAP as an organisation with the ability to carry out international research and to communicate in an effective way to planners across the Commonwealth.

The survey revealed the many challenges being faced by planners and the planning profession against a background of global trends such as world population growth, rural to urban migration, rapid urban development and the large scale expansion of informal settlements within and on the fringes of towns and cities. Box 3.3 sets out some of the challenges being experienced at the time as expressed by planners in their own words.

These vivid comments highlight important points. The lack of maps, so basic to any planning work, was identified by Barbados, Botswana, New Zealand, Sierra Leone and Swaziland. In addition, the lack of planners was also noted, together with

BOX 3.3   CHALLENGES FACED BY PLANNERS IN 1973 IN THEIR OWN WORDS.

Planning legislation has been enacted in all states, though progress has not been uniform. . . . More effective legislation is required in areas of re-development and for regional planning and metropolitan growth control, as are clearer expression and guidance at government level to planning authorities.

Australia

The sale of land has been almost on a world-wide basis and a considerable area has been subdivided and sold in all parts of the world . . . the premature allocation [use] of land to residential purposes pre-empts the use of this land for other purposes in the future, and the problem is of concern.

Bahamas

The public must learn to accept the need for planning and accord the professional planner more recognition. . . . The provision of detailed maps would be an asset.

Barbados

There is already some control of the use of the environment, but coordination of all aspects of planning, economic, spatial and social, needs to be encouraged.

Bermuda

There is little idea of the meaning of Planning among the people. In consequence the priority given to planning is not high. . . . New legislation, more planners, better maps and surveys are needed.

Botswana

Publicity is required to impress upon the people the need for and value of planning.

Cyprus

The knowledge of planning among the general population (and education in it) is virtually non-existent at present.

Fiji

The existing planning legislation was redrafted in 1965, but because of changes of government, the old legislation, enacted in 1945, has continued in force.

Ghana

There is little public participation in the planning process, and it is unlikely that impetus will come from the general public because of the special conditions in Hong Kong.

Hong Kong

Legislation is not yet adequate to promote and regulate physical planning at the three levels, national, state and local.

India

The priority is for more qualified African planners and also the control of the increasing development of shanty towns in and around major towns.

Kenya

Priority is being given to urban centres particularly the re-planning of Blantyre and the planning of Liwonde and Msusu; a survey in the Northern Region and a social survey of traditional housing areas. Work has not infrequently been held up by lack of suitable maps.

Malawi

New legislation appears to be required. . . . It is considered that, at least, 200 new planners are required to meet increasing needs in relation to the population.

Malaysia

There are only three planners working in Malta.

Malta

The [planning] legislation has been useful in exercising some direction and control of urban development, but there remains a problem of ribbon development and communication.

Mauritius

The problems of planning in New Zealand have features in common with other countries eg need for improved legislation, more planners, better maps.

New Zealand

The urgent priorities are more middle level planners, revision of legislation and more comprehensive maps.

Sierra Leone

> With the completion of the long-range Concept Plan (for a population of 4 million to be reached by the 21st century) and the Central Area Sub-Project, current planning activity is mainly focussed on local planning.
>
> Singapore
>
> There is a lack of awareness of the value and need for physical planning.... Up to date mapping is badly needed.
>
> Swaziland
>
> All local planning authorities must prepare plans ... but the strain caused by such things as increase in population, motor traffic and demand for better housing has made it necessary to introduce new development procedures – to reduce administrative delays, emphasise positive planning ... and involve the public more.
>
> United Kingdom
>
> Meanwhile, the population of the towns grows rapidly and is difficult to control. Distribution of public and private services favours urban areas.
>
> Zambia
>
> Source: CAP Archives.

inappropriate legislation. The combination constituted a major obstacle to effective planning across significant parts of the then Commonwealth. The commitment of planners practising under such conditions can only be admired.

Another theme that emerges is the lack of understanding of planning amongst the public. Given the limitations described in the previous paragraph, this should be no surprise. However, it is also a reflection of two interrelated and significant factors. The legacy of colonial planning had made little impact on most of the population, and most of the population did not see planning as a means to improving their access to shelter, health and a good environment. Thus, there was both a lack of a secure platform on which to build planning and a need to create a different type of planning practice that was relevant to the situation in what were the 'developing countries.'

Reinforcing the need to change planning systems was recognition that urban development itself was changing. The flow of international speculative investment into land in Bermuda was effectively shaping the use of land and extraction of resources. Australia recognised the emergence of growth at metropolitan scale. Kenya mentioned the growth of 'shanty towns'; it is surprising that informal housing was not referenced more widely.

Singapore's response made reference to the Concept Plan and the Central Area Sub-Project. These were landmarks pointing the way to a significant departure from the colonial planning tradition and towards an innovative form of planning practice that would make a major contribution to the city state's astounding economic growth in the following decades. A Preliminary Island Plan had been produced in 1955, rooted in British practice and assuming slow, managed growth. It formed the basis for the 1958 Master Plan, a statutory document. However, in 1967 a partnership with UNDP led to the preparation of the Concept Plan, which was adopted in 1971.

> Singapore's path was paved 50 years ago with clear intentions and ambitions. The direction of Singapore's progress and development was charted early on, allowing key action programmes to be identified and swiftly carried out: eradicate poverty; provide safe and permanent housing for the masses; revitalise the city centre; and inject new economic opportunities that would simultaneously create jobs and raise the employment rate.
>
> Choe (2016, p. 19)

The Concept Plan marked a significant break not just with what had gone before but also with much of the planning then on-going in CAP member countries. It was growth-oriented and strategic. It integrated land use and transport, safeguarding land for essential transport infrastructure. New towns were planned at nodes in the transport network – high density residential areas with commercial centres, industrial estates and greenspace. An east-west growth corridor was planned along the southern coast, connecting the airport, the city centre and major industrial estates. The Central Area was identified for urban renewal, commercial expansion and the intersection of the metro lines. Construction of public housing was a key part of the implementation. The 1966 Land Acquisition Act allowed government to acquire private land at market value to support major national developments, making possible the transformation of the central area, where the public sector assembled land and provided incentives to attract private developers and investors. In Singapore, by the early 1970s, planning, social housing and economic development were intertwined.

Extracts from the 1973 survey on the number of planners, planning associations and planning education establishments are given in Table 3.1. The survey showed that of the 27 responses 17 countries and territories had national professional associations in place or being formed but 10 countries had no associations at all. Planning courses were available in 12 countries but 17 countries had no establishments providing planning education. Table 3.1 also shows for comparison purposes, equivalent data for 2018 indicating the scale of growth in the profession over the intervening years.

TABLE 3.1 Select results from CAPs 1973 Survey of Planning in Commonwealth Countries.

Country/Territory	Name of national planning association and date established	Number of members of Association including students. Number of planners in country where no Association exists. (Data from CAP 2018 survey in brackets; Note 2)	Number of planning educational establishments in 2018. (Data from CAP 2018 survey and other sources in brackets; Note 2)
Australia	Royal Australian Planning Institute (1956)	950 (5,165)	10 (24)
Barbados	Barbados Town and Country Planning Society	9 (16)	0
Canada	The Planning Institute of Canada (1918/1919)	885 (6,907)	10 (19)
Cyprus	Association being formed	12 (75)	0
Ghana	Ghana Institute of Planners (1969)	50 (1,394)	1 (3)
Hong Kong	Hong Kong Branch of the RTPI (1963)	36	0
India	Institute of Town Planners India (1951)	1,083 (3,978)	6 (23)
Jamaica	Jamaican Society of Planners (in process of being formed)	10 (30)	0 (1)
Kenya	The Architectural Association of Kenya, Town Planning Chapter (1968)	30 (214)	1
Malaysia	Malaysian Institute of Planners	50 (826)	2 (5)
Malta	No association	3 (12)	0 (1)
Mauritius	No association	4 (32)	0 (1)
New Zealand	New Zealand Planning Institute	195 (2633)	1 (5)
Nigeria	Nigerian Institute of Town Planners (1966)	70 (2,956)	3 (35)

(*Continued*)

TABLE 3.1 (Continued)

Country/Territory	Name of national planning association and date established	Number of members of Association including students. Number of planners in country where no Association exists. (Data from CAP 2018 survey in brackets; Note 2)	Number of planning educational establishments in 2018. (Data from CAP 2018 survey and other sources in brackets; Note 2)
Singapore	Singapore Institute of Planners (1971)	35 (207)	1
Sri Lanka	No association	15 (537)	1
United Kingdom	Royal Town Planning Institute (1914)	8,730 (22,003)	26 (28)

Notes
1. Only a sample of the results is given here
2. Data for 2018 was obtained from a CAP survey of members undertaken in advance of the 2018 CHOGM and published in Oborn and Walters (2020) 'Survey of the Built Environment Professions in the Commonwealth.' The 1973 and 2018 data are not based on exactly the same criteria but broad comparisons are possible.

Source: CAP Archives.

The survey revealed huge differences across the Commonwealth in the number of planners, in the availability of planning education and in the general awareness of planning. The planning profession was shown generally as being poorly resourced; those countries with the smallest planning resources were often the ones expected to receive the most growth where planning would be expected to be in greatest need. In a number of countries colonial-era planning legislation was still to be replaced and so often what planning legislation existed was not appropriate to context. The lack of mapping was recognised as a problem in many locations and still is in some areas.

On a positive note the survey revealed that planning in some form was taking place in all of the countries in the survey and progress was being made in embedding planning as a necessary and valued activity able to help create an improved quality of life for individuals and communities.

CAP's inaugural conference – a major milestone

Following on from CAP's survey of planning in the Commonwealth the second major initiative undertaken by the new organisation was to hold an inaugural conference which took place over a period of six days in 1973 at the India International Institute, New Delhi, India hosted by the Institute of Town Planners India.

The accompanying Photo 3.1 taken at the New Delhi conference shows the predominantly male attendance which reflected the profile of the planning profession at the time which had very few women planners. The Conference brought together planners from a wide range of countries with very different experiences of

PHOTO 3.1 Delegates at CAPs Inaugural Conference, New Delhi, India, 1973. CAP President Arthur Ling (sixth from left front row) and CAP Secretary R.J. Harvey (fourth from left front Row). Country delegates (middle and back rows) from Singapore, Malaysia, India, Fiji, Hong Kong, Nigeria, New Zealand, Australia, Tanzania, Ghana, United Kingdom, Zambia, Canada, Kenya. Delegates representing CAP regions (front row): Americas, South West Asia, South East Asia, Africa, South West Pacific and Europe

Source: CAP archives

planning. It provided a crucial vehicle for discussion of the key planning issues of the day and identified a range of ways in which CAP could take a leading role in the development of the planning profession in years to come such as in the use of new technology, in promoting the value of participation and of planners' education, training and professional development.

The opportunity to meet other planners face to face at CAP conferences was invaluable and was at that time the principal way to share experiences, establish policy positions and help steer the advancement of the planning profession globally (See Photo 3.2). Over the period up to 1988 covered by this chapter some of the major international planning conferences held by CAP are given in Box 3.4; the range of themes reflects the issues important at the time and conferences were often held in parallel with CAP regional meetings.

The growth of CAP in South East Asia

There are few records of CAP's activities over the years following the inaugural conference until Dr Peter Pun from Hong Kong was elected CAP's Asia Regional Representative in 1980 and CAP President in 1984 at CAP's Plenary conference held in

BOX 3.4 CAP CONFERENCES AND KEY THEMES 1973–1988.

1973, India, CAP Inaugural Conference
1974 Kenya, Rural Urban Drift
1974 Barbados, Professional Collaboration
1977 United Kingdom, Education for Planning
1980 Bangladesh, Integrated Rural Development
1981 Hong Kong, Planning in Asia – Present and Future
1982 Cyprus. Planning Legislation
1984 Jamaica, Caribbean Conference of Physical Planners
1986 Tanzania, Urban and Rural Development
1986 Sri Lanka, Urban Planning and The Provision of Shelter
1988 Soloman Islands, Planning and Development in the Pacific

Source: CAP Archives.

PHOTO 3.2 Delegates at CAP Americas Regional Conference, Barbados, 1974. CAP Secretary R.J. Harvey (4th from left back row), CAP President Arthur Ling (5th from left back row). Other delegates from Kenya, Jamaica, India, Singapore, New Zealand, Bahamas, Barbados and St Lucia

Source: Bill Robertson

Canada. Dr Pun was a member of the Hong Kong Institute of Planners (HKIP) and Hong Kong was in the process of transition to a global hub (see Photo 3.3).

Dr Pun is the earliest surviving CAP President and we are hugely fortunate to have received his reflections on his period as president. The following comments from Dr Pun illustrate the burgeoning nature of the planning profession at the time with international linkages facilitated by CAP:

> I became very active when I was elected as the CAP Asia Regional Representative for the period 1980–1984. This appointment allowed me to learn much about the planning and development situation, as well as the availability of university education for urban planners in CAP countries such as Singapore, India, Pakistan and Sri Lanka as well as those in Borneo. CAP offered me opportunities to open my mind toward these countries and their planning circumstances.
>
> Subsequently, I organized a number of CAP planning conferences in various countries in South-East Asia and in Hong Kong. Examples included a conference in 1981 jointly organized by CAP, the HKIP and the newly established Centre of Urban Studies and Urban Planning at the University of Hong Kong. I was also particularly grateful for CAP also inviting participants from mainland China and Taiwan – that was the first time that their planners had participated in an international planning conference. To them and to us in Hong Kong, this was a most rewarding event.
>
> *Dr Peter Pun*

Dr Pun also comments on some of the key challenges experienced at the time including the shortage of planners and planning courses simultaneous with the potential closure of some planning courses due to lack of demand. This was at a time when the benefits of effective planning were not widely recognised including at governmental levels and employment opportunities were limited.

> I gathered very valuable general knowledge about the shortage of urban planners in these parts of Asia and the absence of planning courses at their universities. There were hence not enough well-equipped professional brains to tackle Asian urban planning issues. I was informed that even some of the then existing planning courses were being considered to be abandoned soon, for instance, the one at Singapore, due to inadequate demand. After the conference in 1981, I developed acquaintance with the planners from mainland China and Taiwan and I obtained some useful knowledge concerning their cities.
>
> *Dr Peter Pun*

In the early 1980s in Hong Kong and other parts of Asia there was a heavy reliance on planners and planning education from outside the region including from

Europe and North America. Dr Pun recognised the importance of establishing a planning profession based locally in the region tailored to address the challenges experienced in Hong Kong and elsewhere in Asia, including high density developments. Through his innovative and pioneering work supported by CAP, Dr Pun was instrumental in the establishment of the Centre for Urban Studies and Urban Planning at the University of Hong Kong as he describes here.

> After the conference in 1981, I developed acquaintance with the planners from mainland China and Taiwan and I obtained some useful knowledge concerning their cities.
>
> This experience and information I so acquired enabled me to achieve a most important and positive, but indirect, contribution to planning in South East Asia and beyond. This was a remarkable outcome. In late 1970s, I was involved in an attempt to persuade the University of Hong Kong to establish an urban planning course to train planners who would be able to deal with the urban problems of Hong Kong and, if possible, those in other Asian urban areas. Hitherto, our planners were either foreigners or local people trained in Europe or North America. I proposed to the Vice-Chancellor of the University that the new course should specialize in planning for high-density development (Hong Kong being world famous as an "expert" in this type of development and planners from many other countries looking for opportunities to learn from us), that the course should welcome students from all Asian countries, and China. My subsequent acquaintance with professional people in China somehow generated my own prediction that, as it was starting to open up, China would soon require many more urban planners. Hence, the proposed course would not suffer from the lack of demand.
>
> The university authority was convinced and accepted our proposal. The Centre for Urban Studies and Urban Planning was consequently established in 1981. The Centre was later upgraded to Department which now has great demand from South East Asia countries, mainland China and Hong Kong.
>
> *Dr Peter Pun*

Summary

From the 1970 meeting in London to explore the idea of a CAP through to the end of Dr Pun's presidency in 1988, CAP made significant progress. It became an established Commonwealth professional association, connecting planners in the growing Commonwealth. Building such linkages and helping to establish the planning profession were its main concerns. This was not surprising, given the rarity of such contacts at the time, especially for practitioners, and the relatively new nature of the profession. The lack of records of conference proceedings make it difficult to judge how thought and practice developed amongst members. Did the wider events in the Commonwealth and international events like the 1976 Habitat Conference,

PHOTO 3.3 Hong Kong: Transition from British Colony to Global Hub.
Source: Cliff Hague

discussed in Chapter 2, resonate? Was there engagement with the work of Turner (1972, 1976) whose embrace of informality so influenced the World Bank and helped trigger a host of sites and services schemes across the developing world? These and other questions must be left unanswered for now. What is clear is that CAP was welcomed, filled a void, and was built up and supported by dedicated professionals spread across many Commonwealth countries.

References

Choe, A.F.C. (2016), 'The Early Years of Nation-Building: Reflections on Singapore's Urban History', In Chye Kiang Heng (ed.), *50 Years of Urban Planning in Singapore,* Singapore: World Scientific, pp. 3–21.

Oborn, P. and Walters, J.G. (2020), *Planning for Climate Change and Sustainable Urbanisation: Survey of the Built Environment Professions in the Commonwealth.* Available at https://commonwealthsustainablecities.org/survey/ (Accessed 2 August 2022).

Rathbone, P.R. (1970), *Meeting of Commonwealth Planners 1970,* London: Town Planning Institute.

Turner, J.F.C. (1972), *Freedom to Build: Dweller Control of the Housing Process,* New York: Macmillan.

Turner, J.F.C. (1976), *Housing by People: Towards Autonomy in Building Environments, Ideas in progress,* London: Marion Boyars.

4
1988–2000

New technologies and an existential crisis

Bill Robertson

Preamble

The inauguration of CAP in 1971 was warmly welcomed in NZ. At that time many NZ planners were members of the TPI. The NZPI had recently evolved from an overseas Branch of the TPI and the NZPI then still incorporated an overseas Branch of the TPI. The opportunity for a Commonwealth association and networks was taken up with enthusiasm, with the NZPI becoming a founding member at the first CAP plenary conference in New Delhi in 1973. The second CAP plenary conference held in Auckland in 1976 brought the significance of CAP's planning networks and activity to the attention of many NZ planners.

I became president of the NZPI in 1984 and was appointed to the CAP Executive Committee as the delegate for the CAP SWPR. I was already familiar with Commonwealth activity through my assignment on Colombo Plan Aid to Sarawak 1962–1965. Thus, I looked forward to meeting other Commonwealth planners at the midterm executive meeting in Colombo and developing Pacific planning relationships. My brief

---

BOX 4.1 THE GROWTH OF COMMONWEALTH MEMBERSHIP, 1968–1980.

Between 1968, when Nauru joined and 1980, when Vanuatu became a member, seven other Pacific island nations joined the Commonwealth: Fiji (1970), Tonga (1970), Samoa (1970), Papua New Guinea (1975), Solomon Islands (1978), Tuvalu (1978) and Kiribati (1979). Honiara, where the CAP regional meeting was held, is capital of the Solomon Islands. It is around 755 miles east of Port Moresby, capital of PNG. Funafuti, capital of Tuvalu, sits on a coral atoll, a further 1,360 mi east of Honiara.

DOI: 10.4324/9781003357933-6

from this meeting was to develop a network of support for planners in the far-flung south west Pacific. The holding of this CAP meeting in conjunction with the Sri Lankan town planners' conference energised both the locals and the Commonwealth delegates.

After developing a network of planning contacts and financial support from the CF the first regional meeting of Pacific Island planners was held in Honiara. These Commonwealth planners represented one of the most scattered groups of professionals in any region of the world. All 30 participants were enthusiastic about meeting and their broad experience led to a very productive CAP event covering planning education, professional development, and the establishment of the first PIPA. A *PIPA Newsletter* was agreed and it then provided regular and topical communication on planning in this 'far-flung' region for the next four years. This CAP activity led to PIPA president Donald Kudu advancing the issues and needs of Small Island States at the CAP Hong Kong conference.

A term of change

By the mid-1980s CAP was well established, but it still reflected the conservative nature and structure of professional organisations of the mid-twentieth century. It had top down decision-making with limited regional member input or participation. CAP now had an increased membership of 21 institutes – the majority being developing countries – and a strong representation of women. It was quite different to the small membership and all-male representation at the inaugural conference in 1971. However, the director of the CF was having serious doubts about whether the CF could continue to support CAP. It was time to reflect new Commonwealth development and diversity priorities in the CAP programmes, representation and structure. George Franklin, the CAP secretary and past president, was well aware of current CAP limitations and encouraged a forward approach for the future.

The CAP meeting in 1988 (see Photo 4.1) was held in conjunction with a large conference of Hong Kong and South East Asian planners. The new term began with the CAP executive meeting at the end of the fourth plenary CAP conference in Hong Kong. This meeting focussed on developing a structure and programme that would cope with the rapidly changing global circumstances. I was privileged to be appointed President of CAP and faced an agenda focussed on new initiatives to meet the challenges and opportunities ahead for the Commonwealth. We needed to modernise the administration and structure of CAP, improve communication with members (see Box 4.2) and increase regionally initiated CAP activity. This plenary meeting made some substantive decisions to modernise its operations and change its organisational behaviour and keep CAP organisations and their members more in touch and better informed. It was agreed that the *CAP Newsletter* was in need of upgrading. Funding was obtained from the CIDA, and the new *CAP Newsletter* lifted the visibility and profile of CAP through more regular and effective communication with members over the next four years.

The capability of regional delegates to fully represent and promote CAP activity in their regions was lacking. To reflect this increased expectation, delegates were re-designated regional vice presidents. The CIP contract to host the secretariat was

PHOTO 4.1 Delegates at the CAP Business Meeting, Hong Kong, 1988. President Peter Pun and Secretary-General George Franklin sit in the middle of the front row. Subsequent Presidents, Bill Robertson (back row, third from left) and Jacqui daCosta (middle row, fourth from left) are there, along with Dr Anthony Yeh (Hong Kong), organiser of the planned GIS workshop (back row, second from right). PIPA President, Donald Kudu (Solomon Islands), is middle row, third from right. David Fryer (RTPI) is front row, first from left. Others in the photo were representatives of member organisations in Malaysia, Sri Lanka, Kenya, UK, Bangladesh, Zimbabwe, Cyprus, Barbados, Nigeria, New Zealand, Trinidad and Tobago, Canada, Singapore and Australia.

Source: CAP Archives

BOX 4.2 NEW COMMUNICATION TECHNOLOGIES.

The 1980s saw the first widespread use of technologies that transformed communication. Fax machines allowed printed documents to be sent internationally, cheaply and instantly via a telephone link. Before that such documents relied on airmail delivery, while international phone calls were expensive. Home computers and word processing became common in the 1980s: floppy disks arrived, only to be replaced by CD ROMs.

---

approved as was the appointment of the CIP executive director to also serve as CAP secretary general.

In 1988 technological developments, particularly in the communications, GIS and geospatial fields were advancing rapidly and these offered major advances in planning applications (see Box 4.3). However, a major concern was that LIT was

> **BOX 4.3 THE ADVENT OF REMOTE SENSING.**
>
> Remote sensing developed rapidly in the 1980s, dramatically enhancing the mapping of the earth's surface and resources and enhancing human understanding of the global environment. While aerial photography had existed for some time, satellites replacing planes represented a major breakthrough. Satellites could cover much more space and enabled regular monitoring. Digitisation rather than film also transformed capabilities. The breakthrough had come in 1972 with the launch of Landsat 1, which also included sensors that enabled images of things not visible to the human eye to be taken and analysed.

being driven by supply side providers and that applications in planning and sustainable development were neglected. The adoption of these major technological advances by planners and administrators was also hindered by a lack of training, attention to planning needs, and continual changes in hardware and software. It was agreed that the full potential of LIT for planning purposes needed to be realised through preparation of a comprehensive LIT prospectus to advance this initiative. This was to be the beginning of the first coherent CAP continuing education programme.

This 1988 modernisation of CAP successfully anticipated the direction for change that was to be the objective of the conference of Commonwealth professionals in Sydney in1990 organised by the CF. As president of CAP, I attended and presented a paper (Robertson, 1990). During this conference representatives of 27 CPAs were brought up to date with the future directions and expectations for Commonwealth organisations. The reorganisation of CAP had already positioned it well for these new CF directions. The conference also provided the opportunity for productive bilateral meetings with CASLE, to co-host GIS workshops and with the RAPI Council about them re-joining CAP.

The large joint conference in Kuala Lumpur in 1989 provided a supportive agenda for the CAP programme of activity, particularly the need for assistance in training and technical cooperation, the development of appropriate and coordinated land information systems, the transfer of appropriate technology and the advancement of sustainable development. The CAP Executive Meeting approved a detailed LIT prospectus for implementation (CAP Executive Committee, 1989). The overall aim was to raise the level of knowledge and experience of local officials, especially planners, about the potential and actual use of LIT. This prospectus set out a framework for a comprehensive programme of training, workshops, courses, on-site experience, distance learning and funding/sponsorship for the next two years (1990–1991). It was sent to a wide range of international, Commonwealth and government agencies and generated high levels of interest and enthusiastic endorsement. The Commonwealth of Learning, as one example, agreed to adopt GIS as one of the elements of its strategic plan (see Box 4.4).

> **BOX 4.4 THE ADVENT OF GEOGRAPHICAL INFORMATION SYSTEMS.**
>
> Once upon a time maps were drawn on paper. Planners used to overlay drawn maps, using a light table to illuminate from below, so as to compare two or more factors. This 'sieve mapping' technique would help identify where development was constrained by a combination of factors such as flood risk, underground mining, lack of capacity in the sewerage system etc.
>
> In the 1960s, a Commonwealth country, Canada, with its vast territories to plan and manage, developed a similar but computerised system of overlapping layers, the Canadian Geographic System. This was the forerunner of Geographical Information Systems, but it was not until the 1980s that commercial software became widely available. The American company ESRI launched ARC/INFO for minicomputers in 1982: ARC is the 'architecture' of the system, the geographical base maps and the software that does the processing and output; INFO is the data that is added, e.g. housing condition, household status etc.

During official travel I arranged side meetings in London with the RTPI, CASLE, RICS and the CF on CAP plans and programme of activity. The director of the CF advised that despite earlier doubts he now had a high regard for CAP, particularly its achievements with its workshops and LIT programme for developing countries. CAP now had full CF support for its initiatives, particularly the LIT project.

Progress reports from the CAP secretary general in January and October 1990 recorded good progress on preparation for the Hong Kong LIT/GIS training workshop for January 1991, to be organised by Dr Anthony Yeh and supported by the CF and UNCRD and for a GIS workshop to be held in Trinidad and Tobago and firm commitments for GIS training workshops in Africa and Canada. The secretary general reported a sound position in CAP finances with the receipt of the large CF grant. However the progress report of December 1990 indicated that despite a high level of activity and contact with a significant number of North American sponsorship sources, the secretary general and the consultant who had been working on it had been unable to obtain any funding for the forthcoming LIT Workshop and a planned UN Shelter conference in Canada.

At the Port of Spain plenary conference in 1991 Ms Jacqueline daCosta became CAP's first woman president and also the first president elected with a secret ballot (see Photo 4.2). Other organisational changes included a new position on the executive for the immediate past president, and Africa was accorded two vice presidents. The CIP reported it was comfortable with the relationship between CIP and the CAP secretariat as a semi-autonomous unit in the CIP office. CAP funds were kept in a sub-account of CIP, and as such they were audited by CIP's auditors. However, CIP indicated it felt CIP could be exposed to financial risk and so it would like the CIP National Council to be able to review spending decisions of magnitude related to conferences and the planned workshops on Shelter and LIT. This oversight of CAP finances by the CIP National Council had always been assumed and was formally approved by the CAP Executive Committee. The meeting also recorded its satisfaction in having successfully nominated three member organisation planners for CF Fellowships during the term. The Port of Spain conference provided an effective opportunity for the professional development for local and regional Commonwealth planners.

PHOTO 4.2 Bill Robertson and Jacqueline daCosta.

Source: Bill Robertson

Financial misfortune

Newly elected president daCosta inherited some daunting challenges. CAP was faced with serious difficulties due to an unforeseen debt to the CIP and the consequent hesitance of the CF to grant funds and then their subsequent cessation. In the emergency precipitated by the withdrawal of CIP as CAP's secretariat at the end of 1992, president daCosta had to host the CAP Secretariat through the Town and Country Planning Association of Jamaica, one of CAP's smallest members. That CAP survived this series of 'misfortunes' is a great credit to daCosta's resilience and resourcefulness as president.

The CAP programme of activity had proceeded well over the previous 18 months, but its full implementation was not to be realised. As past president I received a letter from a Canadian consultant in April 1991complaining about unpaid invoices and threatening legal action. This was my first notification that a consultant was being paid from CAP funds, rather than acting as an unpaid volunteer like so many others who gave their time to CAP. I took time to investigate this matter and get as much information as I could. The lack of a written contract was a problem, as it left scope for differences of opinion between the consultant and the CAP secretariat. In due course the consultant was sent a stiff response expressing my concern at the claims for payment, for the payments he had already received and that the honorary role had escalated to the extent it had. I left open the option for a completely thorough professional investigation and audit. There was no response to this letter.

There was more to come. The CAP secretary general reported in October 1991 that he had asked the CF to bear with CAP as a series of unfortunate incidents had caused difficulty. He explained that a cut in Canadian government spending had meant that both the Canadian LIT workshop and the UN Shelter conference had to be cancelled with a forfeiture of advance expenditure for the latter (the sum was 17,500 Canadian dollars). Combined with an overspend on the Port of Spain conference it meant that CAP had to have a loan of 25,000 Canadian dollars from CIP to cover its overdraft, and this would need to be paid back from the CF grant expected for 1991–1992.

The future of CAP

In November 1994 the acting secretary general of CAP wrote to all member associations and advised that efforts to organise a plenary meeting of CAP had not been successful and invited suggestions. Later that year, the secretary general of RTPI told me in my capacity as immediate past president that he had serious concerns about the future of CAP and the RTPI's continued support. In July 1995 he followed up our discussions with a letter in which he observed that his Council had taken the view that CAP had in effect been suspended, and RTPI would no longer wish to continue to pay its subscription. RTPI would be willing to assume responsibility for the secretariat if members felt there was a case for CAP's continued existence and there was no other option. They would be content to let NZ or any other well-established member organisation take on responsibility, provided the same situation never occurred as when CIP withdrew its services. He invited CAP leaders to a meeting: for RTPI continued support three criteria would need to be met. First, a clear wish amongst the membership for CAP to continue. Second, that arrangements for the provision of an effective secretariat were in place. Third, that there would be a president who was capable of guiding CAP through a transitional period and developing a new presidential succession, vision and direction. Mr Fryer thought it would be very difficult to bring in a president who was not fully aware of the situation and problems of CAP. David Fryer had always provided constant and helpful support for CAP, and his premature death in March 1996, just days before the planned meeting with CAP, left a huge gap for Commonwealth planners as well as the RTPI.

A term of transition

Under the capable leadership of its president Jenny Dixon, NZPI offered to host the eighth plenary CAP conference in Auckland later in 1996. A one-off CF grant enabled the attendance of delegates from developing Commonwealth countries. A successful CAP 'Organisation Session' and a two day Commonwealth Planning Symposium was held. Thirty delegates from fourteen member organisations attended. This meeting reviewed the activities of the past term and fully considered the future role and direction of CAP. All delegates were positive about the future of CAP. There was unanimous support for CAP to continue and to relate its role to the current and future Commonwealth environment. Every delegate felt this opportunity for CAP to re-establish itself must not be lost. I was elected president with Robert Schofield – a member of the council of NZPI appointed secretary general – and the NZPI the host for the Secretariat. The confidence in the future of CAP was demonstrated by the RAPI re-joining and by the RTPI accepting its three criteria, for its continued membership had been met. The large Institute of Town Planners, India was represented and subsequently applied to join CAP.

However, there were major challenges ahead in this term. CAP as an association of mainly small organisations that have limited resources was dependent on harnessing external funding to rebuild and undertake initiatives in terms of national and Commonwealth priorities. The credentials and role of CAP needed to be re-established with the CF. Nevertheless, CAP served a unique role for all Commonwealth planners as the only global organisation devoted solely to planning. CAP could become a significant component of the portfolio of Commonwealth organisations that implemented the policies and high level decisions of CHOGMs. Thus CAP was still well placed to play an important role and make good its opportunities if it aligned with developing Commonwealth and UN programmes and priorities. It was critical to again access CF funds regularly to follow up the renewal begun at the plenary conference in Auckland. It was essential that this be a collaborative process involving all CAP members. In June 1998 I sent out a proposal for the 'Development of a CAP Strategic Activity Programme' to start a conversation with all member organisations. This draft strategic outline had as its vision to develop capacity as an overarching CPA that enabled member organisations to use collective capability effectively to contribute high quality planning services to the

BOX 4.5 GLOBALISATION, MARKET PRINCIPLES, CLIMATE AND THE ENVIRONMENT: THE 1997 AND 1999 CHOGMS.

The 1997 CHOGM backed globalisation and 'market principles,' focusing heavily on trade and investment. However, it did include a section on environment. Anticipating the Kyoto UN Summit later that year, it stated 'all countries will need to play their part by pursuing policies that would result in significant reductions of greenhouse gas emissions if we are to solve a global problem that affects us all.' However, in the Declaration from the next CHOGM in 1999 there was no mention of climate, and the one reference to protecting the environment was caveated by stating that this should not impede free trade or trade liberalisation.

Commonwealth community. It also included a Strategic Plan, an Activity spreadsheet for the remainder of the term and a questionnaire seeking information from all member associations on their issues, opportunities and needs.

Over this term there was a good level of contact with Commonwealth organisations through the liaison role in London undertaken for CAP by John Anderson and vice president Cliff Hague and others. This included representation and participation of CAP at UK meetings of CHEC and BEPIC and at UNCHS in Nairobi. Cliff Hague was the CAP accredited representative to the CHOGM in Edinburgh in 1997, where he and his colleagues made a major contribution to a Forum workshop. The RTPI provided strong support to CAP during this term through its new secretary general Robert Upton and international officer Judith Eversley. Good contact was made with the CF and their confidence in CAP slowly revived.

The next CHOGM was in Durban in November 1999. It provided an opportunity to align CAP with the directions and priorities that issue from CHOGM and its supporting meetings. CAP was still having serious difficulty in maintaining a sustainable level of activity without external funding. CAP needed to mount a presence at the 1999 CHOGM and show active support for it directly and through collaboration within BEPIC to strategise for the future. Fortunately CAP was successful in obtaining a CF grant to organise a meeting of our executive in Durban, in conjunction with CHOGM. This meeting was held along with a joint event with the South African Association of Chartered Town Planners. The communiqué from CHOGM identified several priority topics relevant to CAP interests and expertise. The CAP executive confirmed support for these CHOGM directions and its continued involvement in Commonwealth activity and CHEC and BEPIC. It made plans for the next plenary conference and the continuity of the presidency and the secretariat. The task of arranging for the next plenary conference and the next host for the secretariat was allocated to Cliff Hague, the vice president Europe.

Cliff Hague was very effective in arranging the eighth plenary conference that was held in Belfast, Northern Ireland in June 2000 in conjunction with the RTPI annual conference. He also obtained agreement for the establishment of the secretariat for the new term with the RTPI office in Edinburgh. The Belfast conference ended this term with a one-day CAP event on themes relevant to CAP members and a following half-day plenary meeting and elections and a review of strategy and actions for the future. Under Cliff Hague's leadership as president the new term of CAP would ensure its continued role as an important planning organisation.

References

CAP Executive Committee. (1989), 'Land Information Technology: A Key Ingredient for Sustainable Development', *LIT Prospectus for Implementation* (unpublished report).

Robertson, W.A. (1990), *The New Challenge to the Professional Community, Unpublished Paper Presented to the Conference of Commonwealth Professionals*, Sydney: New South Wales.

5
2000–2006

Re-inventing planning for sustainable urbanisation

Cliff Hague

Ideals and institutions

My career has been inspired by the possibilities of planning territories and places to improve the lives of the poor and disadvantaged. That was why I became a planner in the UK in the 1960s. As I have explained elsewhere (Hague, 2017), this commitment was strongly influenced by my childhood in inner Manchester, which imprinted a sense of identity with place and with class. Ideas, research and debate matter. I was lucky enough to be educated to critically analyse received ideas. I became a professional academic, able to challenge – and be challenged by – students and colleagues from diverse backgrounds, while also working close to practice through applied, policy-focused research.

I learned that institutions can make a difference. Working as a planner in Glasgow in the late 1960s revealed the contradictions in a top-down approach to planning 'for the people' and the way a bureaucracy resists ideas that challenge its practices. Then as a volunteer professional advising a pioneering community-based organisation in a deprived Edinburgh neighbourhood during the 1970s and 1980s, I came to understand the potential and the limits of grassroots activism. As a student then academic, I experienced how professional institutions insulated their practice from ethical issues by elevating technical concerns and protection of their 'professionalism' over analysis of the distributional impacts of planning or the potentials of the fuzzy edges of this profession. With others, in the mid-1970s I formed the Radical Institute Group to take on the professional establishment and together, despite opposition, we were able to insert issues of gender and race into Royal Town Planning Institute (RTPI) thinking, and eventually get them to break their institutional links with the planning regime that was delivering apartheid in South Africa.

My involvement with the Commonwealth Association of Planners (CAP) was – and continues to be – built on these foundations. Now more than ever, planners must

DOI: 10.4324/9781003357933-7

use planning as a democratic force for redressing the widening inequalities that are replicated and reinforced in the development of cities and regions. This is central to sustainable urbanisation. If you disagree, please take a moment to consider how and why the climate emergency is playing out or the lessons from the COVID pandemic, or simply open your eyes to the food deserts beyond the extravagance of commercial real estate.

The Commonwealth and CAP are institutions worth investing effort in. For all its limitations and the legacies of colonialism, the Commonwealth is exceptional in its reach, inclusion and values. As a Commonwealth Professional Association, CAP can feed ideas into governments and the UN, as well as reaching other Commonwealth professions and, not least, the planners within CAP's member organisations.

So, simply put, being CAP President enables you to shape an institution that can deliver ideas on the world stage, a voice to advocate urban and territorial planning as a means for sustainable urbanisation and redressing destructive inequalities.

RTPI support to CAP

I represented RTPI at the 1998 Durban meeting mentioned by Bill Robertson in Chapter 4. There Asad Mohammad explained how in Trinidad and Tobago planning was seen as not relevant to the needs of the poor. A planning system had been established after independence in 1955, based on British legislation. It was centralised and an instant anachronism. Gaining planning approvals was slow and cumbersome. There was widespread non-compliance both from the poor and from the very rich. This chimed with my experience in Pakistan, where I had been involved 1992–1994 in a UK-funded project at the University of Engineering and Technology in Lahore that was linked to a slum-upgrading project in Faisalabad (See Photo 5.1). I had also seen on the ground the 'dark side' of planning in the legacy of apartheid when I had addressed the 1995 Club Mykonos workshop to re-structure the profession in South Africa, which was 'a crucial moment for the profession to acknowledge its complicity in creating spatial division during apartheid and to rethink its role in the newly democratic nation' (Jones et al., 2021; Nel and Lewis, 2019, p. 153).

During the late 1990s Robert Upton, the RTPI Secretary-General and I, as CAP vice president for Europe, liaised closely on the future of CAP. By 2000, the RTPI had committed to supporting CAP through provision of the secretariat, with Annette O'Donnell as the part-time administrator, John Anderson as Secretary-General and myself as President.

To make the transition, we needed to hold a business meeting. RTPI Secretary-General Robert Upton and I had a lunch with an official from the then UK Overseas Development Administration (ODA) to put over our medium-term vision for CAP, and were successful in gaining their financial support. This was really crucial. As other chapters show, CAP is always in need of outside funds to deliver major events. Similarly, it is essential to be able to present potential funders with a clear and compelling case. That should not be too difficult for CAP, given the urgency of the need to address sustainable urbanisation and the potential of planning in the Commonwealth for partnerships and knowledge-sharing. However, too often those who control the

PHOTO 5.1 On site in the Faisalabad Area Upgrading Project, 1993. Cliff Hague with residents of a *katchi abadi* (informal settlement) in Faisalabad in a slum improvement project funded by the then UK Overseas Development Administration.

Source: Cliff Hague

purse strings come from backgrounds that know planning only as a local regulatory process. Key gatekeepers like High Commissioners, diplomats or economic policy makers focus at the nation-state level, rather than grasping spatial differences within the country. What can look like progress on key indicators, e.g. on health, may actually conceal increasing in-country inequalities between places and between rich and poor. Furthermore, the benefits of planning are long term, diffuse and not easy to isolate, but funders want clear, short-term, measurable outcomes.

No sustainable development without sustainable urbanisation

On becoming President at the Belfast meeting in 2000, I had two main and related aims. First, to connect CAP to the Istanbul Declaration and Habitat Agenda (UN Conference on Human Settlements, 1996) agreed at Habitat II in 1996. The central theme of the Agenda was 'adequate shelter for all,' reflecting the UN Centre for Human Settlements' (UNCHS) priority focus at the time on housing, and 'sustainable human settlements' (inspired by the Brundtland Report and the UN Environment Summit in Rio in 1992). I had attended Habitat II as RTPI President and been disappointed by how little profile planning and planners had in the event (see Chapter 2). I realised that the local focus of much planning activity, legislation and procedures, understandably defined the outlook of many planning associations, but as a consequence they did not see the global picture. Architects, engineers, environmentalists and others were not constrained in the same way and were able to use internationally shared terms and methods. Furthermore issues of equity and inclusion were central to the Habitat Agenda, but less familiar in mainstream planning practice.

My second aim was to better connect CAP with its members, both to retain support for CAP and also to reach them with the messages about the global need for a more radical, pro-poor planning practice. As an academic I was familiar with email and the internet. Though in some countries and for some practising planners these were still out of reach, things were changing rapidly. The new technology made it much easier for CAP to operate. With help from RTPI, I was able to set up a CAP website. Then, with Annette's help, I started producing CAP Newsletters in digital format, though when we began to include photos some editions took a long time to download, given the limited capacity of some users' computers at the time!

The glue that held my two aims together was the Commonwealth Foundation (CF). Almost my first task was to meet them in London. The previous meeting with Overseas Development Administration (ODA) had shown how essential it was to get face-to-face meetings. I pitched my vision of CAP tied to the Habitat Agenda and asked for trust, and we got £5,000. That got us started, together with Annette chasing members for subscriptions, with some success.

The creation of a CAP Women in Planning Network was another outcome from the Belfast meeting. Olusola Olafemi was its first convenor, and in *CAP News 4* (December 2001) she reported on a survey of women planners she had undertaken (see Box 5.1).

BOX 5.1 WOMEN AND PLANNING IN SOME COMMONWEALTH COUNTRIES, 2001.

There are a few women in the planning profession in Uganda. Thus, their male counterparts who do not understand the specific needs and problems of women take most decisions. . . . It is women who do the children's school run, shopping, cooking and other domestic chores in addition to their professional tasks. The male dominated planning profession does not take cognisance of this in planning decisions and implementation of projects.

Though a few, women professional planners in South Africa are making a difference. Most project allocation procedures in South Africa since 1994 openly discriminate against white men because they were deemed favoured in the past. Women are being given preference in project allocation by the authorities but significant issues remain on the professional level.

In the UK, like in South Africa and Uganda, the decision-makers are predominantly male. In the planning profession, 75% are male and 25% are female. Many people have a dismissive approach to the role of gender (women) in planning.

> Planning has an explicit impact on gender in ensuring equal access to facilities and services. Unfortunately, many women are unaware of their rights due to socio-economic and cultural reasons, and gender issues remain largely ignored. Institutionalisation of a new paradigm that would focus on women's empowerment in housing, land distribution and the categorisation of facilities and services is needed. Women are far less well represented than their male counterparts. The ratio in Zambia can be put roughly at 1 to 8 or 10.
>
> Source: extracts from a report in *CAP News 4* by Olusoma Olafemi.

We also coined the phrase which I tried to repeat at every opportunity: 'No sustainable development without sustainable urbanisation; no sustainable urbanisation without effective planning'. Similarly, it was useful to give people some sense of the scale of the challenge. To do this I included in all my presentations the statistic 'There are 60,000 more people living in Commonwealth cities today than yesterday; tomorrow there will be another 60,000' (See Box 5.2). This was crucial to help non-planning audiences, such as those in the Commonwealth Foundation, grasp why planning matters.

Within a few months, the Queensland Branch of what was then the Royal Australian Planning Institute (RAPI) came forward with the offer to involve CAP in their conference later in 2021. We could link the event to the Commonwealth Peoples' Forum (CPF) that was due to be held alongside the Commonwealth Heads of Government Meeting (CHOGM) in Brisbane. With just a couple of weeks to go, 9/11 happened and nobody knew whether a similar atrocity might be repeated. The CHOGM was postponed, but the CPF along with the RAPI event in the beguilingly named Surfers' Paradise went ahead. We were able to bid successfully to the CF for funds to take delegates from other Commonwealth countries, though when badgering the Foundation I spoken of 'Queensland' or 'Gold Coast,' rather than naming the precise location in case it sounded too much like a beach holiday! This RAPI event proved crucial for generating momentum and mobilising supporters, with Roger Brewster and Alicia Yon being especially active. At the Business Meeting first steps were taken to modernise the constitution.

The same model was worked in 2002. Though CAP was not given a platform role in any plenary in the RTPI Annual Conference in Manchester (despite the conference theme of 'Big Growth'!), we were able to take delegates there, hold another business meeting and, with help from Christine Alvin-Toffler and her colleagues in the Trinidad and Tobago Institute of Planners, to complete the update of the constitution.

CAP was much more to the fore in a two-day workshop in Port of Spain in December 2002 that brought together planners from across the Caribbean, including Guyana, in an event supported by the Canadian International Development

> **BOX 5.2 'PRO-POOR PLANNING – THE GLOBAL CHALLENGE'.**
>
> - Today 60,000 more people are living in Commonwealth cities than yesterday; there will be another 60,000 tomorrow.
> - Poverty is central to the way human settlements are developing: globally one person in six is living in a slum, but it is expected to be one in three by 2033.
> - Through the 1990s local governments could not keep pace with urbanisation: the urban poor lack adequate water and sanitation, land is being lost from agriculture and forestry, climate change is exacerbating run-off and heat island effects.
> - Dispersed, car-dependent development and fossil-fuel intensive lifestyles contribute to emissions that lead to climate change, droughts, flooding and sea level rise that impact on the poor. Special problems for small island states.
> - No sustainable development without sustainable urbanisation. No sustainable urbanisation without fair and effective planning and development management.
> - Pro-poor strategic planning – identify safe and accessible sites; concentrate enforcement efforts on areas at highest risk of disasters; create transport hubs and infrastructure networks as the defining urban structure, but don't set unaffordable minimum standards for development that will follow.
> - Work with the different groups amongst the poor and target strategies that are relevant to their needs and resources – e.g. slum upgrading, sites and services, economic development and the informal sector.
>
> Source: Cliff Hague PowerPoint presentation to the RAPI Queensland Division/CAP conference in Brisbane, 1–2 November 2003.

Agency. The focus was on hazards and disaster mitigation – serious problems in a part of the world subject to extreme weather conditions and seismic activity and where informal settlements have developed in highly vulnerable locations. Here and in subsequent CAP events elsewhere, the 'No sustainable development . . .' strapline could be aligned to local conditions.

CAP also played a significant role in launching the African Planning Association (APA) which was formed in 2006 and operated until 2019 when it became the African Planning Society. The groundwork had been done under the leadership of Christine Platt and the South African Planning Institute (SAPI), backed by CAP, with the launch of the idea at the 2002 Planning Africa conference. CAP was able to support the participation in Planning Africa conferences of delegates from other Commonwealth African planning associations. Member associations were becoming more aware of the Commonwealth dimension. For example, the Kenyans organised a CAP workshop, which drew Ministerial level support and brought in planners from Uganda and Tanzania to share experiences and build an action plan for future co-operation. Nigeria re-joined CAP.

In Brisbane in November 2003 an even more ambitious project was successfully delivered. Roger Brewster and his colleagues who led CAP's work in Queensland were able to access support from the Australian Government's Aid Department (AUSAID) and local consultants which enabled us to bring together planners from the Commonwealth countries in the Pacific to identify their priority needs in terms of professional development and improved practice. Kiribati, Samoa, Fiji, Solomon Isles, Tuvalu, Papua New Guinea, Tonga, Vanuatu and East Timor were represented as well as Australia, New Zealand, Malaysia and experts from Canada and the UK. As with the small island states in the Caribbean, issues of climate change and rising sea levels were a key focus.

A strongly appreciative letter from RAPI followed. Then a couple of months later another letter came saying RAPI were withdrawing from CAP membership! Happily, they soon resumed as members, but it was a sobering reminder of how CAP needs at all times to make sure that leaders of member institutes understand the value of our work. This was not the only setback. An attempt to get funding to pump prime a system of International Planning Aid was turned down by the Overseas Development Administration (ODA). There was also a trip to the inaugural World Planning Schools Congress in the exhausting heat and humidity of Shanghai in July 2001, where I sought to get support for a CAP Network of Planning Schools. The idea fell on stony ground, though I met Carol Archer from Jamaica who proved a valuable addition to our network.

CAP continued to work with member institutes to put on conferences focused on sustainable urbanisation in the Commonwealth and gained support from national politicians. For example, the 2004 event in Kuala Lumpur (see Photo 5.2) was officially opened by the Prime Minister of Malaysia, The Honourable Dato' Seri Abdullah bin Haji Ahmad Badawi.

Re-inventing planning: from Vancouver to the New Urban Agenda

By now CAP had increased its visibility and strengthened its networking. The late John Anderson was able to represent us at the CPFs in Abuja (2003) and Valetta (2005), while also involving CAP fully in the work of Built Environment Professionals in the Commonwealth (BEPIC), where we collaborated with the Commonwealth associations for Architects, Engineers and Surveyors. I was invited to speak at a UN-Habitat workshop in the second World Urban Forum (WUF) in Barcelona in 2004.

PHOTO 5.2 Increasing the presence and visibility of CAP, Kuala Lumpur, 2004. The Honourable Dato' Seri Ong Ka Ting, Malaysia's Minister of Housing and Local Government, presents Cliff Hague with a commemorative pewter plaque at the 2004 CAP conference in Kuala Lumpur.

Source: The Malaysian Planning Department, PlanMalaysia

This became the catalyst for the most ambitious part of my presidency: the aim to use the 2006 WUF as the platform to 'Reinvent Planning' to connect the profession to the interlaced global challenges of sustainable urbanisation, poverty and climate change.

The groundwork was done in a meeting in Edinburgh with Paul Taylor and Shipra Narang from UN-Habitat. Crucially WUF 3 would be held in Vancouver, so Canada would have some influence on the orientation. Through Ron Shishido, the Canadian planners' president at the time, who was also a CAP vice president, along with support within UN-Habitat, we had people who could shape the theme of WUF which became 'Sustainable Cities – Turning Ideas into Action.' Importantly, as CAP President I was given a speaking slot in the closing dialogue session to project the idea of 'Reinventing Planning'.

The lead up to WUF 3 saw CAP work closely with the Canadians to put in place a wider strategy. The Canadian institute would host a World Planning Congress in Vancouver on the cusp of the WUF. CAP would take delegates from member associations. This would be the basis for building a Global Planners' Network (GPN) as a strong international voice for the profession. We could write a 'Reinventing Planning' position paper (Farmer et al., 2006) and have a Vancouver Declaration from the congress (World Planners Congress, 2006) that would establish the GPN and which literally and metaphorically could be waved in the WUF. We could reinforce the messages through a flagship book (Hague et al., 2006), funded by the UK's Overseas Development Administration (ODA).

Thus the final declaration from the WUF (UN-Habitat, 2006) included this statement:

> **Re-inventing planning: applying new paradigms for sustainable urban development.** *The Forum placed a strong emphasis on planning as a tool for urban development and environmental management, and as a means of preventing future slum growth. This view was accepted not just by government officials and urban planners themselves but also by civil society groups that wanted planning to be more inclusive, transparent and ethical. The Forum stressed the important role of planners as agents of change and underlined the importance of sustainability as the backbone of new forms of planning.*

This represented a considerable achievement for CAP. It gave a mandate for future UN Habitat action and gave CAP a new level of visibility in and beyond its member associations and the Commonwealth. The Global Report on Human Settlements for 2009 focused on planning (UN-Habitat, 2009) and was later followed by the International Guidelines on Urban and Territorial Planning (UN-Habitat, 2015), the work on which was led by Christine Platt (see Chapter 6). All these were crucial stepping stones towards Sustainable Development Goal 11 and the New Urban Agenda (UN, 2017). However, CAP was unable to steer the GPN into the truly global organisation we had hoped for (Hague, 2021).

I believe that 2000–2006 was an important period for CAP. Annette O'Donnell did a great job anchoring the administration, and many others (including but not restricted to those named previously) played a key role in staging national or regional events or contributing copy to *CAP News*. CAP's profile was raised and we became a more campaigning body. The internet made it possible to change the way CAP operated. A key lesson was that if its member associations supported CAP strongly, CAP could enhance their voices across the Commonwealth and globally. Last but not least, my presidency ended with the election of a woman from Africa as my successor who would drive CAP forward for the next eight years. The award of an OBE in 2016 (see Photo 5.3) recognised the work that CAP had done.

PHOTO 5.3 CAP's work recognised: Cliff Hague OBE. Cliff Hague and Christine Platt at Australia House with his OBE, February 2017

Source: Christine Platt

References

Farmer, P., Frojmovic, M., Hague, C., Harridge, C., Narang, S., Shishido, R., Siegel, D., Taylor, P. and Vogelij, J. (2006), *Reinventing planning: A New Governance Paradigm for Managing Human Settlements*, Position Paper for the World Planners Congress, Vancouver, 17–20, June 2006, Available at http://globalplannersnetwork.org/wp-content/uploads/2016/10/reinventingplanningenglish-1.pdf (Accessed 6 October 2021).

Hague, C. (2017), 'Challenging Institutions That Reproduce Planning Thought and Practice', In Haselsberger, B. (ed.), *Encounters in Planning Thought: 16 Autobiographical Essays from Key Thinkers in Spatial Planning*, New York and Abingdon: Routledge, pp. 222–241.

Hague, C. (2021), 'Viewpoint: Do Planners Want to Lead the New Urban Agenda, and Are They Being Led by It?' *Town Planning Review*, 92 (6), pp. 677–686, https://doi.org/10.3828/tpr.2021.30.

Hague, C., Wakely, P., Crespin, J. and Jasko, C. (2006), *Reinventing Planning: A Guide to Approaches and Skills*, Rugby: Practical Action.

Jones, P., Andres, L., Denoon-Stevens, S. and Marques, L.M.S. (2021), 'Planning out Abjection? The Role of the Planning Profession in Post-Apartheid South Africa', *Planning Theory*, 21 (1), pp. 35–55, https://doi.org/10.1177/14730952211012429.

Nel, V. and Lewis, M. (2019), 'The Resilience, Adaptability, and Transformation of the South African Planning Profession', In Nunes Silva, C. (ed), *Routledge Handbook of Urban Planning in Africa*, London: Routledge, pp. 149–161.

UN. (2017), *New Urban Agenda*, New York: United Nations. Available at https://habitat3.org/the-new-urban-agenda/ (Accessed 10 February 2023).

UN Conference on Human Settlements. (1996), *Report of the UN Conference on Human Settlements (Habitat II)*, New York: United Nations. Available at https://daccess-ods.un.org/tmp/2466037.27340698.html (Accessed 27 March 2022).

UN-Habitat. (2006), *Report of the Third Session of the World Urban Forum: Vancouver, Canada, June 19–23*, Nairobi: UN-Habitat. Available at https://unhabitat.org/sites/default/files/documents/2019-05/3406_98924_wuf3-report.pdf (Accessed 6 October 2021).

UN-Habitat. (2009), *Planning Sustainable Cities: Global Report on Human Settlements 2009*, Nairobi: UN-Habitat. Available at https://unhabitat.org/planning-sustainable-cities-global-report-on-human-settlements-2009 (Accessed 6 October 2001).

UN-Habitat. (2015), *International Guidelines for Urban and Territorial Planning, Report HS/059/15E*, Nairobi: UN-Habitat. Available at https://unhabitat.org/international-guidelines-on-urban-and-territorial-planning (Accessed 6 October 2021).

World Planners Congress. (2006), Vancouver Declaration, Available at www.globalplannersnetwork.org/wp-content/uploads/2017/08/WPC-declaration-2006-updated-June-2017.pdf (Accessed 6 October 2021).

6
2006–2014

Towards the Sustainable Development Goals and the New Urban Agenda

Christine Platt

Introduction

It is impossible to overstate the enormity of what was achieved in the field of planning in the period which followed Word Urban Forum (WUF) 3 in Vancouver in 2006. It was at this time that the first seeds were sown for what was to follow, leading to the adoption of the Sustainable Development Goals (SDGs) in 2015 and the New Urban Agenda in 2016. It is in this context therefore that the events in CAP in the period between 2006 and 2014 must be measured. It proved to be an extraordinary period of achievement for planners in general and for CAP in particular.

The starting point in 2006 is certainly the events around WUF 3 in Vancouver. CAP held its biennial meeting there at which the presidency passed from Cliff Hague to me. At that meeting I paid tribute to the exceptional work done by Cliff in the six years leading up to 2006 and in particular for the work he had done in building a strong and stable administrative centre for CAP. With a strong centre established, the time had come for CAP to strengthen the member associations and regions, as an organisation can only be as strong as its constituent parts.

The Commonwealth has as its cornerstones the principles of equity, transparency and democracy. These principles informed the approach taken by CAP in our work over the ensuing period.

The Commonwealth therefore represents a unique laboratory of 56 countries from every continent and is a powerful vehicle for developing solutions to the planning challenges of the 21st century, as this chapter demonstrates.

The greatest resource in the Commonwealth is its people. At a function at Marlborough House, around 2011 a High Commissioner argued that the Commonwealth had to re-prioritise its work as it did not have the resources to tackle the multitude of challenges member states face. I argued that this misses the fundamental point that the countries of the Commonwealth are resource-rich in experienced

DOI: 10.4324/9781003357933-8

and talented people who can offer much to the debates and to identifying solutions to the issues requiring attention.

It was recognition of the rich vein of talent which lay within the profession across the Commonwealth that CAP (representing then some 35,000 planners across the world) used from 2006 onwards to develop the informed and inclusive responses which enabled it to enjoy the credibility and success that followed.

The problem with advocacy work is always that it is not possible to know which seed might have fallen on fertile ground, nor to know when a seed may germinate and take root. What is clear however is that the collective efforts of many during the period in the run-up to and after WUF 3 laid the foundation for what was to follow.

WUF 3 was a watershed event for planning globally as the critical message coming from this event was the first ever acknowledgment of planning as a key tool for the strategic coordination of sustainable urbanisation. The UN Habitat report on WUF 3 listed planning as one of four headline issues and recorded 'the important role of planners as agents of change and underlined the importance of sustainability as the backbone of new forms of planning' (UN-Habitat, 2006).

A new groundswell of energy emerged after WUF 3 with the common purpose of 'Reinventing Planning' fit for purpose in the 21st century and to position planning to address the most critical challenges of rapid urbanisation, poverty and climate change. The impetus for this is embodied in the paper *Reinventing Planning* (Farmer, et al., 2006). The sustainable urbanisation agenda began to take on heightened significance.

In 2006 we could not have thought in our wildest dreams that the efforts started then would lead to what came after. They were key to starting a process which led to the adoption of the International Guidelines on Urban and Territorial Planning (IG-UTP) at the Governing Council of UN Habitat (GC) in 2015 (UN-Habitat, 2015) and the adoption by the General Assembly of the United Nations that same year of SDG 11 'Make cities and human settlements inclusive, safe, resilient and sustainable'. This was followed in 2016 by the adoption of the New Urban Agenda at Habitat III (UN, 2017).

In order to prepare CAP to respond to the recognition being given to planning, it was clearly necessary to work with the rich resources which lay in the member associations, using regional leadership as the effective, institutional structure which CAP then had, in the absence of significant central institutional capacity. The regions became key to building the networks needed to respond to the recognition of planning and the mandates which had come our way. The growth in our network was not, however, limited to the Commonwealth as CAP went on to develop strong inter–disciplinary connections and relationships outside the Commonwealth.

The key to reporting on the achievements which followed lies in the way in which partnerships were developed and used.

Grassroots strength

The need to build a strong and credible constituency was the key focus of CAP's activities post-2006. CAP's minimal institutional capacity is far outweighed by the enormous talent with which it is endowed. CAP's role became a facilitator in forging connections and building grassroots partnerships for knowledge sharing and mutual learning, in order to respond to the challenges and opportunities laid at our door.

CAP supported and attended events and meetings in New Zealand, Fiji, Australia, Canada, Barbados, Trinidad and Tobago, Jamaica, Guyana, Uganda, Nigeria, South Africa, Cameroon, Namibia, Singapore, Britain, India and Sri Lanka (See Photo 6.2).

These events all had the core objective of building capacity at grassroots, through the strengthening of pan-Commonwealth and regional linkages. They served also as conduits for the formulation of messages, especially to Heads of Government, using the unique institutionalised structures which the Commonwealth affords us to enable grassroots groups to make a difference. Equally importantly, they enabled CAP to give a voice to planners working around the Commonwealth. The content and outcomes of these events are too numerous to itemise but the following are three of the key areas of success.

Pacific

In April 2007, CAP supported the Pacific Urban Agenda Workshop in Fiji in partnership with the Planning Institute of Australia (PIA) and Commonwealth Local Government Forum (CLGF) The focus of this meeting was the launch of the Pacific Island Planning Association (PIPA) which brought a significant number of Pacific countries into the realm of CAP. The challenges of the small island states are especially urgent in the Pacific where planners face complex issues with minimal resources and little collegiate support. This initiative was a great example of how CAP was able to support PIA and the New Zealand Planning Institute (NZPI) in building linkages and collaboration with planners in their region.

This inclusive and collegiate approach was seen again at a pre-CHOGM *State of Commonwealth Cities Symposium* convened by PIA in Brisbane in 2011. This event was used by the Australian Government to launch the 'State of Australian Cities' report (Australian Government, Department of Transport and Infrastructure, 2011). It brought together ministers of state and planners from throughout the Pacific region and was an example of how CAP and its members are able to use the hosting of CHOGM as a vehicle for the involvement of planners at grassroots in the formulation of messages to our Heads of Government.

Caribbean

The CAP Americas regional conference 'Re-shaping the planning agenda: experiences of small island states' was held in Barbados in 2007. This event brought together representatives from the Caribbean countries and Canada, which not only propelled the Barbados planners onto the world stage but was also the start of a critically important programme to build regional linkages within the profession and with governments in the Caribbean.

A critically important pre-CHOGM workshop 'Partnerships among the State, Civil Society, and the Private Sector in Planning and Development' was held in Trinidad and Tobago in November 2009. It was an outstanding example of how Commonwealth funding can be used as a catalyst to launch a regional initiative, with full government support and exceptional energy and leadership from the local profession. It was an event which warranted special mention many times during the Commonwealth People's Forum which followed. In addition, it demonstrated how committed planners can raise the profile of debate around relevant issues to the point of making national TV newscasts and front–page news in the printed media. It was an example of how linking a CAP event to CHOGM can mobilise political leadership as well as planners in a region. The success of this impressive event was noted by the director of the Commonwealth Foundation and resulted in CAP playing a heightened role in the Commonwealth People's Forum which followed at CHOGM.

It was no surprise that this region gave CAP one if its most significant success stories when with support from CAP, planners from Barbados, Belize, Canada, Guyana, Jamaica and Trinidad and Tobago, working with colleagues from other Caribbean countries, established the Caribbean Urban Forum (CUF). This event has taken place every year since 2011. CUF received very high–level governmental support from the countries within the Caribbean, with the events attended by Prime Ministers and Ministers of State (See Photo 6.1). CAP successfully facilitated the granting of US$80,000 by UN

PHOTO 6.1 Meeting the Minister for Housing and Lands, Barbados 2007 Christine Platt and Richard Gill (CAP representative for Barbados – right) meet the Hon. Reginald R. Farley, MP, Minister for Housing and Lands, Barbados.

Source: Christine Platt

Habitat for the advancement of this work – an example of CAP using its networks and the credibility of planners at grassroots to advance our common objectives.

In 2012 the Caribbean Planners' Association (CPA) was launched in Jamaica, with CAP again able to assist with funding. The CPA has strengthened associations in the region and assisted planners in countries where no association existed to establish one, including in Belize and Guyana.

Africa

CAP has been a supporter of the African Planning Association (APA) since its establishment in 2002. CAP held its biennial business meeting at the Planning Africa Conference in Johannesburg in 2008 at which it facilitated an important workshop with representatives from all of the Commonwealth regions as well as guests from UN Habitat and the *Société Française des Urbanistes*. This workshop explored the 'Lessons, challenges and responses from Reinventing Planning post–Vancouver'.

The messages from this session were visionary and included the need to 'effectively deal with the big issues such as climate change, deepening poverty, increasing slums and the food and energy crisis' and the idea that 'globalisation and its impact on new migrations, densities, heritage and changing sense of place cannot be ignored.' These messages from the planners of the Commonwealth were taken to the WUF 4 in China in 2008 where as President I was the first speaker in the first plenary dialogue session – the inclusive way in which our messages were formulated and hence the credibility which our messages carried had clearly been noted.

As happened in the Caribbean, the support for the APA saw the formation of new associations in Mauritius and Moçambique. In addition, CAP was able to facilitate the granting of funding from UN Habitat for an initial research project on Planning in Africa for the APA.

Position papers

Using these strengthened grassroots connections, CAP was able to bring together planners from different parts of the Commonwealth who were working on the same issues. We developed a process of preparing a discussion paper drafted by a pan-Commonwealth group. This was then sent to member associations for comment, after which the discussion paper was distilled into a position paper on the selected topic.

This achieved many things: it connected colleagues working on the same issues, it gave member associations the opportunity to make input by contributing their own experiences, and then it gave us a position paper, based on solid, collaborative input. These became powerful tools for grassroots knowledge sharing and mutual learning, using the voluntary contributions of committed and knowledgeable people as the basis for this engagement which was always collegiate and about mutual learning, thus reflecting the Commonwealth principles of equity and transparency.

The first CAP discussion paper on 'Gender in Planning and Urban Development' was put out by the Commonwealth Secretariat (CS) and was based on research undertaken for CAP by Alison Todes of South Africa, on Gender Based Planning in the Commonwealth (Malaza et al., 2009). It was presented at the WUF 4 Gender Assembly in Nanjing and was then distilled into a CAP position paper on gender and planning prepared by Carolyn Whitzman of New Zealand for the CAP Women in Planning Network (CAP Women in Planning Network, 2009). This paper formed the focus of a presentation made at the gender session at the Commonwealth People's Forum at CHOGM in 2009. In addition, CAP was asked to chair the gender assembly at WUF 5 in Rio de Janeiro in 2010. CAP went on to secure a Commonwealth Foundation grant to fund further research on Gender

PHOTO 6.2 West Africa Workshop – CAP in Action, 2009. An example of the wide range of activities carried out by CAP and its members in Christine's time as president. Here the Nigerian Institute of Town Planners hosts a CAP workshop on the theme of 'Planning for Liveable Human Settlement'.

Source: Cliff Hague

issues with a 'Gender equity self-assessment tool for local government-planners' completed in 2013 by Dory Reeves of New Zealand (Reeves and Zombori, 2013). It was evident that CAP's initiatives around gender-based planning issues were receiving widespread recognition as well as serving as important learning tools for our members and seriously advancing the objective of the Women in Planning network as an advocacy tool for gender equity within the planning profession as well as in planning practice in the Commonwealth.

This was followed by the preparation of a discussion paper on food security and planning following the CIP conference in 2009. Wayne Caldwell of Canada convened a work group of specialists from South Africa and Australia to draft this paper. This resulted in CF funding being received which was used to distil this work into a position paper on planning and food security in the Commonwealth (Caldwell and Lang, 2014) which became the subject of the first CAP webinar.

The same approach was successfully used when in 2011, Susan Houston of NZPI convened a work group of specialists from Sri Lanka, Samoa and India to prepare a discussion paper on 'Resilience and Planning' based on an online survey (CAP, 2012; Houston et al., 2012). This work was presented at WUF 6 in Naples in 2012 in a joint session with the University College London and the United Nations Inter-Agency Task Force on Disaster Reduction (UN ISDR). It has since been used to highlight good practice, with the Christchurch case study being selected for the UN Habitat IG-UTP (UN-Habitat, 2015). CAP was the key to building the connections which enabled this partnership to happen.

Work was started on two further internal unpublished discussion papers, namely 'Legislation and Planning' and 'Health and the City.' The legislation group was convened by a representative from the RTPI and included representatives from Trinidad and Tobago, Britain, Guyana, Canada, Namibia, Nigeria, South Africa and Australia. Regrettably this initiative did not gain traction and an important opportunity for pan-Commonwealth knowledge sharing was lost.

The 'Health and the City' paper resulted from my being asked to deliver the keynote opening address at the Commonwealth Pharmacists Association conference in 2011 (See Photo 6.3), an unexpected example of inter-disciplinary linkages across the Commonwealth. As a consequence, the Commonwealth Foundation requested CAP to convene a Health and the City event involving over 35 leading planning, health and built environment professionals in London in September 2011.

This very successful event led to the establishment of a work group convened by the RTPI to prepare a discussion paper on 'Health and the City.' Sadly, the impetus for this work appears to have slowed after 2014 although good progress has been made more recently (see RTPI, 2020).

Commonwealth partnerships

CAP developed a very positive relationship with both the Commonwealth Secretariat (CS) and the Commonwealth Foundation (CF) and enjoyed considerable support from both of these organisations over this period.

PHOTO 6.3 Outside the Health and the City Conference, London, 2011. The delegates at the Health and the City Conference in Marlborough House, London. Christine Platt is third from left on the front row with Clive Harridge, second from left.

Source: Christine Platt

CAP continued to serve on ComHabitat and BEPIC but what changed in the period after 2006 was that CAP enjoyed a greatly enhanced role at the governmental and secretariat level. As President of CAP I was invited to address the Inter-Ministerial Commonwealth Consultative Group on Human Settlements (CCGHS) meeting in Nairobi in 2007 on 'Leadership for new approaches to urban planning and development' building on the outcomes of WUF 3. Much of the discussion around the capacity building programme stemmed from this event. CAP went on to play a pivotal role at the Commonwealth People's Forum in 2007 where a call was made in the Kampala Civil Society Statement for the presentation of a State of the Commonwealth Cities Report on a biennial basis at every CHOGM.

The *State of the Commonwealth Cities* work was commenced in 2008 with the preparation of a Scoping Report by Will French of the RTPI and Cliff Hague which assessed the availability of existing data to form the basis of a reporting mechanism to Heads of Government (ComHabitat, 2010). Funding was received for a second phase of the State of the Commonwealth Cities programme with a report prepared by Michel Frojmovic of CIP called 'Urban Challenges: State of Commonwealth Cities Reporting, Indicators and Templates' which was presented at a CAP

EGM in London in March 2011. CAP members from across the Commonwealth were invited to participate in this event. The primary outcome of this event was the document 'Towards a Commonwealth Urban Agenda' which was presented to CCGHS in 2011 – another example of CAP using the Commonwealth conduit between planners working at grassroots and government at the highest level to formulate and deliver key messages.

Regrettably work on the State of the Commonwealth Cities stopped after the CS withdrew all support for this initiative due to a fundamental change in strategic direction. It was in this context that the conversation referred to at the start of this chapter occurred – sadly there was little understanding then of how rich the resources are which reside throughout the Commonwealth and that simple recognition of an issue such as that coming from CHOGM in 2009, noted later, can provide critical leverage for civil society to make a profound contribution using the partnership facilitated by the institutionalised conduits which the Commonwealth offers. Tellingly, this position changed by the time of CHOGM in 2013 with the Commonwealth Statement on the Post-2015 Agenda dealing in paragraph 10 with concerns around the issue of collaboration and partnerships plus an awareness of the 'wealth of knowledge, expertise and experience available within the Commonwealth which remains underutilised' (Commonwealth Secretariat, 2014).

This strengthening of CAP's relationships with the CS and CF was a reflection of the exceptional work being done by the CAP team around the world. The inclusive and transparent way in which CAP was giving a voice to planners at grassroots was seen and acknowledged, and hence CAP's credibility saw us playing a significant role in numerous events.

An impressive example of this was how the work from the Commonwealth Peoples Forum fed into CHOGM in 2009. For the first time planning was recognised by our Heads of Government, with Paragraph 74 of the Port of Spain Communiqué agreed by the Heads of Government reading:

> Heads recognised that rapid urbanisation was posing a significant challenge in many Commonwealth countries, and that new and inclusive approaches to urban planning and management were central to achieving the MDGs.
>
> *(CHOGM, 2009)*

The reference to 'new and inclusive approaches to urban planning' clearly acknowledged the 'Reinventing Planning' agenda that CAP had been advocating since 2006.

These outcomes led to the commencement of CAP's Capacity Building programme stemming from the discussions held at CCGHS and in Barbados in 2007. Capacity building is about more than just a head count and is a multi-faceted issue which includes the training and mentoring of new planners, updating the skills of already qualified planners, optimising planning governance, accreditation and distance learning.

CAP commenced work on its Capacity Building programme with a research project to examine the State of Commonwealth Planning Education, again using a Commonwealth-wide reference group to make critical input. CAP was able to secure a grant of £10,000 to advance this work. Additional funding was made available for a second phase of work which included the first ever survey of planning education in the Commonwealth, presented at the GPEAN conference in Australia in July 2011. A discussion paper 'Do We Want More Sustainable Human Settlements in the Commonwealth? Then Let's Tackle the Capacity Gaps' was prepared by Cliff Hague on this work (Hague, 2012). CAP drafted proposals to take this programme to the next stage which we saw as bench-marking planning education in the Commonwealth, exploring a job exchange programme and distance learning for planners working in remote locations. Regrettably it was at this time that Commonwealth funding was reprioritised and funding became difficult.

A critical feature of this programme was the establishment of a CAP Young Planners' Network, to connect and mobilise planning students and recently qualified professional planners to exchange practice, better understand global challenges and connect directly into CAP's work. CAP was given £12,000 to establish this network which was launched during the meeting in Montreal in 2010. The winners of an essay competition were invited to Montreal. Sadly, two of the winners from Kenya were not able to secure visas despite our best efforts.

During GC in 2011, it became evident that the Commonwealth and the Government of the USA were both researching indicators as a tool for reporting on urban trends and issues. This led to the first ever formal engagement between the CS and the USA Government Department of Housing and Urban Development (HUD), facilitated by CAP, at a workshop in Washington in 2011. This in turn led to the holding of a joint networking event on this topic at WUF 6 in Naples in 2012. This work was then reported on at CHOGM in Perth in 2011 where a statement entitled 'Statement to Heads of Government on the Urban Crisis' was presented by the CAP President during the dialogue session with foreign ministers.

This work was seen as critical as we prepared for the Post-2015 Agenda debates and Habitat III in 2016. CAP invited planners from around the Commonwealth to participate in preparing our organisation for the events we knew were coming. This began with the preparation of a submission in 2013 to the Committee of the Whole which sets the agenda for the Heads of Government meeting and which reflected input from planners in Belize, Canada, Barbados, Kenya, Australia, South Africa, Trinidad and the United Kingdom.

CHOGM was held in Sri Lanka in November 2013 where CAP convened a workshop entitled 'Our Commonwealth Urban Future – Priorities for a Post-2015 development agenda.' The output from this workshop was influential in the final CPF communiqué which called on heads to give priority to urban growth and called for the resumption of the State of the Commonwealth Cities programme. Heads went on to adopt the 'Colombo Declaration on Sustainable, Inclusive and Equitable Development' which talks about the need to promote sustainable development, to address resilience and the need for new international approaches as the context within which sustainable development policies must be pursued (CHOGM, 2013).

Our response to this was to recall the CAP group which drafted the pre-CHOGM statement to draft solutions and a way forward, using the milestones of WUF 7 in 2014, CHOGM in 2015 and Habitat III in 2016 to build a solid foundation to deal with the sustainable development and urban issues which a post-2015 agenda needed to address.

After WUF 7 in April 2014 in Medellin it became apparent that there was an urgent need to advocate for an 'urban' SDG. The CAP post-2015 work group was then asked to prepare a statement on why the Commonwealth needed an SDG addressing urbanisation and human settlements. It made a number of points around the impact of urbanisation on the Commonwealth's ability to develop sustainably, the danger of cities becoming unmanageable, the challenge this presents in small island states and the fact that much of the urbanisation in the Commonwealth is slum-led and undermines sustainable development.

This work was fed into the consultation process of the Open Working Group and submitted to UN Habitat as the UN agency leading on this issue. CAP was invited to attend a civil society consultation in New York in May 2014 at which we were given the opportunity to engage with representatives of governments around the urban SDG issue. An 'urban' SDG was finally adopted at the General Assembly in September 2015.

CAP's credibility can be seen in other engagement such as a meeting between representatives of CS with me as President of CAP to discuss the role of Civil Society organisations in the Commonwealth.

CAP enjoyed substantial and much appreciated financial and logistical support for all of this work with the financial support from the Commonwealth equating to between two to three times our subscription income.

United Nations

In the period after WUF 3 CAP developed a strong and symbiotic partnership with UN Habitat as well as other United Nations agencies.

As President of CAP, I chaired the Plenary Dialogue sessions of Governing Councils 21 and 22, addressed the Dialogue 1 at the WUF 4, served on the WUF 4 Advisory Board in Nanjing and chaired the Gender Assembly and Professionals Forum at WUF 5 in Rio de Janeiro. CAP also attended EGMs to discuss UN Habitat Medium Term Strategic and Institutional Plan 2008–2013. CAP was invited to serve on the World Urban Campaign (WUC) Steering Committee. CAP also chaired the UN Inter-Agency Committee meeting on a Decade of Education for Sustainable Development.

CAP played a pivotal role in resuscitating the Habitat Professionals Forum, leading to chairing the first ever Professionals Forum at WUF 5 in Rio de Janeiro. Being asked to undertake these tasks was all a reflection of the leadership in CAP as well as the credibility which CAP had earned as an inclusive and equitable voice for planners across the Commonwealth – that unique laboratory of 56 countries.

Two Commonwealth projects, identified by CAP, were shortlisted for presentation at the UN Habitat EGM in Rome on the issue of climate change and planning at which I was asked to deliver a keynote address and our CAP colleagues Richard Gill (Barbados) and Rashid Seedat and Florence Mnisi (Johannesburg) were asked to present. The purpose of this meeting was to identify planning case studies for inclusion in the 2009 UN Habitat Global Report on Human Settlements, which was presented at WUF 4 in Nanjing in 2008 (UN-Habitat, 2009).

In 2009, CAP was invited by UN Habitat to co-convene a strategic workshop in Rotterdam on *Urban Planning and Climate Change*. This was a significant development as it was the first time we were partnering with UN Habitat in convening an event. CAP was able to assist in inviting CAP leadership from the Caribbean, Canada, the UK, Africa and the Pacific to participate. It was a privilege to be thanked by UN officials for the exceptional contribution of such knowledgeable and committed colleagues and for 'lending the credibility' of our organisation to UN Habitat's efforts. The primary outcome of this event was a call for proposals to undertake the preparation of a toolkit for Planning for Climate Change. Once again, CAP used our network to circulate this call and the consequence was the awarding of the research project to two Vancouver-based companies: EcoPlan International, Inc. and Compass Resource Management (www.compassrm.com) to develop a guide on planning for climate change which was then tested in numerous Cities and Climate Change Initiative (CCCI) countries around the globe by UN-Habitat. The results of this field-testing formed the basis for *Planning for Climate Change: A Strategic, Values-based Approach for Urban Planners* (UN-Habitat, 2014).

This is an example of how the planners represented by CAP benefitted from CAP's networking and outreach as well as the credibility CAP had earned based on the leadership and constant inclusion of people from across the Commonwealth in the formulating of positions and messages.

Cliff Hague summed this up most appropriately when he said at a CAP event in Lagos 'Having established credibility (and nothing could have been achieved without that), CAP has worked to raise awareness and understanding of the vital role that modern approaches to urban planning can play'.

In yet another unexpected nod of recognition for CAP, as President of CAP I served on the Advisory Panel for the Resilient Cities campaign of the United Nations Inter-Agency Task Force on Disaster Reduction (UN ISDR). Again, it is the constituency which CAP represents which makes it relevant to the UN agencies who otherwise battle to reach people working at grassroots. Important information was made available to CAP members associations from networking and engagement such as this.

In 2013 CAP was invited to attend a UN Civil Society Consultation on the Post-2015 Development Agenda in Geneva. CAP members were invited to comment on the documentation circulated in preparation for that meeting. CAP was acknowledged as a valuable and credible partner because we bring wide-ranging comment from our constituency from all regions of the world. In an email received afterwards, the UN Habitat official who was part of the drafting team stated '(CAP's) strong advocacy made the deliberations within the drafting committee much easier to maintain a strong urbanization presentation in the report'.

As President of CAP I was asked to serve on the Advisory Group for Habitat III. The letter of invitation states

> In recognition of your significant contribution to global urban development efforts, I am pleased to invite the Commonwealth Association of Planners to be a key partner in the preparations for the Third United Nations Conference on Housing and Sustainable Urban Development.
>
> *Habitat III*

CAP was also asked to serve on a UN Habitat advisory group looking at Resilience as UN Habitat believed 'CAP would be an integral link to the global planning professional community'.

CAP also established partnerships with organisations outside the Commonwealth, including with The Prince's Foundation for the Built Environment (PFBE). Following a series of very positive meetings during CHOGM in Kampala in 2007, to explore how we could find synergy between the programmes of the PFBE and CAP, we were invited to a private briefing session for The former Prince of Wales at Clarence House in February 2008. The outcome of this meeting was the signing of a memorandum of agreement between the two organisations. As a consequence of this engagement CAP attended Royal workshops St James and a number of further meetings convened by PFBE in London.

CAP worked with the *Société Française des Urbanistes* (SFU) and SAPI in supporting the *Ordre National des Urbanistes Camerounais* when they convened a francophone planning conference in November 2008.

CAP supported the Global Planners Network (GPN) at the time of its establishment at WUF 3 in Vancouver. CAP hosted the biggest ever meeting of GPN, with representatives from all of the member countries present, in Johannesburg in 2010. GPN was intended to be a global partnership and voice for planners based on the principles of inclusion and equity upheld by CAP. Sadly, the high levels of inclusion at that meeting were not repeated and the traction to advance GPN beyond 2006 and 2008 was lost. GPN was intended to be a global partnership and voice for planners, however, CAP questioned its support of this initiative as GPN drifted away from the principles of inclusion and equity upheld by CAP and drifted into a collaboration at the time between just four of the larger associations.

Administration

None of these achievements would have been possible without the support of our secretary-generals and administrator Annette O'Donnell (See Photo 6.4). As a voluntary association, we rely heavily on these people as our 'institutional memory' and their service has been exceptional. As already noted, Cliff Hague served as Secretary-General from 2006 to 2020, with Clive Harridge taking over from 2010.

During this period Cliff stood down as Secretary-General. In March 2010, when we knew Cliff would be standing down later that year, I gathered together the

PHOTO 6.4 Congratulating Christine Platt on her SAPI Award Clive Harridge (CAP Secretary-General), Annette O'Donnell (CAP Adminstrator) and Dyan Currie (successor CAP President) congratulate Christine Platt, holding her Outstanding Achievement Award from the South African Planning Institute.

Source: Cliff Hague

necessary papers to nominate Cliff for a Royal Honour, in recognition of his exceptional contribution to CAP during ten years of service, vision, leadership and sound thinking. The supporting testimonials from many people in CAP and beyond are in themselves a wonderful reflection of Cliff's contribution. The OBE, which came on 11 October 2016, was richly deserved.

Communication is critical in order to sustain the linkages which made all of the achievements over this period possible. Not only did we circulate numerous pieces of communication, but we upgraded the website and instituted new methods of communication, such as holding quarterly meetings using skype.

Importantly, on 17 November 2014, CAP held its first webinar on the subject of 'Food Security' led by Wayne Caldwell from Canada and Ian Sinclair from Australia. A second webinar on the 'The Sustainable Development Goals (SDGs) & the Urban Agenda' was held on 26 February 2015 with UN Habitat as keynote presenter. The setting up of these webinars was yet another example of CAP making connections between members from across the world to discuss matters of common interest. Importantly, the webinar licence also became a tool available to member associations.

All of these efforts by so many people from so many different places were honoured in many different ways – a tribute to our credibility, built on the principles of inclusion and equity. In January 2011, CAP was awarded the RTPI's President's Special Award for Planning Achievement by President Ann Skippers, who summed up the strong bond we share in CAP when she said the following:

> In recognition of what can be achieved through outstanding cooperation, determination and goodwill, it is my very great privilege and pleasure to award CAP the President's Special Award for Planning Achievement.

In 2012 CAP celebrated its 40th birthday at which tribute was paid to the exceptional work done on a pan-Commonwealth basis by so many people who volunteered their time and expertise. In his book *Beyond a Boundary*, C.L.R. James (1963) speaks of a Trinidadian cricket team showing 'pride and impersonal ambition' which distinguished them from other clubs. I believe this term applies equally to the planners in CAP who have shown passion for what they do, belief in their ability to make a difference, pride in their achievements and above all an 'impersonal ambition' in that nobody stepped forward for personal gain.

This sentiment is worth repeating now at the time of CAP's 50th birthday as I am certain that the success of the past 50 years will continue given the exceptional level of commitment and spirit of volunteerism which typified the period 2006 to 2014.

References

Australian Government, Department of Transport and Infrastructure. (2011), *State of Australian Cities 2011*. Canberra: Major Cities Unit, Department of Transport and Infrastructure. Available at www.infrastructure.gov.au/sites/default/files/migrated/infrastructure/pab/soac/files/00_INFRA1267_MCU_SOAC_2011_FA1.pdf (Accessed 4 April 2022).

Caldwell, W. and Lang, K. (2014), *Perspectives on Planning for Agriculture and Food Security in the Commonwealth*, London: Commonwealth Foundation and CAP.

CAP. (2012), *Commonwealth Association of Planners Survey of Resilience Across the Commonwealth.* Available at https://www.surveymonkey.com/r/SL5MT8R (Accessed 10 February 2023).

CAP Women in Planning Network. (2009), *Position Paper on Gender and Planning Prepared for the CHOGM (Trinidad and Tobago), CAP* (unpublished paper).

CHOGM. (2009), *Commonwealth Heads of Government Meeting: Trinidad and Tobago, 27–29 November 2009.* Available at https://commonwealtheducation.org/resources/ministerial-meeting-communiques/ (Accessed 3 August 2022).

CHOGM. (2013), *Colombo Declaration on Sustainable, Inclusive and Equitable Development*, Available at https://thecommonwealth.org/news/colombo-declaration-sustainable-inclusive-and-equitable-development (Accessed 5 April 2022).

ComHabitat. (2010), *Urban Challenges: Scoping the State of the Commonwealth's Cities*, London: ComHabitat.

Commonwealth Secretariat. (2014), *Commonwealth Heads of Government Statement on the United Nations Post – 2015 Development Agenda*, Available at https://thecommonwealth.org/news/commonwealth-heads-government-united-nations-post-2015-development-agenda (Accessed 5 April 2022).

Farmer, P., Frojmovic, M., Hague, C., Harridge, C., Narang, S., Shishido, R., Siegel, D., Taylor, P. and Vogelij, J. (2006), *Reinventing Planning: A New Governance Paradigm for Managing Human Settlements, Position Paper for the World Planners Congress, Vancouver 17–20 June.* Available at http://globalplannersnetwork.org/wp-content/uploads/2016/10/reinventingplanningenglish-1.pdf (Accessed 5 April 2022).

Hague, C. (2012), *Do We Want More Sustainable Human Settlements in the Commonwealth? Then Let's Tackle the Capacity Gaps* (Unpublished paper for Commonwealth Foundation).

Houston, S., Kohlhase, J. and Narang Suri, S. (2012), *Resilience Planning in the Commonwealth: A Snapshot of Resilience Planning Across the Commonwealth, CAP* (unpublished paper).

James C.L.R. (1963), *Beyond a Boundary*, London: Hutchinson.

Malaza, N., Todes, A. and Williamson, A. with Hague, C. and the Women in Planning Network of the Commonwealth Association of Planners. (2009), *Gender in Planning and Urban Development, Commonwealth Secretariat Discussion Paper 7*, London: Commonwealth Secretariat.

Reeves, D. and Zombori, E. (2013), *Gender Equity Self-Assessment Tool for Local Government Planners* (CAP unpublished paper).

RTPI. (2020), *Enabling Healthy Placemaking, RTPI Research Paper.* Available at https://www.rtpi.org.uk/research/2020/july/enabling-healthy-placemaking/#intro (Accessed 10 February 2023).

UN. (2017), *New Urban Agenda*, New York: United Nations. Available at https://habitat3.org/the-new-urban-agenda/ (Accessed 10 February 2023).

UN-Habitat. (2006), *Report of the Third Session of the World Urban Forum, Vancouver, Canada June 2006.* Nairobi: UN Human Settlements Programme, Available at https://unhabitat.org/sites/default/files/documents/2019-05/3406_98924_wuf3-report.pdf (Accessed 4 April 2022).

UN-Habitat. (2009), *Planning Sustainable Cities: 2009 UN Habitat Global Report on Human Settlements.* Nairobi: UN Human Settlements Programme, Available at https://unhabitat.org/planning-sustainable-cities-global-report-on-human-settlements-2009 (Accessed 4 April 2022).

UN-Habitat. (2014), *Planning for Climate Change: A Strategic, Values-based Approach for Urban Planners, Cities and Climate Change Initiative Tool Series.* Nairobi: UN Human Settlements Programme. Available at https://mirror.unhabitat.org/list.asp?typeid=16&catid=550 (Accessed 3 August 2022).

UN-Habitat. (2015), *International Guidelines on Urban and Territorial Planning*, Nairobi: UN Human Settlements Programme, Available at https://unhabitat.org/international-guidelines-on-urban-and-territorial-planning (Accessed 4 April 2022).

7

2014–2020

Building global partnerships for sustainable urbanisation

Dyan Currie

The 2006–2014 period saw the recognition of planning as fundamental to guiding the world to a sustainable future. The role of planners was acknowledged as critical to research, inform and guide our nations and communities, to help address the global challenges particularly of climate change and rapid urbanisation. The world was changing, and assisted by technology, opportunities arose for CAP and its members to participate more readily, building networks and relationships necessary to support changes and develop guidance, plans and tools to address the key challenges.

I first became involved with CAP through my past role as national President of PIA, the Planning Institute of Australia (2011–2014) where I was connecting with the great work of CAP and the Global Planners Network (GPN). Working with CAP on matters of international policy and advocacy was such an inspiring process that I was happy to accept a nomination for President of CAP, to which I was elected in 2014 at the Singapore CAP Conference of Delegates (Business Meeting).

Embedding the SDGs and the development of the New Urban Agenda shaped this period and provided opportunities for CAP to extend relationships, pursue partnerships and collaborate on planning initiatives both inside and outside the Commonwealth.

In addition to increasing member understanding of the value of CAP and the importance of this international connection for our members, my main focus in my six years as President was on establishing and developing CAP's partnerships around the world. The core external partnership with UN Habitat, the United Nations Human Settlements Programme, involved CAP in major advocacy and policy initiatives. The partnership we developed resulted in the Commonwealth Sustainable Cities Initiative.

UN Habitat partnership

The UN Habitat connections were an early foundation of CAP's work in 2015 and my Presidency. I was privileged to be invited to be part of the drafting and working

DOI: 10.4324/9781003357933-9

groups during the development of the UN Sustainable Development Goals and the New Urban Agenda ahead of Habitat III in Quito, Ecuador in 2016. The UN Habitat events are only held every 20 years so it was an amazing opportunity for participation in a matter as critical for the planning profession as policy at this level. CAP was a central participant in major working groups such as the drafting of the SDG's and related targets and the New Urban Agenda policy document. During this time CAP also continued with critical work as a member of the World Urban Campaign with UN Habitat and I participated in the drafting groups for the document 'The City We Need 2.0.' Multiple CAP members were able to attend Habitat III and undertook amazing work and made significant contributions. In particular, the Royal Town Planning Institute's (RTPI) then President Phil Williams and CEO Trudi Elliott were critical in hosting sessions and attending the joint stand with GPN during this event. Other CAP members who attended and participated in multiple sessions included the Malaysia Institute of Planners and Canadian Institute of Planners. Just under 30,000 people attended Habitat III so it was an important opportunity to highlight the importance of the planning profession across the Commonwealth.

It was a pleasure and privilege to represent and advocate for planning at this level and to collaborate with UN Habitat including the Honourable Maimunah Mohd Sharif, Under Secretary and Executive Director, UN Habitat. The strength of the CAP and UN Habitat relationship is particularly evident in the shared recognition of the importance of the planning profession in contributing to high-quality future cities and communities. I have been able to continue this work as the Co-Chair of UN Habitat's Stakeholder Advisory Group since its establishment in 2019.

Fiji Declaration

Habitat III was followed by the Biennial CAP business meeting in Fiji in November 2016 which allowed CAP the opportunity to focus on the outcomes of Habitat III and to develop a workplan focussed around addressing the challenges of the Sustainable Development Goals and the New Urban Agenda. A core outcome of the business meeting (see Photo 7.1) was the CAP Fiji Declaration which called upon Governments of all Commonwealth nations to help deliver the agreed goals from Habitat III and recognised the crucial role of planners and spatial planning in achieving success. A further core outcome of this conference was the commencement of the formation of the Fiji Planners Association (FiPA). With the assistance of CAP a foundation group of Fijian planners resolved to form a formal association during the CAP Business meeting. CAP offered assistance to the foundation members, in the following years, until the organisation was officially created in 2020. Inaugural President Mere Naulumatua was instrumental in establishing FiPA, with support from the New Zealand Planning Institute (particularly CEO David Curtis and past President Bryce Julyan). Having a professional network is even more important in small communities facing significant challenges and it is wonderful to see this group forming and growing (formally joining CAP in 2021).

PHOTO 7.1 CAP Executive Committee Business Meeting, Sonaisali, Fiji 2016. President Dyan Currie (far centre) presides with Sec. Gen. Clive Harridge (far left) and CAP administrator Annette O'Donnell (far right), flanked by attending CAP vice presidents. Mere Naulumatua, inaugural President of FiPA (pictured far left) alongside then PIA President Brendan Nelson (second from left).

Source: Bryce Julyan

Toolkit for Rapid Urbanisation and Commonwealth Sustainable Cities Initiative partnership

The Fiji conference (Photo 7.2) was also a landmark event for CAP as it hosted the inauguration of the partnership with The Prince's Foundation and the Toolkit for Rapid Urbanisation (now the Rapid Planning Toolkit). The Toolkit was launched by the former Prince of Wales and has been a foundation piece for CAP and our members. This project led to the development of the Commonwealth Sustainable Cities Initiative and our ongoing partnership. The Planning for Rapid Urbanisation initiative was designed to draw on the extensive experience and knowledge within the Commonwealth to coordinate the development of innovative, practical online tools and educational resources to support all those involved in designing towns and cities to prepare for rapid but sustainable urbanisation. This project delivered a free online toolkit which was piloted on the ground to test its utility and confirm its usefulness as a highly valuable tool.

The Toolkit is free to the public and in my view is an outstanding achievement and an example of the assistance that can be provided to our members and communities around the world. Along with others, I was proud to work together with Ben Bolgar, Director at The Prince's Foundation, on this project. Ben's intellect, compassion and commitment to this work were outstanding.

The partners involved in the preparation of the Toolkit have become major partners of CAP over the following years and have established an ongoing working relationship. Our partners in this process (The Prince's Foundation, Commonwealth Association of Architects (CAA), Commonwealth Local Government Forum (CLGF)) expanded discussions and research into the challenges of rapid urbanisation and climate change within the Commonwealth. At the same time, the CAA partnered with CAP and others to undertake a survey of the planning and architecture professions throughout the Commonwealth in an effort to understand the capacity of the built environment professions to address the challenges facing growth in the Commonwealth. The *Survey of the Built Environment Professions in the Commonwealth* (the Commonwealth Association of Architects, the Commonwealth Association of Planners, the Commonwealth Association of Surveying and Land Economy and the Commonwealth Engineers Council, Principal authors: Oborn and Walters (2020)) documented and highlighted the significant capacity shortage of built environment professionals to assist in the creation of sustainable cities into the future. It highlights the need for ongoing advocacy but also a critical need for new solutions. The survey results were launched at CHOGM in London and then in WUF 10 Abu Dhabi (second round of research). The survey was a significant collaborative achievement between CAP and the partners (in particular Peter Oborn and the CAA). The survey can be found at www.commonwealth-planners.org/surveyofplanningbuiltenvironment.

The Commonwealth Sustainable Cities Initiative

The Commonwealth Sustainable Cities Initiative and the ongoing partnership have become a significant area of focus for CAP and critical to CAP's future planning and advocacy roles. The collaboration included co-hosting a major series of webinars (with attendance from around the world) as a precursor event to CHOGM (the latter was sadly deferred due to COVID-19). In an effort to advocate for this initiative and to highlight the scale of work needed around the Commonwealth to achieve sustainable cities in the future, a working partnership of The Association of Commonwealth Universities, CAA, CAP, CLGF and The Prince's Foundation, working in collaboration with the Rwandan Ministry of Infrastructure, the Rwandan Ministry of Local Government worked to develop a series of technical events, a good practice platform and then a Call to Action over the 2019/2020 period.

This work was showcased at WUF 10 in Abu Dhabi where the partnership hosted or participated in six technical events and was referenced in the formal WUF 10 Declaration. This excellent work continues today and is a superb example of the proactive partnerships which adds value to CAP and its members.

The Sustainable Cities Initiative partners' passion, energy and commitment to assisting the members of the Commonwealth to develop high quality future communities is inspiring. In particular I acknowledge the collaboration and contribution of the individuals representing the core partners including Jeremy Cross, Peter Oborn, Alice Preston-Jones, Lucy Slack and Alex Wright.

A further significant event was held in October 2021, on the eve of COP26. At this high level event, involving key Commonwealth partners and The Prince's Foundation, participants considered ways in which the Commonwealth could respond to the 'triple threat' of climate change, rapid urbanisation and the COVID-19 pandemic. In particular, the participants concluded that there is a critical and urgent need for collaboration if the climate change targets are to be met within the limited time now available.

Commonwealth observance day ceremonies

One of the special privileges of leading CAP, being an accredited Commonwealth organisation, was the invitation to attend the annual Commonwealth Service held on Commonwealth Day in Westminster Abbey in the presence of Her late Majesty Queen Elizabeth II followed by a reception at Marlborough House. The 2015 event also included a formal dinner at Clarence House with the former Prince of Wales.

Governance review

CAP undertook a review of our governance processes during my terms as President. This review led to significant changes to the CAP Constitution and improved democratic representation across our membership and modernised access arrangements. These changes were adopted at the Fiji Business meeting in 2016.

PHOTO 7.2 Delegates at the Sustainable Development Conference, Sonaisali, Fiji, Nov. 2016. The CAP Business Meeting held in Fiji, immediately following Habitat III (Quito, Ecuador), resulted in CAPs Fiji Declaration (this can be found at: www.commonwealth-planners.org/cap-fiji-declaration).

Source: Dyan Currie

PHOTO 7.3 CAP Executive Committee at the Business Meeting in Cape Town, South Africa, 2018. Planning Africa Conference 2018.

Source: Dyan Currie

CAP Planning Awards

Another highlight of this period was the development of the CAP Planning Awards for Outstanding Planning Achievement. The inaugural award was given at the Planning Africa conference in Cape Town in November 2018 (Photo 7.3). These awards have continued from that point and have been highly successful in highlighting the excellent work occurring in planning across the Commonwealth (Photo 7.4).

CAP Patron

I was particularly pleased when CAP resolved in 2018 to appoint Trudi Elliott CBE to the inaugural role of CAP Patron. Trudi started at RTPI at the same time as I commenced as PIA President and is an outstanding advocate for RTPI and the planning profession. She has provided wise counsel to CAP and I was grateful for her guidance during my terms. Trudi's expertise and commitment to CAP has been exceptional and she has continued her dedication to the planning profession and CAP after moving on from her role with RTPI. Trudi has led the CAP Planning Awards programme since its inception (initiated by Clive Harridge, Secretary General at the time and Steve Yirenki – Ghana Institute of Planners).

PHOTO 7.4 CAP Awards 2019. John Archer (left) and Phillip Clarke (centre) from One World Link receive an award from Secretary-General Clive Harridge (right) for their work in Bo, Sierra Leone.

Source: Clive Harridge

CAP's international relationships were strengthened during this time, including with the Habitat Professionals Network and the Global Planners Network. These are key areas of partnership for us along with being founding members of the Planners for Climate Action (P4CA) group (inaugurated at WUF 9 in Kuala Lumpur, Malaysia).

Commonwealth Heads of Government Meetings

Participating in the Commonwealth Heads of Government Meetings (CHOGM) including presenting in the Commonwealth People's Forums held alongside the CHOGM sessions in Malta (2015), London (2018) is a highlight as having the opportunity to input into policy at that level is tremendous. While CHOGM 2020 was deferred due to COVID-19, the significant preparatory work was still able to be useful with the Commonwealth Sustainable Initiatives partnership organising a major online series of webinars including participation by the former Prince of Wales. CAP has worked hard over this period to raise the importance of the planning profession as part of the solution to the complex challenges facing the planet.

Young Planners Network

An ongoing focus for the CAP Executive has been developing the Young Planners Network and introducing online learning around the Commonwealth and then contributing to the drafting of the Commonwealth Youth Manifesto in 2018. The CAP Young Planners Network was led by Viral Desai for many years and then by Olafiyin Taiwo. The outstanding commitment of these two Young Planning leaders is to be commended. I remain convinced that the future of our profession is in excellent hands (see Chapter 12).

Women in Planning Network

A second core network is the Women in Planning Network and in 2018 the Women In Planning Manifesto was launched. Kristin Agnello convened the group at this time, which dedicated significant time and energy to assisting women in planning around the globe (see Chapter 9).

Caribbean disaster recovery project

CAP has also worked hard to try to assist members during times of crisis with projects such as the Caribbean disaster recovery project (Kirk et al., 2019a, 2019b) – see Photo 7.5. This project was funded through a grant from the Commonwealth Foundation to undertake a study reviewing the planning responses to the Caribbean hurricanes of 2017 including lessons learnt and tools and mechanisms that could be applied using experiences from around the world. The benefit of this type of work is its transferability. Lessons learnt can be shared across the Commonwealth and may be useful in other countries or regions. For instance, through CAP, planners in the small island nations in

PHOTO 7.5 Hurricane damaged school, Road Town, Tortola, British Virgin Islands, 2018. A CAP team reviewed the planning responses a year after Hurricanes Irma and Maria struck the north-eastern Caribbean in Sept. 2017.

Source: Bryce Julyan

the Pacific were able to exchange knowledge and draw from the comparable experiences in the Caribbean. The work demonstrated the collective ability for CAP to pull together a collaborative, largely voluntary team involving the New Zealand Planning Institute CAP vice president Bryce Julyan and members of the Caribbean Planners Association Dr Asad Mohammed, Dr Perry Polar, Dr Ancil Kirk and Joanna Raynold Arthurton. It was commendable work to deliver this project during a busy period.

World Urban Forums

One of the challenges in working with members located around the world is finding opportunities for face-to-face discussions and international advocacy that is relevant to everyone. The World Urban Forum (WUF) events and processes organised by UN Habitat have been a core opportunity for CAP and our partners to highlight the important challenges posed by the SDGs and to collectively pursue the goal of achieving sustainable cities and communities. Hosting seminars, panels and workshops and organising stands at significant events (WUF events host up to 15,000 people) takes substantial commitment

PHOTO 7.6 CAP partner representatives at WUF9, Kuala Lumpur, Malaysia, 2018. (L-R) Ric Stephens ISOCARP, Jeff Soule APA, Bryce Julyan NZPI-CAP vice president, Dyan Currie CAP President and Eleanor Mohammed CIP-CAP vice president.

Source: Dyan Currie

and support. Consequently, CAP has been very grateful to its core partners over many years for co-hosting opportunities. Our members have participated in organising the main events (WUF 9 in Malaysia including Malaysian Institute of Planners members on the organising committee), submitted and hosting a range of seminars, networking events and presentations and hosted combined stands to highlight the work of the planning profession. CAP was active and represented at WUF 9 Malaysia (Photo 7.6) and WUF 10 Abu Dhabi during my Presidency, supported and made possible by our members, who have regularly worked so hard to ensure our profession was showcased at these events. CAP's participation at these events was enabled through the selfless efforts of our member organisations particularly RTPI, CIP, MIP, NZPI and our partners in the Commonwealth Sustainable Cities Initiative.

Other partnerships

CAP also has partnerships outside the Commonwealth such as the Global Planners Network, which includes the American Planning Association (APA) and International Federation of Housing and Planning (IFHP). In the spirit of global collaboration these partners generously share knowledge and experience from different sectors and have been incredible supporters of combined sessions and functions at international events. This has helped spread the workload and build the profile of CAP (see Photo 7.7).

PHOTO 7.7 The five presidents at CIP Centenary celebrations, Ottawa, Canada, July 2019. (L-R) Kurt Christiansen APA, Dyan Currie CAP, Eleanor Mohammed CIP, Ian Tant RTPI and Steve O'Connor PIA.

Source: Ian Tant

Acknowledgements

The Commonwealth covers the globe and CAP is a volunteer organisation. It relies on the support of its members and relationships with its partners. CAP only functions and operates through the efforts of its volunteers.

The CAP Executive Committee attend meetings late at night and early in the morning to accommodate the various time-zones. It is these individuals – from planning organisations around the world – that give time and effort to improve and enhance our collective knowledge, tools and skills so that the communities we live and work in are better off.

The 2014–2020 years consolidated the role of planners and value of planning in shaping a future that enables sustainable urbanisation. Building on the SDGs this period saw the establishment of guiding principles to shape this future such as the New Urban Agenda. CAP was active in this process and participated through the dedication and remarkable efforts of the members and volunteers as well as through our collaboration with key partners. As CAPs 50th year loomed the focus on sustainable urbanisation for our cities and settlements was supported by enduring relationships, key partnerships and best practice – informed by strong principles embedded in our education and practice amongst our members.

References

Kirk, A., Julyan, B. and Reynold, J. (2019a), *Review of National and Local Area Planning Methodologies in the Eastern Caribbean. Cap.* Available at www.commonwealth-planners org/_files/ugd/25734f_1428c4718b6f46c0ba617a836c466619.pdf (Accessed 9 March 2023).

Kirk, A., Julyan, B. and Reynold, J. (2019b), *Summary Report of OECS Land Use Planning Methodology Review Workshop, 27–28 Nov 2018. Cap.* Available at www.commonwealth-planners.org/_files/ugd/25734f_51178fc3c9ac4e48804ab04594343377.pdf (Accessed 9 March 2023).

Oborn, P. and Walters, J.G. (2020), *Planning for Climate Change and Rapid Urbanisation: Survey of the Built Environment Professions in the Commonwealth, Survey Results.* Available at https://commonwealthsustainablecities.org/survey/ (Accessed 2 August 2022).

8
2020–2022

The road to the Kigali Declaration on sustainable urbanisation and beyond

Eleanor Mohammed and Kelley Moore

Continuing advocacy during a pandemic

As the past president of the Canadian Institute of Planners (CIP) and their representative to the Global Planners Network, I recognised the power of CAP as an advocate for planning, the capacity of the profession and the importance of delivering the UN2030 Agenda for Sustainable Development and the New Urban Agenda (NUA) and in taking Climate Action. Throughout my four-year term at CIP, I had many opportunities to collaborate with CAP and to develop international relationships at important events such as the Habitat III conference in Quito, the UN-Habitat World Urban Forums (WUFs) in Kuala Lumpur (2018) and Abu Dhabi (2019) and the Caribbean Urban Forums in Caribbean Community and Common Market (CARICOM) cities.

By my election to CAP President in 2020, the COVID-19 pandemic had completely shifted how organisations, our partners and members conducted business and operations. Everything moved online – including the CAP Business Meeting where I was elected. Central business districts emptied and many planners found themselves working from home. This helped bring CAP members together and led to greater participation of the national representatives at regular meetings.

Continuing the work of previous presidents, advocacy has been an important element of my work. Representing CAP, I became co-chair of the UN-Habitat Professionals Forum (HPF), and amidst other things developed new terms of reference for the Forum. This put in place an important foundation that will allow professional planners and planning to have a greater influence in the initiatives implemented by UN-Habitat.

Building new partnerships for sustainable urbanisation

In the early 2020s CAP continues to participate in a number of UN-Habitat initiatives, including Planners for Climate Action (P4CA), the World Urban Campaign

(WUC) working groups and Urban Thinker Campuses. CAP has been a keynote, panellist and moderator at a number of WUC Urban Thinker Campuses which have promoted planning globally and provided key content that is being used in UN-Habitat's review of the NUA.

Partnerships have been widened to include the Urban Economy Forum (UEF) and the World Urban Pavilion in Canada. The UEF is an international organisation that engages with the United Nations (UN) system, city leaders, academia, civil society and the private sector to build capacities and global networks for the Sustainable Development Goals (SDGs), particularly SDG 11 – Sustainable Cities and Communities, by leading global dialogues on sustainable urban resources. Through the UEF, CAP has a platform to share important planning perspectives and approaches to addressing and localising the SDGs across the Commonwealth and beyond.

The World Urban Pavilion is a global hub for that dialogue to be centred, along with the exchange of urban knowledge and innovation. The Pavilion is supported by UN-Habitat and the Canadian Mortgage and Housing Corporation, and CAP has been a key partner in the launch of the Women's Secretariat within the Pavilion.

However, the most important work of CAP in relation to sustainable urbanisation and climate action is being done in collaboration with partner Commonwealth organisations through the Commonwealth Sustainable Cities Initiative (CSCI) and the Call to Action (CTA) on sustainable cities (Commonwealth Sustainable Cities, 2022). As Dyan Currie explained in Chapter 7, the CTA was developed and facilitated through a collaboration with Commonwealth partners – the Commonwealth Local Government Forum (CLGF), the Association of Commonwealth Universities (ACU) and the Commonwealth Association of Architects (CAA) in close collaboration with The Prince's Foundation and the government of Rwanda.

The CTA was launched in February 2021. It shares key areas of concern with the NUA, underpinned by common principles and objectives with urgent need for:

- Sustainable urbanisation and climate action to be embedded in policies to support the achievement of the NUA and SDGs.
- Dialogue to define, implement and sustain new collaborative ways of working across the Commonwealth and beyond.
- A commitment to implementation of practical action to support sustainable cities and human settlements supported by enabling institutional and intergovernmental mechanisms.

Alongside the launch of the CTA, CAP and its partners created the Commonwealth Sustainable Urbanisation Online Programme comprised of twelve online webinars convened in June to September 2021 during the pandemic. These attracted more than 2,000 participants from all regions of the Commonwealth and from non-Commonwealth countries including Bahrain, Iraq, Nepal and the Philippines.

Work has continued on the Rapid Planning Toolkit for Urban Expansion (see Photo 8.1). The Toolkit is a four-step process which aims to provide a simple and streamlined

PHOTO 8.1 The Rapid Planning Toolkit in action. Rapid Planning Toolkit site meeting with Bo City Council representatives facilitated by One World Link. Bo, Sierra Leone, 2019.

Source: Philip Clarke, One World Link

methodology to shape sustainable urban growth despite the scale and pace of urbanisation. It was piloted in Sierra Leone, The Gambia and a small village in Bangladesh – and extended into Ghana. In collaboration with the University College of Estate Management at the University of Reading and with support from CSCI partners, The Prince's Foundation created an online platform that guides users through learning about – and implementation of – the Toolkit. In 2022 it was being tested in five Commonwealth countries – Trinidad and Tobago, Pakistan, Malaysia, Zambia and Fiji. Each location has representation from a mix of sectors including architects, planners, academics, engineers, surveyors, local government and youth.

CAP also collaborated in online events in July 2021 under the title of 'Building Better Data,' aimed at improving the quality and availability of data to support sustainable urbanisation in the Commonwealth. The events were held in collaboration with the CAA, International Growth Centre, Ordnance Survey and Nesta Challenges.

At the heart of the CSCI and the CTA is the Survey of Built Environment Professionals. Under Dyan Currie's presidency, CAP partnered with CAA, the Commonwealth Association of Surveying and Land Economy (CASLE) and the Commonwealth Engineering Council (CEC) to undertake the first survey in 2017 and a follow-up in

2020, with another follow-up planned in 2022/2023. The survey revealed a critical shortfall in professional capacity to respond to the demands of rapid urbanisation and climate change in many Commonwealth countries. For example, the average ratio of planners per thousand head of population in the United Kingdom and Canada is 0.330 and 0.167 respectively, whereas in Nigeria, Pakistan and Tanzania it is 0.008, 0.006 and 0.006 respectively (Oborn and Walters, 2020, p. 24).

Kigali 2022 – putting sustainable urbanisation on the agenda

In October 2021 on the eve of COP26, a high-level event was convened by key Commonwealth partners and The Prince's Foundation to consider ways in which the Commonwealth could respond to the 'triple threat' of climate change, rapid urbanisation and the COVID-19 pandemic and the need for collaboration if the targets in the SDGs and NUA are to be met within the limited time available.

The initial purpose – and one of the key targets – in the work of the CSCI and the CTA was to leverage the Commonwealth Heads of Government Meeting (CHOGM) in Kigali, Rwanda to centre sustainable urbanisation and climate action in Commonwealth conversations on our collective future. The CHOGM was deferred in 2021 for a year due to COVID-19, when the CSCI partners finally had our chance to shine. CAP joined with its partners in leading *A Call to Action on Sustainable Urbanisation Across the Commonwealth Official Side-Event*, over two days in the wings of the Kigali CHOGM (see Photo 8.2).

This side-event provided an exceptional opportunity to convene key Commonwealth stakeholders, to review the CTA, share good practices, explore opportunities to mobilise the Commonwealth and identify priorities and actions to advance the CTA during CHOGM and at the upcoming 11th UN-Habitat WUF, the 27th UN Climate Change Conference (COP27) and other future high-level global events. Panellists attended from across the globe and discussed, engaged and debated:

- How we leave no one behind and move forward together.
- Empowering cities.
- Closing the gaps of capacity, data, evidence and policy.
- Cities as centres of economic growth and securing long-term finance.
- Accelerating climate action.
- Urban water resilience.

We were honoured to host the executive director of UN-Habitat, Maimunah Modh Sharif and the government of Rwanda, Minister of Infrastructure Dr Ernest Nsabimana, along with many other international ministers, mayors and high-level officials and professionals from government, the private sector and civil society.

In addition to this side-event, CAP and the CSCI partners shared four important launches to implement the CTA and to address sustainable urbanisation and climate action. The first was the Commonwealth Youth for Sustainable Urbanisation

PHOTO 8.2 At the side-event, CHOGM, Kigali, Rwanda 2022. Kelley Moore, Ms Maimunah Mohd Sharif, Eleanor Mohammed and Olafiyin Taiwo.

Source: Eleanor Mohammed

(CYSU). With 60% of the population of the Commonwealth under the age of 30, CYSU aims to empower Commonwealth Youth to support, contribute to and advocate for sustainable urbanisation and climate action in the Commonwealth and to explore ways that cities and human settlements can better reflect the needs of youth.

Nearly 50% of the projected increase in the world's urban population to 2050 is forecast to be in Commonwealth countries (that's 1 billion additional urban dwellers by 2050). That growth is expected particularly in African Commonwealth cities. To acknowledge this and support CAP members in addressing this massive challenge, a new CAP East Africa Network (CAPEAN) was also launched during the 2022 CHOGM. This network is being locally led in East Africa and their terms of reference were being developed at the time of writing this book. The same day as the launch of the CAPEAN, the Rwanda Urban Planning Institute also became an official member of CAP.

Partnerships connecting professionals, governments and civil society remain crucial. To advance the CTA, the third launch at the 2022 CHOGM was *The Kigali Commitment*. Twenty Commonwealth Built Environment organisations endorsed the *Commitment to Collaborate in support of the Call to Action on Sustainable Urbanisation across the Commonwealth*, with the intent to expand in the following year. Signatory organisations pledged to:

- To invite and bring together all the Commonwealth Built Environment Professions to engage in the implementation of the CTA.

- To champion the CTA, sustainable urbanisation and climate action and ensure it is at the heart of all Built Environment Professional ethics, standards, data, principles and policies.
- To promote and develop dialogue in each of our respective jurisdictions to define and develop a new way of working towards transparent and accountable multi-level governance in addressing sustainable urbanisation and climate change.
- To lead the development of new partnerships and strategies within and between the public, private and non-profit sectors and all levels of government to achieve a Commonwealth-led response to the challenges and opportunities of sustainable urbanisation and climate change.
- To come together between – and at – CHOGM to review progress and look at future opportunities to take practical action to address sustainable urbanisation, climate change and SDGs.
- To promote and celebrate the Built Environment Professions as experts in sustainable urbanisation and in taking climate action and to jointly advocate for the CTA to Commonwealth Heads of Government and other associated international organisations.

I am optimistic and excited to see where this leads and how it can positively impact the implementation of the CTA.

The fourth launch was for a new alliance with Practical Action, World Resources Institute, WaterAid, The Prince's Foundation and the CSCI partners to accelerate action on climate and urban water resilience in towns and cities across Africa (Practical Action, 2022).

In a great measure of the CSCI's and the CTA's success, on completion of CHOGM, the Heads of Government adopted the Kigali Declaration to prioritise a greater focus on sustainable urbanisation to address the impacts of rapid urbanisation and climate change in the Commonwealth, to ensure liveable cities, towns and villages for all Commonwealth citizens (Commonwealth Secretariat, 2022a). Potentially, this is a major step forward for the Commonwealth.

Just days after Kigali, I represented at the UN-Habitat WUF11 in Katowice. Our aim was to gain further impetus on the CTA and to promote our Women in Planning Network, Young Planners Networks and new East Africa Network. The CAP team and I were speakers and panellists in over ten events. As a speaker for the World Urban Campaign 'City We Need Now' special event, I was able to share the successes of CHOGM and further actions that CAP is taking to implement the SDGs and the NUA. At WUF11 we created new partnerships for implementing the CTA, including additional on-the-ground projects for East Africa.

In the same week, the Leaders of the Group of 7 (G7) rich nations, which include Canada and the UK, met in Elmau, Germany. Here too there was a landmark declaration on sustainable urbanisation (see box 8.1).

After decades of campaigning by scientists, professionals and civil society, might 2022 prove a turning point? Certainly, at CHOGM and WUF, CAP accompanied

> **BOX 8.1 G7 ENGAGES WITH SUSTAINABLE URBAN DEVELOPMENT.**
>
> *51. Recognising the particular strain multiple crises have put on developing countries we reaffirm our strong commitment to put the 2030 Agenda for Sustainable Development and the Addis Ababa Action Agenda at the centre of our agendas to mainstream sustainable development across all policy priorities. We will accelerate our efforts to achieve the Sustainable Development Goals by 2030 by mobilising all sectors and levels of society.*
>
> *56. Cities are places of diversity and identity, exchange and integration, creativity, and solidarity. They are crucial to driving prosperity and ensuring equal opportunities for all. We acknowledge the significant role of cities, their associations, and networks as actors in our transformation towards sustainable development. We commit to foster exchange among and with cities. We task our relevant Ministers to develop a joint understanding of good urban development policy to be adopted at the first ever G7 Ministerial Meeting for Sustainable Urban Development, and to decide on joint initiatives for unlocking the full potential of cities to promote social, cultural, technological, climate-neutral, economic, and democratic innovation for the common good.*
>
> Source: (G7 (2022).

by its partner Commonwealth organisations, took to governments our messages about the importance of delivering sustainable urbanisation and climate action and provoked a more positive response than ever before. However, if the Kigali Declaration marks the end of the beginning for CAP's role in promoting planning for sustainable urbanisation and climate action, the 2020s must become the beginning of a long process of delivery across the Commonwealth and for all peoples and communities around the globe.

Decolonisation and anti-racism

The modern Commonwealth is centred on free and equal voluntary cooperation of independent countries. CAP must continue to be grounded in equity, diversity, inclusion and anti-racism, so that professional planners and the practice of planning around the world better reflects the communities we serve and the organisations and individuals who make up our membership.

To move forward, we also need to look back as a profession on the impact of colonialism and how our profession grew out of a land settlement and governing system that marginalized Black, Indigenous and People of Colour.

In 2006, the United Nations Declaration on the Rights of Indigenous Peoples called for an end to systemic discrimination, recognition for inherent right to self-determination and honouring of promises made to First Peoples at the time of settlement.

> Indigenous peoples have suffered from historic injustices as a result of, inter alia, their colonialization and dispossession of their lands, territories and resources, thus preventing them from exercising, in particular, their right to development in accordance with their own needs and interests . . . [there is] the urgent need to respect and promote the rights of indigenous peoples affirmed in treaties, agreements and other constructive arrangements.
>
> UN General Assembly, 2007, p. 3

There are pockets of progress towards this end emerging in planning throughout the Commonwealth (see Box 8.2). Some have been celebrated in CAP's annual Awards.

One of the UN's founding purposes is to promote and encourage respect for human rights and fundamental freedoms for all without distinction as to race, sex, language or religion (UN-Habitat, 2020). An end to racism and racial discrimination is also enshrined in the Universal Declaration of Human Rights. As decreed in the Commonwealth Charter, Member Countries and CAP as an accredited Commonwealth Organisation are:

> fully committed to the Universal Declaration of Human Rights and other relevant human rights covenants and international instruments. We are committed to equality and respect for the protection and promotion of civil, political, economic, social and cultural rights, including the right to development, for all without discrimination on any grounds as the foundations of peaceful, just and stable societies.

BOX 8.2 CANADA PUTS RECONCILIATION WITH INDIGENOUS PEOPLE INTO ITS PLANNING.

In 2015, the Canadian Truth and Reconciliation Commission released their 94 Calls to Action calling for all levels of government to fully adopt and implement the UN Declaration on the Rights of Indigenous People. In 2016, the Government of Canada endorsed this direction. In 2019, the CIP Board of Directors released the *Policy on Planning Practice and Reconciliation* as a guide for planners leading discussions to foster respectful relationships and reconciliation through the planning process.

We note that these rights are universal, indivisible, interdependent and interrelated and cannot be implemented selectively. We are implacably opposed to all forms of discrimination, whether rooted in gender, race, colour, creed, political belief or other grounds.

Commonwealth Secretariat, 2022b

Professional planning standards are being updated to acknowledge the importance of representation and to reflect the pivotal role planners have in building relationships with Black, Indigenous and People of Colour founded upon mutual respect, trust, dialogue and meaningful engagement (Canadian Institute of Planners, 2019). As we reconcile our past, planners are listening, supporting, taking action and emerging as champions for human rights and anti-racism in the formation of laws, policies and engagement practices (see Box 8.3).

While great strides are being made, there is still much to be done. Addressing equity, diversity, inclusion, and anti-racism is not a singular project or working group; it requires on-going efforts by all.

The road ahead

CAP recognises that the challenges of today and the future require solutions, innovation, collaborative policy development and technology adaptation from a variety of perspectives, geographic locations, cultural backgrounds and social contexts. Through the partnerships established between Commonwealth nations and beyond,

---

BOX 8.3   MOVES TOWARDS EQUITY, DIVERSITY AND INCLUSION.

In Queensland, Australia, the 2016 Planning Act introduced a provision requiring the consideration of Aboriginal and Torres Strait Islander people's knowledge, culture and tradition as an integral part of advancing the purpose of the Act. This was strongly supported by the Queensland Division of the Planning Institute of Australia (Harwood and Wensing, 2017).

The Women in Planning Network of the Planning Institute of Australian produced a discussion paper on gender equity that also acknowledged 'the strength, resilience and contributions of our Aboriginal and Torres Strait Islander peoples, and the eternal and spiritual connection they hold for their lands, waters, cultures and beliefs' (Thorpe et al., 2021, p. 2).

The Royal Town Planning Institute (2020) published its Equality, Diversity and Inclusivity Action Plan.

The CIP (2020) produced its Equity, Diversity, and Inclusion Roadmap.

Sources: as identified in the box.

we are stronger together. Moving into the future, CAP will continue to build strategic partnerships to promote and support systematic positive change to embed human rights, sustainable urbanisation and climate change mitigation and adaptation. We will continue to seek and create tools to assist planners and communities in developing sustainable human settlements. The world needs planners more than ever.

References

Canadian Institute of Planners. (2019), *Policy on Planning Practice and Reconciliation*. Ottawa: CIP. Available at www.cip-icu.ca/Indigenous-Planning# (Accessed 18 May 2022).

Canadian Institute of Planners. (2020), *Equality, Diversity and Inclusion Roadmap*, Available at www.cip-icu.ca/Topics/Equity-Diversity-and-Inclusion (Accessed 12 July 2022).

Commonwealth Secretariat. (2022a), *CHOGM 2022 Communiqué, Leaders' Statement, and Declarations on Delivering a Common Future*, Available at https://thecommonwealth.org/news/chogm-2022-communique-leaders-statement-and-declarations-delivering-common (Accessed 10 March 2023).

Commonwealth Secretariat. (2022b), *Commonwealth Charter*, Available at https://thecommonwealth.org/charter (Accessed 12 July 2022).

Commonwealth Sustainable Cities. (2022), *Call to Action on Sustainable Urbanisation Across the Commonwealth*, Available at https://commonwealthsustainablecities.org/calltoaction/ (Accessed 6 August 2022).

G7. (2022), *G7 Leaders' Communiqué*, Available at https://pm.gc.ca/en/news/statements/2022/06/28/g7-leaders-communique (Accessed 11 July 2022).

Harwood, S. and Wensing, E. (2017), *Background Report on Draft Aboriginal and Torres Strait Islander Planning Policy*, Cairns: James Cook University.

Oborn, P. and Walters, J.G. (2020), *Planning for Climate Change and Rapid Urbanisation: Survey of the Built Environment Professions in the Commonwealth*, Survey Results. Available at https://commonwealthsustainablecities.org/survey/ (Accessed 2 August 2022).

Practical Action. (2022), *New Opportunity to Help Billions of City Residents Cope with Climate Change*, Available at https://practicalaction.org/news-media/2022/06/21/new-opportunity-to-help-billions-of-city-residents-cope-with-climate-change/ (Accessed 11 July 2022).

Royal Town Planning Institute. (2020), *Change – Equality, Diversity and Inclusivity Action Plan*, Available at www.rtpi.org.uk/media/4157/equality-diversity-and-inclusivity-plan.pdf (Accessed 12 July 2022).

Thorpe, A., McCabe, A., Johnson, C., Hobbs, E., Bailey, M. and Hartigan, M. (2021), *Developing a National Gender Equity Policy for the Planning Profession: A Discussion Paper*. Barton, ACT: Planning Institute of Australia Women in Planning Network.

UN General Assembly. (2007), *United Nations Declaration on the Rights of Indigenous Peoples: Resolution/adopted by the General Assembly*, 2 October, A/RES/61/295, Available at www.refworld.org/docid/471355a82.html (Accessed 12 July 2022).

UN Habitat. (2020), *Statement by UN Habitat on Racism and Discrimination*. Available at https://unhabitat.org/statement-by-un-habitat-on-racism-and-discrimination (Accessed 12 July 2022).

9

GENDER AND SUSTAINABLE URBANISATION – THE WORK OF THE CAP WOMEN IN PLANNING NETWORK

Jua Cilliers and Kristin Agnello

A solid foundation from which CAP continues to build (as it heads into its second half century) is its support for Women in Planning. The Commonwealth Women in Planning Network (CWIP) has been established for over two decades and is a global network which supports the role (and contribution) of Women in Planning.

Background (why Women in Planning globally?)

Women have been vocal about the different needs in the urban environment, but these needs have not necessarily been recognised because, as Greed (2003) states, the planning profession has historically been male dominated. While this comment was applied to the profession worldwide this is also true in the Commonwealth. Preliminary findings from the Commonwealth Association of Planners' *Survey of the Planning Profession in the Commonwealth* (Currie et al., 2018) revealed a significant gender imbalance in the planning profession. There were substantial variations in ratios of male and female planners across the Commonwealth, with the highest proportion of female planners being in Belize 70%, Fiji 54%, Barbados 54%, and Zambia 48% and the lowest proportions in Malta 15%, Nigeria 25%, South Africa 30%, Namibia 38% and the UK 38%.

The women's liberation movement in the 1970s and 1980s triggered a number of challenges from a feminist perspective to the planning profession and to mainstream practice.

Ways in which patriarchy was embedded in built environment practice were specifically confronted and a call to advocate for change become more prominent. This was especially apparent through the work of the Women's Design Service – providing advice and advocacy for more inclusive planning – and the work of the Greater London Council (GLC) women's committees in seeking to address inequalities. The 1990s saw academics start to publish in this field; for example, Clara Greed (1996) and Little (1994).

DOI: 10.4324/9781003357933-11

This work (and thinking) was reflected in practice with the creation of the RTPI Practice Advice Note 12 Planning for Women (1995). Slowly but surely, there was some progress towards the understanding that the cities of the 21st century require gender-transformative urban planning to ensure that urban infrastructure can support good governance and safety for all citizens, irrespective of gender or issues of identity (Ortiz Escalante and Gutiérrez Valdivia, 2015).

Current reality (status of Women in Planning globally)

As with most professions, feminist discussions in urban and regional planning have become more prominent (Hendler, 2005). The view of urban planning from a gender perspective is likewise better understood from the starting point that women are experts about the places they live and that women, as with all other groups which constitute being 'users of the space,' should contribute to shaping these spaces (Ortiz Escalante and Gutiérrez Valdivia, 2015).

There has also been some progress moving away from the broad feminist critique of planning (Ritzdorf, 1994; Roy, 2001; Saarikoski, 2002) towards more of an appreciation of a feminist approach as a conceptual framework to deliver broader social justice for all (Speak, 2012). As feminist-informed literature increased, especially in relation to housing (Gilroy and Woods, 1994), land use (Reed, 1997), safety (Wekerle and Whitzman, 1995) and philosophical approaches to planning (Roy, 2001, Saarikoski, 2002), it became more evident that it is not enough for feminism to be a guiding principle of urban planning but that it should be a practical tool for action to make further progress in this space.

'Feminist ideology must not only describe the world to be built but must provide the tools with which to build it' (Speak, 2012). This realisation laid the foundation for a global movement towards collectively creating such a framework and supporting tools. There is a renewed understanding that women have a fundamental role to play as designers of – and active participants in – the built environment, as well as in advancing the Sustainable Development Goals (SDGs), the New Urban Agenda (NUA) and the International Guidelines for Urban and Territorial Planning (IGUTP). There is a broader appreciation for the role that women can play in developing policies and in shaping decision-making processes, which will lead to more effective, inclusive and sustainable environments and community-wide resilience.

CWIP history (development and leadership)

The CWIP was established in 2001 under the leadership of Olusola Olufemi from the University of the Witwatersrand, Johannesburg, South Africa with the support of Alicia Yon from Australia, amongst others. One of the first things it did was seek information from member organisations about the impact of planning on gender, impact of gender on planning, role of gender in planning and suggested roles of gender in planning. Some of the responses are shown in Box 9.1.

In 2004 at the Kuala Lumpur Business Meeting, it was agreed that the CWIP should be regionalised to reflect the regional nature of CAP. Dr Roxana Hafiz

> **BOX 9.1 ATTITUDES TOWARDS WOMEN IN PLANNING IN SOME COMMONWEALTH COUNTRIES, 2000.**
>
> Jean Hillier responded: 'In Western Australia we are at the stage of making women more visible by informing planning officers that women have different needs from men in the built environment and women experience the built environment differently. We have not yet begun to enter the stage of celebrating women's diversity and considering the different needs of different groups of women-aged, pregnant, ethnicity etc. . . .Too often women lose their gender awareness when they enter the planning office at the start of the working day. They are taught (in education and practice) that planning is neutral and too often blindly accept this and continue to plan in what is effectively a male stream manner.'
>
> From the UK, Dory Reeves reported: 'Many people have a dismissive approach to the role of gender (women) in planning. It is disregarded by others who see social inclusion as the catch all.'
>
> J. Babarinde emailed that in Zambia 'socio-economic and indeed psychological barriers, given the hazardous nature of the built environment professions, hinder women from being involved.'
>
> From South Africa, R.Taylor provided insight and hope: 'a woman got up to say at a meeting that men were often away from home and it was the women who had their fingers on the pulse of what was going on. This statement changed the composition of the committee to reflect better gender balance. There is thus positive news in terms of gender at grassroots and in terms of planning education.'
>
> Source: Olufemi (2001).

from the Bangladesh University of Engineering and Technology took on the leadership of the network with support from Pamela Ayebare for the East Africa region, Dr Carol Archer for the Caribbean region and Alicia Yon for the Australia-Pacific region. In 2005, reflecting the growing profile of CAP and the CWIP, Alicia Yon represented CWIP at the 49th Session of the UN Commission for Status of Women in New York. Shortly afterwards the Commonwealth Secretariat launched its own Plan of Action to promote the Commonwealth's commitment to gender equality.

In 2006 Alicia Yon of Australia was elected as convenor of the CWIP and in the same year the UN Habitat sponsored her to attend a three-day workshop on gendering land tools which followed on from discussions held at the Vancouver World Urban Forum (also held in 2006). CWIP also took on a key role during the UN Habitat Conference of 2006 entitled *State of Safety in World Cities* which was held in Monterrey, Mexico. CWIP was invited to host a session and Alicia Yon took the lead on this international event which had a focus on safer cities for women. This

> **BOX 9.2 HOW PLANNING CAN SUPPORT WOMEN LIVING IN SLUMS.**
>
> Urban areas provide women with better employment opportunities than do rural areas. Pro-urban planning policies are thus more likely to benefit women than those seeking to halt urban growth. However, urban labour markets often remain segmented along gender lines; many poor women find jobs as housemaids, cleaners or vendors. Can they get housing, or access public transport to reach these jobs? If health and sanitation services and infrastructure in slums can be upgraded, women are likely to be prime beneficiaries since they fetch water and spend most time in the slum.
>
> Malaza et al. (2009), p. 1

was one of the best-attended sessions at the conference and CWIP was consequently invited to be a partner of the 2008 World Urban Forum.

Meanwhile, support from the Commonwealth Foundation enabled CAP to commission work on Good Practice in Gender in Planning. Professor Alison Todes led a team from the University of Witwatersrand that carried out the commission. She presented findings in the Women and Harmonious Cities Roundtable at the 2008 WUF in Nanjing. The work also led to the publication by the Commonwealth Secretariat of a discussion paper on 'Gender in Urban Planning and Development' (Malaza et al., 2009), see Box 9.2.

In 2008 the CWIP Strategic Plan (2008 to 2010) was adopted at the CAP Business Meeting held in Johannesburg that year. In 2014, at the CAP Business Meeting held in Singapore, Alicia Yon was re-appointed as convenor of the CWIP.

In 2018, Kristin Agnello became the convenor of the CWIP committee and served till 2021. At the start of her term CWIP drafted a manifesto in conversation with a diverse group of planners and built-environment professionals from across the Commonwealth, including planners in urban and rural communities, planners representing Aboriginal communities and professionals from international, gender-based civil society organisations. This manifesto was circulated to all CAP vice-presidents for review and comment on behalf of all member organisations before it was adopted and signed at the CAP Business Meeting, held in Cape Town, South Africa on 14 October 2018 (see Photo 9.1).

The manifesto (CAP, 2018) serves as the foundation for ongoing international collaboration and as a global call to action to governments, professionals, academics, organisations, individuals and stakeholders. It provides referenced examples of ways in which gender inequality is experienced in the built environment (see Box 9.3). It includes a call to equalise the gender balance within the planning profession by actively and consciously encouraging girls and women to pursue science, technology, engineering, arts and mathematics (STEAM) studies and careers; providing

PHOTO 9.1 The Commonwealth Women in Planning Network Manifesto was adopted in 2018 at the CAP Business Meeting, SAPI Conference, Cape Town, South Africa. L-R: Deputy Minister Andries Nel, Co-operative Governance and Traditional Affairs, South Africa; Jua Cilliers, author; Minister Maite Nkoana-Mashabanes, Minister of International Relations, South Africa; Christine Platt, author; Selna Cornelius, Lecturer North-West University, South Africa; Zinea Huston, PhD Student North-West University, South Africa.

Source: Jua Cilliers

BOX 9.3 GENDER-BASED ISSUES THAT NEED TO BE TACKLED IN PLANNING FOR SUSTAINABLE URBANISATION.

How places are planned can exacerbate or tackle:

- Gender-based violence and vulnerability of women in public spaces.
- Limited physical and social mobility, including unequal access to jobs, training, education, and land or financial capital for entrepreneurial activities.
- Prolongation of discriminatory social norms and policies, including limited rights to land title and use.
- Decreased housing security and access to affordable housing.
- Limited or inconsistent access to and use of public amenities, including public transportation, parks, roads and sanitation services, particularly for breastfeeding mothers and women travelling alone.

- Inhospitable environments and lack of proximity contribute to uneven distribution of responsibilities for the burden of care and limitations for women.
- Limitations regarding girls' and women's pursuit of non-traditional careers.
- Under-representation of women in the built environment professions.
- Increased workload or burdens resulting from climate change-related impacts (e.g. increased walking distances to fetch water and greater risk of mortality from natural disasters).

Source: CAP (2018, p. 2).

mentorship and support to women working in the built environment professions and endorsing merit-based appointments of women to high-profile leadership, governance and political positions. The manifesto serves as a call to planners worldwide to assume a leadership role, positioning themselves as ambassadors for women and girls and calling for gender-inclusive, responsive, sustainable and equitable built environments in the face of global challenges. It actively pursues a gender-balanced work force in the planning profession by attracting and retaining female talent and supporting merit-based appointments for women to high-profile and leadership planning, policy, and political positions.

In 2021 Jua Cilliers took over as convenor to further expand its reach and impact. At the time of writing the CWIP continues with its aim to provide an intersectional, gender-based lens through which we can examine the built environment, advance the Sustainable Development Goals and support women working in the planning profession. To ensure inclusiveness and equality – as advocated for by the Beijing Declaration, the 2030 Agenda, the NUA and the Paris Agreement – the CWIP is now focused on gender equality and the participation of women in shaping the built environment. It does this by recognising the potential of intersectional, gender-inclusive planning, policy and design that contributes positively to achieving global economic, social, cultural and environmental objectives.

CWIP goals and objectives (manifesto and action plan)

CWIP has a vision to ensure all self-identified women and girls have the social, economic and political power to shape our shared built environment. CWIP calls to national, regional and local governments, academic institutions, public and private organisations, practitioners, citizens and stakeholders of all genders to ally and engage with women – as planners, designers and equal participants in the built environment – through gender-inclusive policies, practices and partnerships.

CWIP has also expressed a shared commitment to recognising the crucial role that women play as designers of – and active participants in – the built environment. Through its endorsement of the CWIP Manifesto, CAP has affirmed the fundamental role of women in achieving and advancing all 17 of the SDGs, the NUA and the IGUTP. CWIP objectives are further advanced in the Commonwealth through CAP's 2016 Fiji Declaration on sustainable, resilient and inclusive human settlements. Within these broader aims the current goals of the CWIP include – but are not limited to – the following:

- Advance the UN SDGs (in particular Goal 5: Gender Equality, Goal 11: Sustainable Cities and Communities and Goal 17: Partnerships for the Goals) through planning practice and research.
- Advance partnerships with CAP member organisations, partners and friends of CAP, including UN Women, Women in Cities International, Women Transforming Cities and others to enhance our collaborative thinking.
- Provide a collaborative platform to support women in planning and other emerging professionals working in the built environment.
- Promote relevant publications written by CWIP members (including blog entries, journal articles, student research, white papers and books) to advance information-sharing and collaboration among international planning professionals.
- Develop a toolkit for professional planners to assist them in applying a gender lens to planning projects and research around the globe.

CWIP progress to date (projects, networks, impacts)

Since its endorsement by CAP in 2018, the CWIP Manifesto has been formally endorsed by the Canadian Institute of Planners, the Royal Town Planning Institute, the Ghana Institute of Planners, the Barbados Town Planning Institute and the New Zealand Planning Institute. In 2019, CWIP launched social media

PHOTO 9.2 Women in Planning event in South Africa, 2020.
Source: Jua Cilliers

Gender and sustainable urbanisation 133

campaigns on Facebook, LinkedIn and Twitter. In collaboration with the Commonwealth Young Planners Network, CWIP supported an informal mentorship programme to establish connections between women mentees and mentors. CWIP has been active in promoting its manifesto and advocating for women's equitable contribution to the design and management of the built environment, including:

- Advocating for women's equity in the built environment at two world design summits (Montréal, 2017 and Saint-Étienne, 2019).
- Acting as signatory of the unprecedented Montréal Design Declaration in 2017.
- Contributing three 'Women in Planning' case studies to a publication released at the 64th UN Commission on the Status of Women (2020) – the event was cancelled due to COVID-19 pandemic, but the publication was released.
- Advocating for women's equity in the built environment at the 65th UN Commission on the Status of Women event in 2021, and promoting the CWIP Manifesto at the World Design Summit (2019).
- Co-authoring an encyclopaedia chapter on 'Feminist Planning' in the Palgrave Encyclopedia of Urban and Rural Futures (2020).

CWIP future vision (plans)

A future plan for CWIP includes (amongst others) creating a Women in Planning Network Advisory Group comprised of CAP member representatives and other partner organisations. Such a group is envisioned to have status at an international

PHOTO 9.3 Promoting a Women in Planning Open Event in Australia, 2021.
Source: Jua Cilliers

level to serve as a resource for governmental, intergovernmental, non-governmental and civil society organisations, as well as practicing professionals, academic institutions and other stakeholders.

Another goal is to advance advocacy for the development and implementation of gender-inclusive land access, control and use policies across the Commonwealth. Eventually the aim would be to develop a toolkit of sustainable processes to support women's access, ownership and use of fertile lands for agricultural activities as a means of addressing poverty, inequality and vulnerability. This would also align with a goal to develop, maintain and enhance partnerships with CAP member organisations, UN Women, Women in Cities International, Women Transforming Cities and other organisations pursuing similar gender-related objectives in the built environment. The CWIP can in this way demonstrate and support the relationships, objectives and indicators between SDG 5: Gender Equality and the other 16 Global Goals, with a particular focus on SDG 11: Sustainable Cities and Communities.

Ultimately the network envisions contributing to planning education, specifically by focussing on gender-responsive planning toolkits, as well as supporting new platforms and curricula for planning education and research dissemination. CWIP recognise and promote training on gender responsive planning for people already working professionally as part of continuing professional learning requirements.

As we enter the second 50 years of CAP the CWIP initiative provides a strong foundation from which we continue to strive to achieve the goal of gender equality. Through this, along with other collaborations, we move closer to the common goal of more sustainable cities and communities.

References

CAP. (2018), *Commonwealth Women in Planning Network Manifesto,* Available at www.commonwealth-planners.org/cwip-network. (Accessed 5 August 2022).

Currie, D., Fenner, R. and Harridge, C. (2018), *Planning for Rapid Urbanisation: Survey of the Planning Profession in the Commonwealth – Preliminary Findings,* Available at www.commonwealth-planners.org/publications-1 (Accessed 4 August 2022).

Gilroy, R. and Woods, R. (1994), *Housing Women,* London: Routledge

Greed, C. (1996), *Promise or Progress: Women and Planning, Built Environment, 1978,* Marcham: Alexandrine Press.

Greed, C.H. (2003), *Women and Planning: Creating Gendered Realities,* London: Routledge.

Hendler, S. (2005), 'Towards a Feminist Code of Planning Ethics', *Planning Theory & Practice,* 6 (1), pp. 53–69.

Little, J. (1994), *Gender, Planning and the Policy Process,* Oxford: Pergamon.

Malaza, N., Todes, A. and Williamson, A. with Hague, C. and the Women in Planning Network of the Commonwealth Association of Planners. (2009), 'Gender in Planning and Urban Development', *Commonwealth Secretariat Discussion Paper 7,* London: Commonwealth Secretariat.

Olufemi, O. (2001), 'CAP Women in Planning Network', *CAP News,* (4), pp. 17–20.

Ortiz Escalante, S. and Gutiérrez Valdivia, B. (2015), 'Planning from below: Using Feminist Participatory Methods to Increase Women's Participation in Urban Planning' *Gender & Development,* 23 (1), pp. 113–126.

Reed, M. (1997), 'Seeing Trees: Engendering Environmental and Land use Planning', *Canadian Geographer*, 14 (4), pp. 398–414.

Ritzdorf, M. (1994), 'A Feminist analysis of Gender and Residential Zoning in the United States', In Altman, I. and Churchman, A. (eds.), *Women and the Environment*, New York: Plenum Press, pp. 255–280.

Roy, A. (2001), 'A "public" Muse: On Planning Convictions and Feminist Contentions', *Journal of Planning Education and Research*, 21 (2), pp. 109–126.

Saarikoski, H. (2002), 'Naturalized Epistemology and Dilemmas of Planning Practice', *Journal of Planning Education and Research*, 22 (1), pp. 3–14.

Speak, S. (2012), 'Planning for the Needs of Urban Poor in the Global South: The Value of a feminist Approach', *Planning Theory*, 11 (4), pp. 343–360.

Wekerle, G. and Whitzman, C. (1995), *Safe Cities*, New York: Van Nostrand Reinhold.

PART 3
The next 50 years

Introduction

CAP has come a long way in its first half-century and particularly in the past 20 years in the scale of its ambitions and the realisation of what the organisation can achieve by working with partners on a global stage – particularly UN Habitat – and across the Commonwealth with The Prince's Foundation and fellow Commonwealth bodies. At a high level, we have recognised the abilities of planning to contribute to addressing major global challenges and have succeeded to a significant degree in getting this message across at the level of the United Nations, the Commonwealth Heads of Government and even the G7. So far, so good.

However, planning is essentially forward-looking. Planners come into the profession with a view of making things better than they are. While keeping the best of what we inherit from the past (but by conservation – managing change – rather than by preservation), we nevertheless see the things that can and often should be done better. So, in preparing this history of CAP and its first 50 years, we cannot leave it as simply an account of what has happened: we need to critically assess what has been achieved, what remains to be done and how we improve the world around us.

And there is much to be done. Two decades into the 21st century, the evidence is stark of the problems posed by the need to feed and house a growing world population which is increasingly urban while addressing the impacts of human demands on the planet in climate change and biodiversity loss.

Part 3 of the book therefore considers the challenges facing planning and planners in the coming decades in delivering sustainable urbanisation. We start in Chapter 10 with an overview by Cliff Hague (UK) and Christine Platt (South Africa) of where we stand in the early 2020s. They recognise the challenges in terms of the substantive, real-world problems to be faced (climate change, rapid urbanisation,

DOI: 10.4324/9781003357933-12

poverty, ill-health, poor housing) but they also identify the procedural challenges for planners, working with and for communities, including indigenous peoples, when acting within legislative frameworks that are often out-dated and based inappropriately in colonial approaches and with widespread shortages of resources.

The subsequent chapters provide the opportunity for authors from different backgrounds and perspectives to consider how planning should tackle the challenges of sustainable urbanisation in the coming decades. In Chapter 11, Vijay Krishnarayan, the former director of the Commonwealth Foundation, who has lived and worked in the Caribbean, sets out his views on the social, economic, technical, environmental and political challenges for planning. In each of these areas, Vijay notes the significance of civic engagement and sees successful planners of the future as convenors and facilitators that bring people and diverse interests together to negotiate a better future.

Speaking for the over 60% of the Commonwealth population that is under 30 years of age, Olafiyin Taiwo, from the UK (but with a background in Nigeria), looks to the mainstreaming of youth into planning processes and writes of their roles as innovative disruptors, drivers and catalysts for important institutional changes. In Chapter 12, she identifies the need for locally relevant solutions to planning challenges and touches on the role of planning education in developing the professional resources of the future.

Appropriately, therefore, in Chapter 13 Professor Barbara Norman of Australia sets out her thoughts on the challenges facing planning from the perspective of a planning educator. She identifies a number of key trends for the coming decades, including increasingly community-based approaches to city and local design (echoing Vijay's thoughts). Reflecting the efforts that CAP made to spread such tools in the 1990s, she identifies the availability in the future of a wider range of digital tools for planning and design. Importantly, Barbara also discusses the requirement for evolved design responses to pandemics, changing lifestyles and working practices – and the need in places to resettle urban communities to respond to the impacts of climate change. In concluding her comments, Barbara highlights the value of the connections and shared understanding that CAP can bring to planning education.

Finally, in Chapter 14, the Endpiece, we seek to draw lessons from the history of CAP set out in Part 2 of the book and reflect on the challenges foreseen in Part 3, drawing out four key themes of: colonialism, land and planning – the Commonwealth in relation to sustainable urbanisation; CAP and planning history; activism and agency and beyond the SDGs – knowledge, attitudes and skills for the future. This critical review of what CAP has done and the nature of the written history and of the limitations of a volunteer-operated organisation leads to a recognition of the need for a 21st-century sense of professionalism that provides ladders into planning for those who cannot afford or cannot access Masters-degree level training. Ultimately, whatever the successes to date (including lasting for its first 50 years), there is no room for complacency when so much remains to be done.

10

PLANNING FOR SUSTAINABLE URBANISATION

Issues and challenges

Cliff Hague and Christine Platt

Planning – a 'fundamental driver' for sustainable urbanisation

The need to plan for a sustainable urban future is now acknowledged across and beyond the Commonwealth. Sustainable Development Goal (SDG) 11 calls upon all nations to 'Make cities and human settlements inclusive, safe, resilient and sustainable.' We have International Guidelines for Urban and Territorial Planning (IGUTP) (UN Habitat, 2015a). These are endorsed in the New Urban Agenda (NUA) (UN, 2017), which was adopted at Habitat III and signed by 167 nations. The NUA makes it clear that urban and territorial planning has a vital role to play in delivering prosperity, a liveable environment and social equity.

CAP can be proud of the part it played in achieving these outcomes by making the connections among sustainable development, urbanisation and planning. In the landmark 'Re-inventing Planning' paper (Farmer et al., 2006) prepared for the World Planning Congress and World Urban Forum (WUF) 3 we argued that 'planning is central to a new paradigm for governance of human settlements.' The paper called for planning to be 'inclusive and pro-poor,' better linked to budgets and a way to reduce vulnerability to natural disasters (see Photos 10.1 and 10.2). Ten years later, the NUA identified planning as a 'fundamental driver of change.' It committed to 'Reinvigorating long-term and integrated urban and territorial planning and design in order to optimize the spatial dimension of the urban form and deliver the positive outcomes of urbanization' (para.15c (iii)). The need for age- and gender-responsive planning was stressed; also 'We will reinforce the link between fiscal systems and urban planning' (para.137). A proactive, planning-based approach was endorsed to enhance resilience in the face of disasters.

In short, CAP sought a mandate for a more ambitious, integrated and inclusive form of planning. That mandate has been given at the highest level of multilateralism through the NUA and SDGs. We have to achieve SDG 11 and its targets by 2030, with

DOI: 10.4324/9781003357933-13

PHOTO 10.1 Natural disasters – hurricane damage in Tortola, British Virgin Islands, 2018. The Caribbean islands are vulnerable to hurricanes. In 2018, Hurricane Irma became the most powerful storm since records began to cross the Atlantic Ocean. Hurricane Maria followed weeks later. In the British Virgin Isles they inflicted damage estimated to be four times the gross domestic product.

Source: Bryce Julyan

PHOTO 10.2 Natural disasters – Tsunami threat, Fiji at venue of CAP business meeting. Many small island Commonwealth states have to live with the threat of tsunamis which can cause huge damage. Planning can mitigate their impacts.

Source: Clive Harridge

Planning for sustainable urbanisation **141**

PHOTO 10.3 Car-oriented growth, Gaborone, Botswana. Downtown in Gaborone, Botswana which, although still quite a small city, is growing rapidly but not necessarily sustainably.

Source: Cliff Hague

just six further years to implement the NUA. Will we be able to report that planning in the Commonwealth delivered? Will Commonwealth planners have led the world – or failed to rise to the UN's challenges? The rate of urbanisation is expected to level off in the 2040s, but urban development is long lasting and a huge legacy of poorly planned and unsustainable urban growth could endure to the 2070s (see Photo 10.3). For the Commonwealth and for the world, the window of opportunity to make a difference is closing: we do not have the luxury of waiting another 50 years. Therefore, the immediate challenge for the planners of the Commonwealth is to embrace the role expected of us in accelerating the implementation of these international sustainable urbanisation accords. As the 2020s draw to a close, nations will formulate successor documents to the SDGs and the NUA. CAP member associations should now know what is expected of planning. They need to act and to demonstrate practical impacts. The hard work is just beginning: unless it is done quickly, it will be too late.

A difficult but necessary transition

Since CAP was established world population has more than doubled, and for the first time a majority of people on the planet live in cities. New industrial methods, globalisation and a new world order reversed the pattern of production imprinted by the colonial era. Cities have been reshaped into globally connected places of commercial, retail, tourism and entertainment experiences, and in Africa and Asia the urban areas have been utterly transformed in scale. Changes have been happening all along the urban-rural continuum, from the metropolitan conurbations, to the secondary cities and in the emerging urban clusters (see Photo 10.4). Agri-business continues to

PHOTO 10.4 Emerging urban clusters blur urban-rural differences, Ncepheni, Kwa-Zulu Natal, South Africa. Ncepheni's growth takes a very different form than that in Calgary (see Photo 2.5) or similar cities in the Commonwealth but typifies what is happening in many African Commonwealth nations. Ncepheni is developing with surrounding 'urban' areas Masotsheni, Ngedla and Magaga as part of an emerging urban cluster in a deeply rural setting. This dynamic poses questions about how planners understand the urban-rural continuum and social, environmental, functional and economic relationships across it. It also challenges our thinking about how to plan this new embryonic urbanisation. It poses critical questions as to how planners should respond in a new and often difficult context.

Source: Christine Platt

displace traditional farming jobs while constructing global supply chains. People have migrated from rural regions, while the average size of farms has increased.

The digital revolution is driving many of these profound changes and will disrupt planning practices. 'We have now entered an era of "digital by default" where the dramatic spread of computational resources has pervaded every aspect of our society' (Batty and Yang, 2022, p. 1). This 'fourth industrial revolution' is not yet over (see Box 10.1).

Despite – or maybe even because of – this era of oil-fuelled splurge of unsustainable consumption and development, with its towering temples to commerce in large urban centres, the closing years of CAP's first five decades were marked by deep anxieties. COVID-19 showed how fragile life could be but also how profound and destructive are inequalities within and between countries. It became impossible to ignore the evidence of climate change but also to forge the international solidarity and urgency needed for mitigation and adaptation.

Yet planning systems changed surprisingly little through the 50 years. Generally, they were adapted rather than fundamentally rethought. They have been slow to

> **BOX 10.1 A DIGITAL FUTURE ANTICIPATED BY THE PLANNING INSTITUTE OF AUSTRALIA.**
>
> It is clear that planning will change significantly from the impact of digitization. Be it digital tools for community engagement, digital visualization and augmentation, the use of artificial intelligence to apply planning codes and policies, and the ability for real time monitoring of the impact of decision-making through sensors and big data.
>
> David Williams, Chief Executive Officer, Planning Institute of Australia
>
> Source: invited comment submitted to CAP for this book.

> **BOX 10.2 ATTITUDES TOWARDS PLANNING IN INDIA.**
>
> Until the recent past Urban Planning was not a priority sector for the Central Government and Urban Planning and Development was a State subject, and hence not much emphasis was given to this sector.
>
> Pradeep Kapoor, Secretary General, Institute of Town Planners, India
>
> Source: invited comment submitted to CAP for this book.

digitise. In some countries planning powers were diluted as governments sought to de-regulate development of land and property. In many rapidly urbanising countries, statutory masterplans could not keep pace with the rate of development or address the needs of the poor, and planning simply ceased to matter to politicians and senior administrators (see Box 10.2). The disconnect between traditional planning approaches and the wider pace of change is key to understanding the ambitions in SDG11, the International Guidelines and the NUA to re-orient planning practice to 21st-century realities.

Public administration, at national and local levels, too often has remained entrenched in ministerial and departmental silos. With the scope of planning prescribed in legislation, many planners find themselves locked within such silos. Thus unplanned urbanisation has occurred against a backdrop of outdated planning systems and under-investment in planning skills. There is a gap, reflected in planning education, between the aspirations of those advocating for new ways of planning and the constraints enforced by the narrow technocratic focus of much practice in market-driven systems.

Faced with a complex, multi-faceted world, where everything affects everything else, the public policy response needs to be smarter, better integrated and more than ever to be inspired by the core Commonwealth values, such as human

> **BOX 10.3   STATEMENT FROM CANADIAN INSTITUTE OF PLANNERS/INSTITUTE CANADIEN DES URBANISTES, 2022**
>
> CIP believes the Canadian planning profession must be representative of the society it works in, which is supported by its Equity, Diversity, and Inclusion Roadmap and policy on Indigenous reconciliation. CAP also has a key role in championing this (e.g. through its support of the United Nations Declaration on the Rights of Indigenous Peoples and acknowledgement of colonial histories) and helping to address systemic racism and discrimination in our governance systems, practices, and policies.
>
> Source: invited comment submitted to CAP for this book.

rights, democracy, international peace and security and tolerance and understanding (see Box 10.3). Equity, transparency and democracy need to be the foundations on which the Commonwealth builds the future for all its citizens. Civil society action must also play a larger role. The Commonwealth – and Commonwealth planners – can be and need to be accelerators of change.

Scoping the challenge

UN-Habitat (2020a, p. 3) observes that there is now a realisation that 'while cities hold the key to solving many of the world's sustainability challenges, the current model of urban development is unsustainable.' Building sustainable cities, addressing poverty, the threat of inadequate water, food and energy security and delivering sanitation and shelter define the challenge.

> As the world continues to urbanize, sustainable development depends increasingly on the successful management of urban growth, especially in low-income and lower-middle-income countries where the pace of urbanization is projected to be the fastest. Many countries will face challenges in meeting the needs of their growing urban populations, including for housing, transportation, energy systems and other infrastructure, as well as for employment and basic services such as education and health care.
>
> *UN Department of Economic and Social Affairs, 2018*

Matters like housing, transport, employment and basic services are the building blocks of human settlements and feature regularly in land use and development plans. However, the failures to meet such needs – and recognise whose needs are not being met and why – have been less frequently addressed by planners. A fundamental point must be grasped: poverty excludes people, and how cities are planned or not planned impacts on poverty. Planning systems and practices now need to embrace a human-rights-based approach (Hague et al., 2018). This means empowering vulnerable and marginalised groups; non-discrimination, participation and inclusion; accountability and the rule of law. Human rights are indivisible, not to be traded off, and they are universal: homelessness is as much a denial of human rights in Montreal or Melbourne as it is in Mumbai or Mombasa.

Unplanned urbanisation has created extensive areas around the peripheries of Commonwealth cities where inadequate infrastructure means that transport connectivity is poor and traffic congestion is endemic, which in turn undermines the efficiency of labour markets. Many of these areas are vulnerable to the worst impacts of climate change. Public spaces are lacking, and farm land and biodiversity are lost. Basic public services are absent and even in rich countries have been downgraded.

In much of the Commonwealth, these challenges to where – and how – development is planned are set against the backdrop of rapid urbanisation that is slum-led, with women a significant proportion of the heads of slum households. Often such development takes place on sites that are vulnerable to hazards. There are two fundamental points, therefore. First, that the long period during which urban planning was marginalised and ineffective has bequeathed a legacy that will be problematic for decades to come. Second, planned urbanisation is essential: it is preventative medicine. While the COVID-19 pandemic saw some reverse migration, as people moved back from cities to rural areas where living costs were cheaper and there were family support networks, the expectation of strong urban growth across less-developed Commonwealth regions remains, with India and Nigeria accounting for a significant proportion of the overall numbers (UN-Habitat, 2020a, p. xvi). While the absolute numbers are much less in the Commonwealth's small island states, urban growth combines with the limited land area and direct exposure to rising sea levels to create significant challenges there too.

The climate emergency compounds the need for action on cities and human settlements. The Intergovernmental Panel on Climate Change (2021) reported that climate change is already creating weather and climate extremes in every region across the globe, with observed changes such as heatwaves, heavy precipitation, drought and tropical cyclones. Continued global warming is projected to further intensify global monsoon precipitation and the severity of wet and dry events.

It is difficult if not impossible to think of any Commonwealth country that will not be adversely affected in some way. The vulnerability to rising sea levels of people and property in the 707 Commonwealth urban settlements located within the Low Elevation Coastal Zones is obvious (ComHabitat, 2010). In many small Commonwealth states the main city, which houses a significant proportion of the population and is the main economic driver, is in that zone. Managed retreat from areas vulnerable to extreme weather events and inundation and a more ecologically aware approach to planning settlements is a challenge planners will face in several Commonwealth countries in the next 50 years (see Box 10.4).

Similarly, countries that have contributed least to the climate emergency are the most vulnerable to its effects. Small island states, especially small island developing

> **BOX 10.4 PLANNED RETREAT FROM THE COAST AND A BLUE-GREEN NETWORK APPROACH TO PLANNING: BELMOPAN, BELIZE.**
>
> After Hurricane Hattie and a tidal wave in 1961 caused great damage to Belize City, a decision was taken to build a new capital inland and on higher ground. Thus the construction of Belmopan began in 1970, influenced by British New Town planning. In 2016 UN-Habitat in collaboration with the Belmopan City Council and other local stakeholders undertook a blue-green network planning approach for Belmopan, creating strategies for managing urban flood risk, enhancing the garden city character and promoting economic development. This city-wide strategy is based on the network of existing natural systems, multi-modal transit systems and public spaces in order to improve connectivity spatially and socially.
>
> Source: Mayr et al. (2017).

states, exemplify this inequity. Continued rise in sea levels is judged by the IPCC to be 'very likely.' Combined with storm surges and waves it will result in coastal inundation, the retreat of sandy coasts and potential saltwater intrusion into aquifers. Around the coasts of Africa, the rise in sea levels over the past three decades has exceeded the global mean. Continued rise seems 'virtually certain' creating increased frequency and severity of flooding in low lying areas.

The Commonwealth can make a difference if its political leaders can grasp the multi-faceted importance of urbanisation to the international development agenda, connecting urgent concerns such as climate, food security, carbon reduction and gender equality through place-based actions. For example, research on SDG performance in Africa found that 'Good health is most strongly related to Sustainable cities' (Tschudin, 2022, p. 27). The rising profile of an urban focus in policy has been driven by the Group of 77+China coalition of countries, many of which are experiencing rapid urbanisation (UN-Habitat, 2020a, p. 3), while, as at COP-26, some of the larger and richer Commonwealth countries have been less enthusiastic. Looking ahead, the case still needs to be made at the highest levels in the Commonwealth. Hopefully the Kigali Declaration will prove a turning point. While urban growth is slower in the highly urbanised countries, it is still happening and will continue. Cities there are spreading at a rate greater than their rate of demographic growth and will not escape from the consequences of climate change and widening inequalities.

Looking to the next 50 years, a focus on building resilience is needed, but that does not mean 'bouncing back' to some past state. Rather, it means the capacity to adapt to the kind of challenges sketched earlier that require new, not old solutions. Critically too, resilience must be seen in its fullest sense of encompassing social, economic and environmental resilience and as essential to peacekeeping in a world of diminishing natural resources.

Despite the general pattern of urban growth, there will also be some 'shrinking cities.' Places based economically on extractive industry are particularly vulnerable: many of the UK's former coalfields have never recovered from the closures and associated wider decline in the 1980s. South Africa's Free State Goldfields tell a similar story. Some 180,000 worked in the mines in Matjhabeng, in the mid-1980s, but the figure was less than 30,000 by 2013 (Marais, 2013). The population also declined sharply from 180,000 in 1990 to 36,000 in 2010, as many workers emigrated (Marais and Cloete, 2016). In such situations drawing a land use map is not enough. Planners need to be proactive and creative. They need to use planning tools which allow them to think and act in strategic ways and which enable them to integrate complex and interconnected issues.

While the details will vary in line with the diversity within the Commonwealth, we need to implement the new, re-invented forms of planning, which can deliver sustainable urbanisation and growth without all the negative side effects. This planning needs to be international in outlook and focused on equity, because inequalities lie at the root of so many problematic aspects of urbanisation as we face the next half century. Health gaps, migration, hazards, food scarcity, social unrest and women's safety are just some examples. Planners across the Commonwealth need to be driven by passion and by skills to make quick impacts on the ground. What might they do?

Accelerating the delivery of sustainable urbanisation

The Commonwealth, as a well-connected laboratory of 54 diverse countries, is uniquely positioned to build on the commitments of our Governments to the SDGs and SDG 11 in particular, as well as the NUA. Many clauses of the NUA expressly recognise planning as a key tool to achieve the 'what.' with specific mention of the IGUTP in Clause 90. We also know the 'how' – it was clearly argued in Farmer et al. (2006) and the IGUTP which both set out what is needed to make planning fit for purpose.

Outmoded planning systems have struggled to cope with rapid, slum-led urbanisation for a number of reasons. Fundamentally, infrastructure has lagged behind development. In part this is because of the cost of sewers, water and transport systems in relation to affordability by poor migrants, but it also reflects the failure of plans to anticipate and provide for urban expansion and to use infrastructure to steer development. In turn this is part of wider fiscal and governance weaknesses in states, which impact particularly on health and education services for the poor.

Containment of urban growth was deeply embedded in colonial planning, together with discriminatory forms of spatial segregation. In 2013, 84% of governments in less-developed regions had policies to lower migration from rural to urban areas (UN, 2013). With the best of intentions to be comprehensive, plan-making has often involved extensive and time-consuming data collection. In situations of slow change this did not matter much, but rapid urban growth can make master plans outdated before they are published.

The problems can be compounded by the legacy of colonial era planning. In the late 1940s the British Colonial Office produced a template for planning legislation to be used across the colonies in Africa and the Caribbean. Even when countries introduced new post-colonial planning legislation, much of the first round mirrored previous laws. This has changed in the 21st century, with further law reform being undertaken. Tanzania revised its planning legislation in 2007: the objectives of the system now include ensuring 'security and equity in access to land resources.' However, much still needs to be done to align planning legislation with the NUA. This issue requires pan-Commonwealth attention. Berrisford (2013) argued that reform of planning legislation in Africa for example needs to be responsive to the majority affected, which is the urban poor (see Box 10.5). He put forward broad principles, in particular that the priority should be to set realistic minimum development standards to ensure basic health and safety.

Professional planners are unevenly distributed across the Commonwealth (Oborn and Walters, 2020). They are primarily located in the countries where rates of urbanisation and the threats from climate change are much less than in the Commonwealth countries where their skills are most urgently needed. Within countries, trained planners tend to be concentrated in the capital cities, though the highest rates of urbanisation are in secondary cities, which are also often economic drivers in their region. In the NUA (para.102) governments committed to 'strive to improve capacity for urban planning and design and the provision of training for urban planners at the national, subnational and local levels.' Commonwealth countries need to work on this.

The issues are qualitative too. A qualification to become a professional planner takes time and money; therefore planners too often are not representative of the cities for which they plan. The uneven distribution of planning education facilities across the Commonwealth compounds this problem. Change will take time,

---

BOX 10.5 PLANNING LAW IN AFRICA.

Planning law has a poor record in Africa. Legislation designed to protect the public from the negative aspects of urban land development has all too often been used by the state to enhance the value of land owned by the wealthy – and to penalise and intimidate the disadvantaged. Laws to protect public spaces and facilities that enhance civic life are seldom implemented as intended. In a context of insecure and unpredictable land rights, planning law is a major fault line running through society.

Source: Berrisford (2013, p. 1).

so action is needed to tap into the practical knowledge of community organisers amongst the poor and marginalised to produce and support 'barefoot planners.' Online, face-to-face mentoring can be used. A proactive Commonwealth should play a leading role in creating such networks. Together with re-deployment of existing planners to work to deliver the NUA, this could make a difference.

More of the same is not enough. However, as Watson (2016, p. 441) observed, planning systems are often 'embedded in institutions and politics not necessarily oriented in the direction of the values of the SDGs or the NUA. Planning systems suffer from strong historical inertia and are not easily changed owing, often, to vested interests, especially in land.'

Yet change is happening and experiences need to be shared. South Africa pioneered a system of Integrated Development Plans as part of its post-conflict recovery from apartheid. In particular, the IDPs brought improvements into rural areas that had previously been left in deep poverty without basic public services. The IDPs accelerated service delivery by focusing in a cross-cutting manner on consultation, strategic planning and delivery (Gueli et al., 2007). The Compendium of Inspiring Practices (UN Habitat, 2015b) and the book *Leading Change* (Hague et al., 2018) provide many other practical examples of approaches to pursue. Similarly, the CAP annual awards for outstanding planning practice demonstrate how planners can become change agents and deliver the SDGs through planning practice; see, for example, Box 10.6. Such new approaches need quickly to become mainstream.

The Commonwealth could and should lead the change that is needed now and in the years to come. The NUA advocates a reinvigorated planning and integrated urban and territorial planning. Adoption and implementation of these approaches needs now to be accelerated across the whole Commonwealth, and to this end robust methodologies must be developed that can enable rapid planning. This is not

---

BOX 10.6 PLANNING FOR REGENERATION AND RECOVERY: WAIMAKARIRI DISTRICT COUNCIL, NEW ZEALAND.

Following the 2010 and 2011 earthquakes in Canterbury, NZ, Waimakariri District Council undertook numerous community engagement, recovery and regeneration planning exercises, including the preparation of a Draft Recovery Plan for the worst affected areas. It is an example of resilience planning, responding to complex land use and technical requirements, the needs of multiple stakeholders and an exhausted and polarized public in a relatively short time frame. Disaster recovery is an international issue and other Commonwealth countries could learn from this council's work. Planners played a leading role and thoroughly linked the work to the SDGs.

Source: CAP (2019).

as forbidding as it may sound. Where to develop and where not to develop is often obvious. Avoid areas of environmental risk, important biodiversity, good agricultural land, cultural and natural heritage and favour areas where infrastructure can be provided and which provide access to essential services and economic opportunities. An infrastructure-led approach can work with informality to steer the broad pattern of development, without trying unrealistically to manage the detail.

Informal settlement upgrading

The legacy of the surge in informal settlements will be a challenge for decades to come as they remain a home to impoverished people and a vital receiving environment for poor migrants. Upgrading of such areas needs to be recognised as an essential part of adaptation to climate change, since often they are vulnerable in numerous ways, e.g. house insulation, landslides, flooding, fire risk etc. Planning powers often have been used to clear such areas, causing displacement and victimising the inhabitants (see Photo 10.5). Too often planners have failed to oppose such actions (Kamete, 2007). Upgrading schemes have generally proved a better solution, though results vary widely (Satterthwaite and Sverdlik, 2021).

PHOTO 10.5 Informal densification in a Slum Relocation Colony, Mandanpur Khadar Colony, Delhi, India. People from unauthorised informal settlements have been evicted and relocated to Slum Relocation Colonies like this one. There are over 50 of these in Delhi, home to around 10% of citizens. Originally, the development was single storey and semi-formalised, but storeys have been added – informal densification to meet demand for affordable shelter in the city. For more see Hague (2019).

Source: Cliff Hague

> **BOX 10.7 MAPPING INFORMAL NEIGHBOURHOODS: NAIROBI.**
>
> Much of the Nairobi slum Mathari was unmapped until activist cartographers walked round and typed landmarks into hand-held GPS devices. They mapped things like informal schools, storefront churches and day care centres, as well as dark corners with no streetlights, illegal dumping grounds and broken manholes. The exercise produced practical benefits. Residents used them to get improved lighting or help find pathways to install water connections.
>
> Source: Warner (2013).

Involvement of residents is crucial, as reflected many times in the NUA. Residents are a key resource: usually they know their area and their own needs better than officials do. Too often informal settlements have been simply overlooked by government bodies. In such situations volunteer professional support can make a difference, as Box 10.7 shows.

Partnerships between public agencies and private service providers are essential. There is an important role here for planners, but they need appropriate skills – in community development and organisation, along with design and knowhow in civil engineering, which should then be passed on to residents. Planners in future will need to care more about the social consequences of physical upgrading schemes, recognising that higher rents or house prices can lead to economic eviction for poor residents unless measures are in place to prevent that.

Smart city technologies have a role to play. Mobile phone technologies and apps can, for example, provide platforms that enable local businesses to reach customers in and beyond the informal settlement or put residents in quick contact with employment opportunities. There are already initiatives which should provide valuable lessons to build on. For example, there is a partnership between UN-Habitat and Planet Smart City that is operating in two of the largest informal settlements in Nairobi (UN-Habitat, 2020b). Such technologies seem sure to play an increasing role in the coming decades.

A transition to a circular economy means that in rich countries planning will also need to shift its focus away from new development and towards conservation and maintenance of existing infrastructure, including housing and open space. There as elsewhere, community wealth-building practices are needed to recycle resources and wealth within the community.

Urban-rural continuum

The past five decades saw multiple new levels of connection across all points on the urban-rural continuum. Migrants maintain connections to the countryside, e.g. by sending home remittances, keeping in touch through mobile phones or even returning 'home' for periods if employment opportunities are scarce. Similarly, rural regions became increasingly entangled in global flows of investment and global markets for their products.

This hyper-connectivity seems likely to extend into the future but with the twist that food security is likely to become an increasing concern. The World Bank says that to feed an anticipated nine billion people by 2050, the world will need to produce 50% more food, but climate change could cut crop yields by 25% (Greaves et al., 2017). Already, the problems are severe in some Commonwealth countries; for example, 50% of the population in Ghana experiences moderate or severe food shortages, while in Kenya the 2018 figure was 64.3% and rising (World Bank, 2022). Yet Africa has 60% of the world's uncultivated arable land and the potential to feed itself while also exporting agricultural produce (Kofi Annan Foundation, 2021).

Rural planning has had a limited remit and lacked relevance in many parts of the Commonwealth. Agriculture has been outside its scope, while limited demand for development has meant that there was little priority attached to plan-making. New inclusive and strategic approaches based on the principles of urban and territorial planning are needed to redress this imbalance. Planning needs to address water security, waste management as well as the protection of high value agricultural land, forests and biodiversity, all within the context of moving to a circular economy and in a way that understands urban and rural not as separate entities but as an integrated system. However, this will require political will and again new knowledge and updated ecological and data skills for many planners.

The aim must be to look for synergies, connecting more sustainable agricultural practices to rural development programmes with villages and small towns forming hubs in networks of services and distribution. In particular, the role of women in rural development needs to be recognised. Many good examples exist to draw on from across the Commonwealth, one of which is work done in the North East Region of Ghana (see Photo 10.6) where a planner worked with two women's groups to boost production of orange-flesh sweet potatoes, a project highly commended in the 2019 CAP Awards for Outstanding Planning Practice (CAP, 2019). This reinforces a point made earlier, that the need is not just for more planners but for more planners doing innovative things.

Urban agriculture looks set to play a more prominent role in food systems and is likely to feature increasingly in the work of planners. However, urban land scarcity can mean that urban agriculture widens inequalities. While prioritising urban agriculture in long-term planning efforts, planners will also need to develop mutually respectful relationships with food justice organisations and urban agriculture participants from diverse backgrounds and guard against the threats of gentrification and displacement from urban agriculture (Horst et al., 2017).

The next 50 years – issues and challenges for the Commonwealth and for Commonwealth planners

The coming decades will present multiple and inter-connected challenges for the Commonwealth and for Commonwealth planners. The diversity of the Commonwealth is rightly celebrated and is potentially a great strength – uniting countries

PHOTO 10.6   Women preparing to have the crop weighed: Orange Flesh Sweet Potato project, Ghana. A member of CAP's Women in Planning Network, Belinda Bukari, led this rural development project, working with women's Saving and Loans Associations to create economic and nutritional benefits for the villagers. Belinda skilfully persuaded traditionally patriarchal leaders to give the women access to fertile land.

Source: Belinda Bukari

large and small – and embracing different religions and cultures. However, part of that diversity is also inequality between and within Commonwealth countries. Any future prospectus for Commonwealth development needs to address this issue, not least because the climate emergency threatens to penalise the poorest for the actions (and inactions) of the richest. A rights-based approach to planning is needed, advancing the clearly enunciated principles on which planning fit for purpose in the 21st century can be practised.

If the Commonwealth prospers as a multi-lateral grouping building on its values and principles, its focus needs to shift to the Commonwealth as a whole and away from a focus on London. If that happens, the challenges posed by urbanisation are likely to receive greater attention. Such a shift of the gaze is also needed in those countries where long-standing regional and intra-urban inequalities have been increased by the era of austerity urbanism which has marginalised planning and realigned it with the property development industry. As the World Cities Report 2022 noted, 'Modern urban planning has achieved limited success in equitably distributing resources. Profound inequalities have existed in cities for several decades, persist in the present and will possibly continue into the future without urgent changes in the way cities are planned' (UN Habitat, 2022, p. xxiii).

The Commonwealth is exceptionally well placed to share ideas and knowhow and to lead the world in using urban and regional development to take people out of poverty, tackle the climate emergency and associated food insecurity and build a healthy and democratic future. If political leaders grasp this, the cohesion of the Commonwealth and its global profile will be enhanced and the lives of millions of its citizens will be improved. CAP needs to be a leading voice for an inclusive and practical vision for that future. As Ritta Khiba from the Namibia Council of Town and Regional Planners commented to the authors of this book 'We need to create a platform where more research is done on the built environment issues, share the success stories.'

Planning in the future will change, as different issues are prioritised, and new concerns come to the fore. Technological change will reconfigure settlement patterns and transport systems but also will impact on how planning is done. Digitisation will make deep inroads into traditional practices. More information will be available in real time, enriching the planning process by facilitating simulations and virtual reality assessments with algorithms replacing much of the work currently done in development management, while also making enforcement potentially much more effective. However, as the team behind Future Street (see Photo 10.7) observe, 'The Smart City agenda needs to be driven by people, not technology. The

PHOTO 10.7 Future Street, a scale demonstration embedding green and smart infrastructure and technology, Sydney, New South Wales, Australia. On 12–15 October, 2017 this 50m transformation of a street was visited by thousands of Sydneysiders able to directly experience what a street might be like in future, with electric cars, autonomous shuttles, smart poles and vertical farming. For more see Place Design Group, (2022).

Source: Place Design Group

question is, how can we use technology and big data to make our cities better places to live?' (Toon, 2022).

Above all, the future of planning across the Commonwealth will largely be shaped by rethinking forms of governance. Top-down traditions that came with colonial planning systems and assumptions of effective states are not appropriate. Power has increasingly shifted to globalised companies, while states have shrunk. In much of the Commonwealth basic public services, including planning, never really reached areas where many citizens live. Recent research that covered ten cities in five Commonwealth countries in Africa and Asia found that 'Although most cities boast they have a master plan, neighbourhood planning is rare and almost always benefits only the rich and the emerging middle class' (Wang and Kintrea, 2020).

There is going to be an increasing need for community-driven local interventions that can deliver immediate benefits. Tactical urbanism (see, e.g. Carmichael, 2020) is already a practice that can be built upon, and similar small-scale initiatives exist in many communities across the Commonwealth. They are part of building resilience, which, as the South African Cities Network (2011) argued, requires innovation, creativity and long term commitment.

To build on the Kigali Declaration of 2022, the Commonwealth needs to:

- Use the Commonwealth Fund for Technical Cooperation to support sustainable urbanisation projects.
- Establish a Commonwealth Urban Observatory, as a virtual network with a hub in Africa or Asia, to evaluate and share practice.
- Work with UN-Habitat to get a Commonwealth 'cut' of their data.
- Convene a meeting of Commonwealth Sustainable Development Ministers every two years in the wings of the WUF.
- Pump prime the establishment of a system of Commonwealth Planning Aid, mobilising volunteers and information technology to train barefoot planners.

None of these are costly and they do not need to take long to set in place.

Looking 50 years ahead, the real challenge is terrifyingly immediate. What matters is not where planning in the Commonwealth might be 50 years from now but rather reinventing the way we do planning *now* to accelerate the delivery of a sustainable urban future; we have only two decades to achieve this. The NUA represents a statement of faith in the idea of planning. CAP needs to be a passionate and informed advocate to drive the response to this by accelerating change, making the connections and sharing experiences. CAP played a significant role in getting sustainable urbanisation on the global agenda in the 21st century, now planners need to use their skills within and beyond formal governmental and commercial structures to put those ideas into practice. How the Commonwealth addresses the intertwined crises of urbanisation, poverty, inequality and the climate emergency will determine whether it still exists in 2072.

References

Batty, M. and Yang, W. (2022), *A Digital Future for Planning: Spatial Planning Re-imagined*, London: Digital Task Force for Planning, Available at https://digital4planning.com/wp-content/uploads/2022/02/A-Digital-Future-for-Planning-Full-Report-Web.pdf (Accessed 21 February 2022).

Berrisford, S. (2013), *How to Make Planning Law Work for Africa, Counterpoints*, London: African Research Institute, Available at www.africaresearchinstitute.org/newsite/publications/planning-law-in-africa/ (Accessed 23 July 2022).

CAP. (2019), *2019 CAP Awards: Winners Announced*, Available at https://a08f9366-f017-4982-8fe9-473d83d2b075.filesusr.com/ugd/25734f_99c0bf0f52764affa8cccf04b79ae454.pdf (Accessed 6 January, 2022).

Carmichael, J. (2020), *Tactical Urbanism: Making It Happen*, Available at www.arup.com/perspectives/publications/research/section/tactical-urbanism (Accessed 23 July 2022).

ComHabitat. (2010), *Urban Challenges: Scoping the State of the Commonwealth's Cities*, London: ComHabitat.

Farmer, P., Frojmovic, M., Hague, C., Harridge, C., Narang, S., Shishido, R., Siegel, D., Taylor, P. and Vogelij, J. (2006), *Reinventing Planning: A New Governance Paradigm for Managing Human Settlements, Position Paper for Debate Leading to the World Planners Congress, Vancouver 17–20 June*. Available at www.globalplannersnetwork.org/wp-content/uploads/2016/10/reinventingplanningenglish-1.pdf (Accessed 7 February 2022).

Greaves, S., Faunce, L. and Cocco, F. (2017), 'A world Perspective on Food Shortages', *Financial Times*, Available at www.ft.com/content/9d2b0b36-f784-11e6-9516-2d969e0d3b65. (Accessed 5 January 2022).

Gueli, R., Liebenberg, S. and van Huyssteen, E. (2007), 'Integrated Development Planning in South Africa: Lessons for International Peacebuilding?' *African Journal on Conflict Resolution*, 7 (1), pp. 89–112, https://gsdrc.org/document-library/integrated-development-planning-in-south-africa-lessons-for-international-peacebuilding/ (Accessed 16 February 2022).

Hague, C. (2019), *Delhi – Colonial Planning, Slums and Gated Communities*. Available at www.centreforsustainablecities.ac.uk/news/delhi-colonial-planning-slums-gatedcommunities/ (Accessed 19 August 2022).

Hague, C., Platt, C. and Taylor, P. (2018), *Leading Change: Delivering the New Urban Agenda through Urban and Territorial Planning*, Kuala Lumpur: UN Habitat, Republic of South Africa Department of Human Settlements and South African Local Government Association, Available at https://unhabitat.org/leading-change-delivering-the-new-urban-agenda-through-urban-and-territorial-planning (Accessed 5 August 2022).

Horst, M., McClintock, N. and Hoey, L. (2017), 'The Intersection of Planning, Urban Agriculture and Food Justice: A review of the literature', *Journal of the American Planning Association*, 83 (3), pp. 277–295, https://doi.org/10.1080/01944363.2017.1322914.

Intergovernmental Panel on Climate Change. (2021), *Climate Change 2021: The Physical Science Basis. Contribution of Working Group I to the Sixth Assessment Report of the Intergovernmental Panel on Climate Change* (Masson-Delmotte, V., P. Zhai, A. Pirani, S.L. Connors, C. Péan, S. Berger, N. Caud, Y. Chen, L. Goldfarb, M.I. Gomis, M. Huang, K. Leitzell, E. Lonnoy, J.B.R. Matthews, T.K. Maycock, T. Waterfield, O. Yelekçi, R. Yu, and B. Zhou (eds.)), Cambridge: Cambridge University Press, Available at www.ipcc.ch/report/ar6/wg1/ (Accessed 23 July 2022).

Kamete, A.Y. (2007), 'Cold-Hearted, Negligent and Spineless? Planning, Planners and the (R)Ejection of "Filth" in Urban Zimbabwe', *International Planning Studies*, 12 (2), pp. 153–171, https://doi.org/10.1080/13563470701477959.

Kofi Annan Foundation. (2021), *News and Media: Combatting Hunger*, Available at www.kofi-annanfoundation.org/combatting-hunger/orange-fleshed-sweet-potato-ghana/ (Accessed 5 January 2022).

Marais, L. (2013), 'The impact of mine downscaling on the Free State Goldfields', *Urban Forum*, 24(4), pp. 503–521, https://doi.org/10.1007/s12132-013-9191-3.

Marais, L. and Cloete, J. (2016), 'Patterns of Territorial Development and Inequality from South Africa's Periphery: Evidence from the Free State Province', *Working Paper Series No. 188*, Santiago, Chile: RIMISP, https://doi.org/10.13140/RG.2.1.4754.3284.

Mayr, M., Alonso, C. and Rouse, C. (2017), *Blue-green Network Planning as a Spatial Development and Climate-Resilient Strategy – The Case of Belmopan, Belize, Paper to Caribbean Urban Forum, 15–19 May 2017*, Belize City: Belize, Available at https://unhabitat.org/blue-green-network-planning-as-a-spatial-development-and-climate-resilient-strategy-the-case-of-belmopan-belize-urban-development-and-climate-resilience-through-blue-green-network-infrastructure (Accessed 23 July 2022).

Oborn, P. and Walters, J.G. (2020), *Planning for Climate Change and Rapid Urbanisation: Survey of the Built Environment Professions in the Commonwealth, Survey Results*. Available at https://commonwealthsustainablecities.org/survey/ (Accessed 2 August 2022).

Place Design Group. (2022), *Future Street*, Available at https://placedesigngroup.com/projects/future-street/ (Accessed 30 August 2022).

Satterthwaite, D. and Sverdlik, A. (2021), 'The Implications of Informal Settlement Upgrading Programs for Access to Water, Sanitation and Public Health', *Global Public Health*, https://doi.org/10.1093/acrefore/9780190632366.013.317.

South African Cities Network. (2011), *2011 State of SA Cities Report*, Johannesburg: South African Cities Network.

Toon, B. (2022), *Website Enquiry – Place Design Group, E-mail from Lisa Evans to Cliff Hague, 30 August 2022*.

Tschudin, A. (2022), *Strengthening the Capacity of African Countries to Design and Implement Policies that Promote the Nexus between Peace, Humanitarian Work, Development and Human Rights for an Accelerated Implementation of the SDGs*, New York: UN Office of the Special Advisor on Africa.

UN. (2013), *World Population Policies 2013*, New York: Department of Economic and Social Affairs.

UN. (2017), *New Urban Agenda, Resolution adopted by the General Assembly on 23 December 2016*, 71/256, Available at https://uploads.habitat3.org/hb3/New-Urban-Agenda-GA-Adopted-68th-Plenary-N1646655-E.pdf (Accessed 3 January 2022).

UN Department of Economic and Social Affairs. (2018), *68% of the World Population Projected to Live in Urban Areas by 2050, says UN*, Available at www.un.org/development/desa/en/news/population/2018-revision-of-world-urbanization-prospects.html (Accessed 7 February 2022).

UN-Habitat. (2015a), *International Guidelines on Urban and Territorial Planning*, Nairobi: UN Human Settlements Programme, Available at https://unhabitat.org/books/international-guidelines-on-urban-and-territorial-planning/ (Accessed 31 December 2021).

UN-Habitat. (2015b), *International Guidelines on Urban and Territorial Planning: Towards a Compendium of Inspiring Practices*, Nairobi: UN Human Settlements Programme, Available at https://cpbuse1.wpmucdn.com/blogs.uoregon.edu/dist/f/13542/files/2016/09/International-Guidelines-Compendium-Inspiring-Practices-1pimrn1.pdf (Accessed 16 February 2022).

UN-Habitat. (2020a), *World Cities Report: The Value of Sustainable Urbanisation*. Nairobi: UN Human Settlements Programme, 2020. Available at https://unhabitat.org/sites/default/files/2020/10/wcr_2020_report.pdf (Accessed 31 December 2021).

UN-Habitat. (2020b), *Planet Smart City Partners with UN-Habitat on Slum Upgrading Initiatives in Kenya*. Available at https://unhabitat.org/planet-smart-city-partners-with-un-habitat-on-slum-upgrading-initiatives-in-kenya (Accessed 5 January 2022).

UN-Habitat. (2022), *Envisaging the Future of Cities, World Cities Report 2022*, Nairobi: UN Human Settlements Programme, Available at https://unhabitat.org/wcr/ (Accessed 23 July 2022).

Wang, Y.P. and Kintrea, K. (2020), *Neighbourhood Inequality and Division Undermining Drive for Sustainable Cities*, Available at www.centreforsustainablecities.ac.uk/news/neighbourhood-inequality-and-division-undermining-drive-for-sustainable-cities (Accessed 6 January 2022).

Warner, G. (2013), *In Kenya, Using Tech to Put An "Invisible" Slum on the Map*, Available at www.npr.org/blogs/parallels/2013/07/17/202656235/in-kenya-using-tech-to-put-an-invisible-slum-onthe-map (Accessed 31 March 2022).

Watson, V. (2016), 'Locating Planning in the New Urban Agenda of the Urban Sustainable Development Goal', *Planning Theory*, 15 (4), pp. 435–448, https://doi/10.1177/1473095216660786.

World Bank. (2022), *Data: Prevalence of Moderate or Severe Food Insecurity in the Population*, Available at https://data.worldbank.org/indicator/SN.ITK.MSFI.ZS?end=2018&start=2015&view=chart (Accessed 5 January 2022).

11

PLANNERS WILL NOT BE THE MAN IN THE HORNED RIMMED GLASSES

The future is civil not civic

Vijay Krishnarayan

I was pleased to be asked to contribute to this publication – particularly since I did not come to practice as a professional planner. The invitation provides me with an opportunity to congratulate the Commonwealth Association of Planners (CAP) on 50 years of achievement and challenge them to continue their excellent work as we look forward to its next semicentennial.

As I reflected on the theme for this chapter, I cast my mind back to 1972 and considered how far planning as a discipline in the Commonwealth has come since then. My recollection is of a profession that was largely male, that largely looked to Britain for its cues – the associations of planners (where they existed across the Commonwealth) having been established largely in the image of the Royal Town Planning Institute (RTPI). It was tempting to dismiss the task of looking to the next 50 years as a fool's errand. I resisted, reminding myself (courtesy of some stirring British public information films of the 1950s and 1960s) that the very essence of planning is aspirational and forward-looking. It taps into our deeply held need to make tomorrow better. It is inherently optimistic.

Fifty years on we can see that progress has been made. My father travelled from Trinidad and Tobago to train as an architect in the 1960s. He returned in 1976 as a qualified built-environment professional and helped establish the Trinidad and Tobago Institute of Architects. He was angry that he had to be a member of the Royal Institute of British Architects to practice in Trinidad. The same was true for planners. The Trinidad and Tobago Society of Planners was established in 1975. Over the past 50 years, different traditions of planning have emerged. It has become a much more plural profession, but is it able to meet the coming challenges?

I was asked originally to look at this question from a civil society point of view. That is because I drifted into the role of Director-General of the Commonwealth Foundation (the Commonwealth's agency for civil society) having been heavily

PHOTO 11.1 Vijay Krishnarayan and Clive Harridge meeting at a reception at the Foreign and Commonwealth Office, London.

Source: Clive Harridge

influenced by planning. The Foundation was established by member states in 1966 as a testimony to the idea that the Commonwealth is more than an association of governments and is as much an institution of peoples and cultures. The Foundation strengthens civic participation in development and democracy through its programmes and grant-making.

I studied planning – but realised after eight weeks at college that I did not have what it takes to work in development control (acknowledging that not all planners work in 'DC' but that was certainly a dominant theme at the time). But I was excited by the way that planning made provision for consultation and participation (this was radical in 1983 – when the dominance of the market was having a profound impact on planning practice).

In this chapter, I aim to identify the significant issues that planners in the Commonwealth will have to address: the social, economic, technical, environmental and political.

The social

In the coming years, I can see the public becoming increasingly involved in planning processes. While this is common practice now – it will change. The shape of society will change. At the moment we often make reference to the fact that two-thirds of the Commonwealth's population is under the age of 30. Over the next 50 years, that narrative will change as the demographic balance shifts to an ageing population (a trend already apparent in Asia). This will have many implications for public policy, including planning for housing, transport and health.

The practice of planning will continue to evolve and find new ways of engaging with citizens, who will find new ways of organising themselves. As society changes so will civil society. It will reform as citizens increasingly enjoy access to information and data that was previously seen as the preserve of the professionals. In response, planners will be called on to re-invent themselves as interlocutors and facilitators.

The economic

Imagining the ways in which we will work for a living seems always to have been clouded by fears of a dystopian future. These may be black-and-white images of workers attending a production line in an automaton trance or narratives of insecure employment in an increasingly atomised society. These imaginings have their basis in reality. Digitalisation and globalisation have changed profoundly the way we work and these trends have been accentuated by Covid. But planning has an essential part to play in helping to address the uncertainties that will be even more apparent over the coming years. As an instrument of public policy, planning will have to help deliver decent work and the ability to skill up and to retire.

By 2072 the world of work will have been completely transformed by technological innovations and demographic shifts. Globalisation will continue to evolve and shape the way we produce and consume goods and services. Back in 1972,

PHOTO 11.2 Climate change protest in Trafalgar Square, London. Public protests urging businesses, governments and people to take climate action are increasingly prevalent in many parts of the Commonwealth.

Source: Clive Harridge

industrial strategy and structure planning were widely accepted but over the following ten years lost ground. I think their time will come again as the demand for locally produced and delivered services continues to grow. Value chains will come under increasing scrutiny as the demand for locally produced and delivered products continues to grow. Local economic development will increasingly be seen as a means of generating wealth and delivering development in response to consumer preferences, changes in the workforce and climate change. In this context, planners will be the convenors that bring together public and private stakeholders (while understanding that the division between the two is already blurred and this will continue) to plan for local economies.

The technical

Much has been made of the impact of digitalisation and this is often seen as synonymous with technological change. I think this misses a wider appreciation of the impact of technology on the future. Artificial intelligence, virtual reality and bitcoin will all continue to shape the way we live. There will soon be a universal expectation of good connectivity. This has already had an impact on work patterns and the way services are delivered. A new normal is already emerging in the global north and this will spread.

The new frontiers for technology will focus on the realms beyond the digital. This will include new ways of producing energy and new kinds of building materials. I can recall the impact that cheaply available Portland cement and steel had on planning in the 1960s and 1970s. The decarbonisation of materials will see a new blend of ancient and modern materials, including cellulose and rammed earth. In turn, this will shape the scale and layout of buildings. This will call on planners to liaise between architects, engineers and politicians as new technologies are applied to the built environment.

The environmental

In 1972 an awareness of climate change was nascent. John Stanley Sawyer (a British meteorologist born in 1916) wrote an article for *Nature* magazine (Sawyer, 1972), which predicted climate change due to increased levels of carbon dioxide in the atmosphere. There is now no credible disagreement with this fact and planners all over the Commonwealth treat climate change as a matter of course. To date, these responses can be characterised as responsive, aimed at coping with expected change based on modelling that reveals the impacts, for example, on coastlines.

The challenge for planners in the coming period will be to find ways that enable people to live with nature and the environment rather than compete with or battle it. The multiple challenges of climate, Covid and commerce have reminded us of the importance of building resilience. This means more than

PHOTO 11.3 Community-based watershed management study visit, Trinidad and Tobago. Vijay Krishnarayan (centre back to camera) on a site visit in Port of Spain, 2001 listening to a speaker (right) from Water and Sewerage Authority of Trinidad and Tobago (WASA). Others are people from across the Caribbean.

Source: Vijay Krishnarayan

planning so that we can bounce back from shocks – which are ever-present and likely to occur with increasing regularity. It means planning so that we are able to continue to progress with equity and sustainability. Planners have a role to play in bringing longitudinal perspective in the face of short-term and short-sighted development proposals.

The political

The relationship between central and local government (where the majority of planners are employed) has changed dramatically over the past 50 years. There has always been tension but there has been a decisive shift towards centralisation across the Commonwealth – with powers increasingly vested in ministers and quasi-governmental agencies. This has led to bad planning decisions (if good decisions are characterised, for example, by inclusive participation and accountable institutions). In general, people are more distrustful of their institutions than they were 50 years

PHOTO 11.4 Public Protest, New Delhi, India.

Source: Christine Platt

ago. Institutions will have to respond to citizen activism, which will demand that decisions be taken nearer to the people directly affected. As the social contract between the state and citizens evolves, this will be one of its new features.

Some municipal governments have already proven to be more agile than their national counterparts. For example, as institutions plan for a Net Zero future, it is city governments that are leading the way and demonstrating leadership. The trend towards greater urbanisation will see city governments grow in stature and authority. This is where innovation will take place in policy development and delivery. Global policy agendas will be increasingly set by city governments. Planners will be called on to make the connections between agencies and stakeholders bringing systems thinking to decision-making processes.

On civil society

In each of the realms I have mentioned, civic participation is a significant feature and they intersect. The trend is towards decision-making by referenda and the implicit framing of policy in terms of binary choices. Technical advances will continue to make it easier for citizens to express their policy preferences digitally. But increased choice and access to information via technology do not have to be reductive. They can also enable greater transparency and more open governance. Which centralising administration does not seek to shut down social media as a means of shutting people down or covering misdemeanours up? People will increasingly rely on civil society institutions to help them navigate the wealth of information.

The issue of trust is central to the future of civil society and the way that it will interact with other institutions (including planning). As information becomes increasingly available, people will look for help as they seek to make sense of the choices they are presented with. Indeed, they may also look for allies as they reject the choices they are presented with and formulate new options. There is no guarantee that civil society as currently constructed will be the repositories of people's trust.

Over the space of 40 years, I have seen the term 'NGO' go from valorised to vilified. While it is true that this has been aided and abetted by those with no interest in social justice, it has to be acknowledged that some civil society organisations have been found wanting in terms of accountability and probity – and they have provided a useful stick for detractors to beat the whole sector with. But in the agora people will continue to seek out leaders and spokespeople who are authentic and trusted. In 50 years, these may look new (e.g., individuals and brands) as well as traditional (e.g., media organisations, churches).

One of the reasons I took issue with planning as an undergraduate was because it was presented by some as a mechanism for mediating interests – community on one side and developers on the other. It was implied that this was an equitable relationship. I disagreed. There is a tradition of civil society support for people as they engage with interests that have access to far greater resources. As long as that planning paradigm prevails, the need for civil society as a means of advising, organising and advocating community interests in that system will remain.

If the Commonwealth is going to continue to be an association of peoples it will place civic participation as a determinant of sustainable development at the heart of its mission. This is enshrined in Clause 16 of the Charter of the Commonwealth which states:

> We recognise the important role that civil society plays in our communities and countries as partners in promoting and supporting Commonwealth values and principles, including the freedom of association and peaceful assembly, and in achieving development goals.
>
> *Commonwealth Secretariat, 2012*

I feel sure that the institution will continue to grapple with finding a balance between the interests of member governments and the interests of the civic as these are not always aligned. Civil society will (rightly in my view) continue to demand space in Commonwealth processes and this will be harder and harder to resist as the logic of civic participation resonates ever stronger.

Conclusion

I am wary when I see the William Gibson quote, which posits that 'The future is already here – it's just not evenly distributed' (Gibson, 2001). I hesitate because I know that the quote implies that we lack the agency to make the future better. At the same time, I look around and see things that I sense will be commonplace in 2072 – a shorter working week, a universal basic income, plant-based diets, self-driving cars. Planners will be instrumental both in accelerating these trends and managing them. But they will do so from a different vantage point. Planners will not be the man in horned rimmed glasses holding the felt-tip pen as was perhaps the case in 1972 (I commend the film *Tomorrow's Canberra* from the Film Australia Collection. It was made by the Commonwealth Film Unit in 1972 and describes the planning of Canberra as Australia's national capital at the time). Instead, they will be the convenors and facilitators that bring people and diverse interests together to negotiate a better future. They will be judged not on the basis of their technocratic expertise or mastery of data but on their ability to make development better for people and the planet.

References

Commonwealth Secretariat. (2012), *Charter of the Commonwealth*, London: Commonwealth Secretariat.
Gibson, W. (2001), 'Quoted in The Economist', *The Economist*. London: The Economist. https://www.economist.com/business/2001/06/21/broadband-blues
Sawyer, J. (1972), 'Man-made Carbon Dioxide and the Greenhouse. Effect', *Nature*, 239, pp. 23–26.

12

YOUNG PEOPLE DRIVING SUSTAINABLE URBANISATION

Olafiyin Taiwo

The Commonwealth represents a third of the world population on all continents and over 60% of this demographic are under the age of 30. The United Nations predicted an increase in the world's population in urban areas to over 68% by 2050 whilst over 50% of this increment will occur in the Commonwealth (United Nations et al., 2018). Population growth requires access to essential basic services and adequate infrastructure for sustenance. Planning is therefore very important to facilitating and delivering practical solutions that address the present challenges and adequately provide for the demands of the future.

Beyond improving the physical characteristics of spaces to make better places, the potential of planning to improve the quality of life and human settlement is infinite. Despite the diversities of states in the Commonwealth, the lived experiences of young people across these states are significantly similar. The fact that young people navigate a series of life's critical transitions in a shorter timeframe than any other age group demands that adequate attention is given to ensure their environment provides the physical, social, economic and other amenities needed to achieve independence that is beneficial to the society. Yet, the active involvement of youth in planning, place-shaping and policymaking remains a serious challenge in several commonwealth states.

The need for planning to deliver well-designed, resource-efficient human settlements that create a sense of place, identity and belonging for all demographic group is challenged across all regions of the Commonwealth. Whilst it cannot be affirmed that planning delivered on these expectations in the last few decades, the next five decades present the opportunity to learn from the past, robustly engage stakeholders and revolutionise rapidly for the future.

Rapid urbanisation to sustainable urbanisation

There are increased uncertainties about the future of young people in cities particularly given the extensive impact of rapid urbanisation on a variety of aspects,

DOI: 10.4324/9781003357933-15

PHOTO 12.1 Olafiyin Taiwo at CHOGM, Kigali, Rwanda 2022. Olafiyin addresses the Youth Forum at the Commonwealth Heads of Government Meeting in Kigali, Rwanda, June 2022.

Source: Commonwealth Youth for Sustainable Urbanisation Network

including economic, social and environmental aspects. The poorly planned expansion of cities exposes residents to increased social instability. As widening inequalities become more visible, urban violence and social unrest are becoming a common phenomenon in some Commonwealth cities. The quality of life and well-being of the youth especially in settlements with large youth populations affects the stability and security of these cities and human settlements.

PHOTO 12.2 Testing the Rapid Planning Toolkit, Bo, Sierra Leone. Rapid Planning Toolkit Workshop facilitated by One World Link, Bo Sierra Leone, December 2017.

Source: Jane Knight, One World Link

The unprecedented inflow of people to urban areas is particularly strong in disaster-prone regions and outpaces urban planning which might lead to high-risk exposure with a potential for the creation of new risks. Rapid urbanisation raises serious concern for the increasing number of young people who will live in urban areas. Young people will continue to be affected by these challenges in a series of real and significant ways, with ripple effects on their ability to live their daily lives and achieve future aspirations.

Over the next five decades, the role of young planners as the voice of young people in place-shaping and policy development processes will become more apparent. Young planners are increasingly engaging in policy debates and advocating for opportunities to contribute effectively to decision-making. Drawing from their lived experiences as both skilled professionals and young people, young planners are able to better identify the barriers to engagement and also to offer advice to mitigate the challenges. Given the pace at which this movement is growing, it is anticipated that appropriate mainstreaming of youth into planning processes and procedures will be witnessed within the next 50 years across most Commonwealth states.

Cities will continue to remain the main centres of culture, innovation, economic development, entrepreneurship and human development. The increasing youth population in the Commonwealth if utilised suitably provides the opportunity to maximise Commonwealth cities' potential as hubs for improved economic outcomes, creativity, prosperity, better living conditions and better access to services.

Young people as innovative disruptors, drivers, and catalysts for important institutional changes will facilitate the evolution of planning approaches in the

PHOTO 12.3 Young planner speaking up Viral Desai, first leader of the CAP Young Planners Network, addresses the Commonwealth Sustainable Cities meeting in Canada House, London in 2018.

Source: Clive Harridge

Commonwealth in the next few decades. Advanced information technology and digital transformation are likely tools that young planners will employ to explore productive and innovative ways of maximising the advantages of urbanisation whilst addressing the associated challenges against a backdrop of progressively global developments.

Planning education

The survey of the built environment professions in the Commonwealth found that there is lack of educational and institutional capacity to grow the professions fast enough and increasing recognition of weakness in built environment policy in many Commonwealth countries (Oborn and Walters, 2020).

Given the skills shortage, the role of planning education in addressing these issues and responding to future demands cannot be disregarded. These findings suggest a need for a radical transformation of planning education in many Commonwealth countries, particularly because the quality of planning education varies significantly. Several aspects of planning education will be evaluated in order to increase the capacity of planning education to respond effectively to the demands of the profession. Emerging trends in delivery modes will shape how planning education will be delivered. The future of planning education is that of solid theoretical frameworks, continued research, and high-quality professional preparation and practice.

Regardless of the delivery modes, a strong multidisciplinary approach with an intergenerational perspective in planning education is expected to emerge within the next five decades. It will involve the interaction of diverse populations of older professionals, intermediate professionals and younger planning students in knowledge-building exchanges that are designed to strengthen the reputation of the planning profession and benefit the Commonwealth as a whole. This intergenerational perspective will provide a broader understanding of the nature of planning and address the challenges of economic, social and political implications of the professional preparation of planning students for practice in the field for the future.

Interdisciplinary and cross-sectoral working

Cities and human settlements function through complex, interdependent and multidimensional systems that interface between several disciplines and sectors. They have been influenced by silo policies, strategies and systems in competing directions resulting in mismanagement of resources, duplication of responsibilities and wastage. Professional distrust, resistance to collaboration and lack of shared vision have led to devastating outcomes for the vulnerable in cities and human settlements across different commonwealth countries, particularly children, youth and older people.

It is vital that all relevant stakeholders are involved in the process of planning the cities and human settlements for better outcomes. The interconnectedness and complexity of the challenges in cities and human settlements require that the added benefit of solutions should lead to multiple benefits for different sectors and on different scales. Furthermore, collaboration facilitates the shared ownership of risks and costs which also creates possibilities for innovative and quality solutions.

Young planners have recognised the need for multi-disciplinary nature of solutions to ensure that they are capable of withstanding unexpected challenges and have the flexibility to adapt to new situations. They have joined forces with their counterparts from other built environment professions and sectors to create platforms for engagement and collaboration.

As young people become increasingly drawn to tackling social issues, these platforms for engagement provide opportunities for the present generation of young people and young professionals to interact with older experienced professional groups and sectors on cross-cutting themes and will continue to inspire the next generation of young people and young professionals. The Commonwealth Sustainable Cities Initiative (2022) and the Commonwealth Youth for Sustainable Urbanisation (Commonwealth Youth Programme, 2022) are setting the pace in this regard. These initiatives provide platforms for discourse, engagement and knowledge sharing among relevant built environment disciplines, institutions and other actors. These forms of collaborations will spread across the Commonwealth and influence planning significantly.

An increasingly multigenerational professional setting will be witnessed across the Commonwealth. This has a significant potential for innovation, advancement, productivity, social cohesion and value transfer. Creating opportunities for young planners to advance while also ensuring experienced professionals, whose wealth of skills, experience and values cannot be easily replaced, are involved in transforming cities and human settlement is critical. The interaction and collaboration among young planners and veteran professionals that are not limited to the built environment profession will be witnessed as young people increasingly question the existing conventional approach and demand for the realisation of a more equitable society.

Disaster risk reduction and climate change

Planning is critical to managing the risks from hazards and vulnerabilities. There is no one-size-fits-all. What works in a particular context and at a specific point in time does not guarantee the universal effectiveness of the approach. Whilst climate change is acknowledged as a global issue, the scope and scale of challenges and impact differ significantly at local levels. Several Commonwealth cities and human settlements are among the world's most vulnerable to climate risks and disasters.

Climate change and the frequency of disasters necessitate the strategic integration of disaster risk management and climate adaptation into planning particularly at subnational and local government levels. The development of climate action plans for several local government areas in the Commonwealth is widely accepted. However, the governance and policy development processes of these plans have excluded considerable input from planning. An implication of this exclusion is the possibility that climate action plans and policies might create new challenges and adverse repercussions on the delivery of strategic outcomes that can improve the quality of life and experiences of the most vulnerable in the local communities.

Research studies and reports are recognising the importance of planning in vulnerability reduction and climate adaptation. The mainstreaming of disaster risk reduction and climate change actions into existing or future plans, strategies and processes that cut across strategic, physical, sectoral and spatial development plans demands the leadership input of planners. The next decades will see young planners taking the reins and leading in the protection of the environment for sustainable cities and human settlements whilst establishing their expertise in areas and disciplines outside the norms of planning.

Inclusive planning

The growing severity of environmental and social problems and the continued marginalisation of the different demographic groups in policy development and planning has reached a tipping point. In general, women, girls, children, young people, people with disabilities and older people encounter significant social and economic disadvantages. Key characteristics of the cities and human settlements relating to security, access, safety, mobility, climate resilience and health create disproportionate liabilities for the most vulnerable and reaffirm the challenges encountered by these demographic groups. Establishing a critical approach to planning that addresses the needs of the different groups is fundamental to creating safe and secure cities and human settlements and perhaps is unavoidable.

Given that demographic groups interact with and experience the cities and human settlements differently, the demand to contribute to the planning process and decision-making of their local communities will increase dramatically in the future. Citizens and residents will be more interested in actively shaping their communities beyond traditional engagement. This inclusion would not by any means undermine the importance and relevance of land use planning. It would complement land use planning in maximising the potential of physical resources for local economic, social and environmental benefits whilst ensuring efficiency, sustainability and equity during the planning process

Therefore, planning processes will evolve to accommodate the participation of citizens and residents in the decision-making, visioning, design and implementation of the plans, policies and strategies in cities and human settlements. This evolution will be enhanced by technological advancement. It is anticipated that there would be a systematic departure from strictly land-use planning to more spatial planning to ensure that land can continue to be managed sustainably for future generations.

Developing locally relevant solutions

The cities and human settlements that will function in the future are those that consider meeting the needs and well-being of the local communities at the core of their innovation and functions. There are different plausible concepts about how to

PHOTO 12.4   Youth Forum at CHOGM, Kigali, Rwanda 2022. Members of the Commonwealth Youth Forum celebrate their involvement in the Commonwealth Heads of Government Meeting in Kigali, Rwanda, June 2022. Included in the group are Olafiyin Taiwo, third from right and Alice Preston-Jones of The Prince's Foundation, second from right.

Source: Commonwealth Youth for Sustainable Urbanisation Network

shape towns and cities such as smart city, compact city, 15-minute city, knowledge city, creative city or transit-oriented development among others. Each concept has its own merits and disadvantages. Adopting a particular concept is bound to create new complications, given the diversity of the population, the differing capacities, available resources, the range of political contexts and other local nuances. There is limited evidence on the capacity of a singular concept to promote equity and inclusion for sustainable cities and human settlements. Planners will create innovative systemic models with local knowledge in order to assess and adapt to the relevant characteristics of the many concepts to the specific spatial context in order to meet the needs of the present whilst enriching the future.

Conclusion

It is anticipated that the next five decades will be a new era of significance for planning and the planning profession globally but particularly in the Commonwealth countries as the present young population will lead to a significant demographic change. It is an era that will make the most valuable impact on cities and human settlements. With active youth engagement, intergenerational culture and multi-disciplinary approaches, planning will progress to take on additional responsibilities whilst championing the fundamental principles of integrating social, economic and environmental considerations into cities and human settlements.

References

Commonwealth Sustainable Cities Initiative. (2022), *Planning for Climate Change and Rapid Urbanisation: Commonwealth Sustainable Cities Initiative,* Available at https://commonwealth-sustainablecities.org (Accessed 5 August 2022).

Commonwealth Youth Programme. (2022), *Commonwealth Youth for Sustainable Urbanisation,* Available at https://commonwealthsustainablecities.org/youth/ (Accessed 5 August 2022)

Oborn, P. and Walters, J.G. (2020), *Planning for Climate Change and Rapid Urbanisation: Survey of the Built Environment Professions in the Commonwealth, Survey Results.* Available at https://commonwealthsustainablecities.org/survey/ (Accessed 2 August 2022).

United Nations Department of Economic and Social Affairs, Population Division. (2018), *World Urbanization Prospects: The 2018 Revision,* New York: United Nations, Available at www.un.org/development/desa/publications/2018-revision-of-world-urbanization-prospects.html (Accessed 5 August 2022).

13

EDUCATION FOR PLANNING A SUSTAINABLE FUTURE

Barbara Norman

Introduction

The Commonwealth Association of Planners (CAP) has been instrumental in building capacity in urban planning education in both developed and developing countries across the Commonwealth. As the mission for CAP states, CAP 'seeks to focus and develop the skills of urban and regional planners across the Commonwealth to meet the challenges of urbanisation and the sustainable development of human settlements.'

Over the last 50 years the nature of planning education has changed significantly, growing from a focus on the form and structure of a city to a more triple bottom line approach to urban planning and management; planning education for the constant challenges of rapid urbanisation such as housing, transport, water, energy, services and protection of the urban environment and heritage. There are also new challenges with climate change, technology, the nature of work, the circular economy and global pandemics (RTPI, 2021).

These urban planning challenges, current and future, need to be considered in planning for over two billion people (United Nations Department of Social and Economic Affairs, Population Division, 2022, p. i) most of who will live in urban settlements. The increasing complexity of planning for more sustainable and climate-sensitive cities has implications for the current and future training of urban planners and capacity building more broadly for decision makers at all levels of government.

Current and future challenges

Educating current and future urban planners is an ongoing and exciting proposition.

Two of the biggest global challenges are urbanisation and climate change, and good urban planning is central to addressing both. Urban planning has the unique role of 'connecting the dots' and providing integrated spatial solutions. Training planners is

DOI: 10.4324/9781003357933-16

unique in providing the necessary skills for thinking laterally, spatially and holistically. It is also fundamentally about public good and a better place for people and the planet.

Urbanisation is occurring at a rapid rate particularly in India, African and Asia. Many countries within the Commonwealth are dealing with everyday issues of escalating demand for basic housing, transport and access to essential community services. Clean water and energy are vital to the health of these communities. The contribution of urban planning is the ability to understand the urban environment in a spatial context and bring together the social, economic and environmental considerations in a dynamic and evolving context. Equipping planners with skills to think laterally and problem solve is critical to developing innovative urban solutions (Gurran et al., 2008).

Skills in spatial and local planning supported by national urban policy are essential to effectively managing the pace of urbanisation. Skills in community involvement in developing urban plans and local solutions are vital as is monitoring and evaluation during implementation. The pace of change is also placing pressures on qualified urban planners who need ongoing professional development and support – skills in critical thinking, communications, leadership and ethics. A deeper understanding by urban planners of urban poverty and informal settlements in developing countries will be essential given that is where much of the urban growth will occur in the 21st century, potentially gained through case studies and in-country experience.

Climate change is already affecting communities particularly in coastal regions (see Photo 13.1), where for historical reasons, most urban communities are located (IPCC, 2021; IPCC, 2022). The impact of coastal flooding has cost lives and displaced communities in the Pacific region with the future threat of permanent relocation facing Commonwealth island nations. Skills for urban planners will need to be enhanced to better plan for these climate risks such as scenario planning, competent knowledge of climate change science and its implications and possible spatial solutions (Norman et al., 2021). No longer are planners dealing with a relatively certain landscape but a dynamic one. So, skills in planning for risk management will be imperative. Communications skills will be critical in working with communities facing climate induced resettlement (Norman, 2022, Chapter 4).

Housing over two billion people by 2050 is a daunting prospect. More than half the global urban population currently lives in urban settlements of less than one million people. Most of the urban population lives in Africa, India and Asia (Norman, 2018). Therefore, urban planners are tackling urban problems across the urban hierarchy from global cities to villages and hamlets. The nature of housing varies considerably responding to place, the local culture of the communities and the availability of resources. In this context it is really important that CAP and kindred organisations provide affordable and accessible ongoing training and sharing of leading practice, for example, the mentoring programmes by urban planning associations for young planners and the CAP Young Planners Network supporting colleagues throughout the Commonwealth. Providing sufficient training and support in rural and remote regions is particularly important as often there may be only one planner operating in isolation and facing complex problems (see Box 13.1). Smart technology provides

PHOTO 13.1 The vulnerability of coastal settlements and livelihoods, Sri Lanka. It is not only large cities that are vulnerable to rising sea levels and more intense weather. Many fishing communities such as this one live by the shore, barely above sea level.

Source: Christine Platt

BOX 13.1   CHALLENGES IN RURAL MUNICIPALITIES IN SOUTH AFRICA.

While metropolitan areas have a large number of registered planning staff (42 on average), smaller municipalities are typically understaffed, with the rural municipalities typically only employing a single registered planner for all planning work (Municipal Demarcation Board 2012). This poses major challenges for planning educators expected to train planners able to work in a wide range of contexts, with highly variable levels of support in place.

Denoon-Stevens et al., 2022

the opportunity to develop online, affordable, on-the job-training in rural and remote communities or rapidly expanding cities in developing countries. Increased recognition of prior experience in the field would facilitate the urgent need for accredited planners in under-resourced urban environments.

Infrastructure is an ever-growing demand for an increasingly urban world. However, the nature of infrastructure is changing with smart technology, climate change and environmental protection. Social inclusion is a high priority placing emphasis on effective access and local distribution. Food security and urban gardens are re-emerging as well as local energy microgrids. Urban planners will need to work in interdisciplinary teams to develop future climate resilient plans including affordable net zero carbon housing solutions, green infrastructure (wetlands, biodiversity, community solar farms) and sustainable development options. Opportunities to be connected to international smart digital platforms will assist planning students to gain experience in collaboration and current research, for example the Urban Climate Change Research Network with regional nodes across the globe (UCCRN, 2022).

Transport will change rapidly and in many ways has the potential to transform urban futures. The current electrification of transport systems will continue with electric trains, buses and cars significantly cleaning up air pollution, particularly in developing countries. New innovative smart modes of transit will emerge, providing greater flexibility and access for poorer communities. Equally lessons can be learned and shared with more developed cities by urban communities still reliant on less-energy-intensive transport modes.

Coupled with more flexible transit systems is the changing nature of work, accelerated by the impacts of COVID-19. The traditional understanding of 'journey to work' is being tested with global corporations and universities adopting a 3:2 model of three days in the office and two days home based. The implications are far reaching with an increasing focus on neighbourhood design and services. Local liveability such as safe walking and cycling is becoming a priority along with shared local community hubs with smart technology for local access. All of this must be planned to ensure all local communities have access to the necessary services to run local enterprise and community health and education services.

Resettlement of urban communities is an issue many decision makers and politicians are choosing to ignore as it is seen as being in the 'too hard basket.' However, with the impacts of climate change, resettlement is a reality for some communities already beginning to plan to move (Lopez-Carr and Marter-Kenyon, 2015). A recent planning example can be found in Queensland Australia where a community, having been flooded three times in three years, elected to move to higher ground. The township of Grantham successfully moved the town to higher ground with community and government support (Moore, 2020). Educating planners in digital GIS, scenario planning and community planning is important and occurring in some urban planning schools as well as providing 'studio' opportunities to work in interdisciplinary teams with scientists, economists and social scientists. Web based

PHOTO 13.2   Devastation caused by the 2004 tsunami in Sri Lanka. On 26 December 2004 an Indian Ocean earthquake triggered a tsunami that hurtled into Sri Lanka's east and south coasts, killing over 35,000 people, destroying 100,000 houses and displacing half a million people. In March 2005 CAP and the Planning Institute of Australia participated in a Sri Lankan government-supported reconstruction workshop that paved the way for a five-year re-planning project with local planners, funded by AusAID and the Red Cross

Source: Cliff Hague

'urban labs' are providing the opportunity for online sharing of leading practice and knowledge on urban management. The international CAP Awards celebrate the best in the field with active participation from developing nations.

Natural disasters are likely to become more frequent and are a field where planning can make a difference; see, for example Photo 13.2. A recent example, although not directly connected to climate change, is the dramatic volcanic eruption in Tonga that triggered a tsunami and carpeted the small low-lying islands with volcanic ash. While the main island capital of Nuku'alofa can survive after clean-up and aid, some of the very small surrounding community islands were completely inundated with every house demolished (Menon et al., 2022). This example provides an insight into what planners may be dealing with in the future and the complexities involved (clean water, food, health, energy, communications, emergency shelter). The Tonga example was exacerbated by the risk of outside volunteers bringing COVID-19 to a group of islands basically Covid free, so immediate assistance was required via air drop etc. to protect the affected communities. In this respect planning education needs to be focused on resilience and to teach planners the skills to respond appropriately, skills in working with communities in country and adapting planning solutions to be culturally appropriate. Early involvement of indigenous communities in the planning process is essential.

> **BOX 13.2 AN EXAMPLE OF AN URBAN LAB: ROYAL MELBOURNE INSTITUTE OF TECHNOLOGY UNIVERSITY.**
>
> The Healthy Liveable Cities Lab at the RMIT University recognises that 'Creating healthy, liveable and sustainable cities is a major challenge in the face of population growth, social inequalities, traffic congestion, increases in non-communicable diseases and climate change.' The Lab aims to contribute to academic research but also to inform policies and practices to create healthy and sustainable cities. A multidisciplinary research team drawn from architecture, behavioural science, econometrics, geography, geospatial and computer science, health economics, public health, social epidemiology, sociology, sociology ecology and transport and urban planning examines the influence of city design and planning on health and well-being.
>
> The priority areas are stated as:
>
> - To explore the nexus between place, health and well-being, with a particular focus on spatial disadvantage, by developing health-related spatial indicators locally, nationally and globally.
> - To simulate, model and assess the health impacts of local and state planning policies and interventions, including transport, land use and health impact.
> - To influence future policies to improve population health outcomes.
>
> Source: RMIT Centre for Urban Research (2022).

Health and well-being have come into sharp relief as a result of COVID-19. It's a full circle for planning education given the origins of the RTPI in1914 being driven, in part, by the need for improved health and sanitation at the time. The healthy cities movement of the 1970s and 1980s has seen a resurgence with healthy city urban labs (see Box 13.2), revisiting the powerful links between urban planning and design and active living. Adding to this has been growing urban pollution through urban congestion and most recently catastrophic wildfires particularly in Australia (see Photo 13.3) and California. Advocacy skills for planners are increasingly important for influencing public policy and political decisions to improve land use planning decisions in an urbanising world.

These impacts on health and well-being are driving planners to rethink the location and design of urban settlements (Norman et al., 2021). Similarly, urban planning education needs to be updated to reflect these potentially transformational changes to the urban landscape. Several national planning associations, including the United Kingdom, Canada, Australia and New Zealand, have now made climate change statements and support embedding climate change considerations into city

PHOTO 13.3 Wildfire damage, New South Wales, Australia. Professor Barbara Norman investigating the immediate impact of a catastrophic wildfire in southeast New South Wales, February 2020.

Source: Associate Professor Hitomi Nakanishi

plans and processes. This in turn will flow through to professional accreditation and planning education requirements. CAP can play a valuable role in extending urban planning for climate change across Commonwealth nations through professional cooperation and education.

The digital world has provided urban planners with an exciting array of new technologies for tracking and analysing urban activity to feed into better planning. Smart technology has also expanded the opportunities for community engagement and a greater reach to parts of the community that may not have previously engaged in the future design of their neighbourhood/town (e.g. three dimensional visualisation of development proposals for public comment). The advent of the smart city has allowed for greater efficiencies (water, energy, communications) and enabled more flexible arrangements for home-based work. Urban planners now need good digital skills training to be able to analyse and engage with the integrity of the data and use it appropriately and ethically.

The circular economy is a trend that is expected to only increase with more understanding by society that reuse of everything is fundamental to a more sustainable future. Some of the other changes mentioned previously will facilitate this, such as smart technology enabling a greater sharing of resources such as transport (shared mobility), energy for buildings (community solar farms), materials and green infrastructure (community green spaces including wetlands). The transformation of our cities in the future through 'softer' connectivity means that urban planners will need to be more mindful of not only the physical infrastructure but possibly significant behavioural change in how cities operate in the future.

Capacity building has always been central to CAP's mission. The aforementioned issues are illustrative of the range of challenges facing urban planners in the 21st century. The issues include longstanding matters such as housing and transport as well as new challenges such as climate change and global pandemics. With all these changes comes the need for new skills and wider capacity building for decision makers and community leaders. As well, the nature of training and the mode of delivery will continue to evolve taking advantage of the digital world. The use of remote learning tools, podcasts, webinars and online degrees, has the ability to transform how CAP can reach rural and remote communities in developing countries that are part of the Commonwealth network – a future programme for CAP? A positive example, also discussed in previous chapters, is the 'Rapid Planning Toolkit' developed by The Prince's Foundation with CAP and others which provides an online free resource for urban communities in developing countries particularly where there is a lack of trained planners (Princes Foundation, 2022). Importantly it enables in-country training supported by invited specialists as required in an affordable and accessible way. Of course, there are limitations where digital communications are minimal but this is also changing very rapidly as costs are driven downwards through solar cells and increasing digital connectivity.

Conclusions: CAP 50 years on

The Commonwealth Association of Planners has provided an important global network for sharing the latest in knowledge and practice to Commonwealth nations. This global network has been an enormous strength and will continue to make a very positive contribution over the next 50 years. From a planning educator's perspective, the challenges outlined earlier present new opportunities for collaboration and partnerships in capacity building and education in urban and regional planning for sustainable urbanisation.

There will always be shared concerns across the nations, playing out differently in developed and developing countries, depending on the pattern of urbanisation, urban governance, cultural context and environmental imperatives. In my view, one way towards sustainable urbanisation will be through a continuing dialogue of sharing experience and developing innovative models of planning education that are accessible to all communities.

In summary, some of the key trends over the next 50 years that will need to be considered in the planning and design of future urban settlements and therefore in the training of urban planners may include:

1. Increasing community-based approaches to city and local design.
2. Nature-based solutions becoming central to urban futures.
3. A wider range of smart digital tools for planning and designing urban settlements.
4. Redesigning of cities with significant change to journey to work patterns.
5. Resettlement of urban communities due to impacts of climate change.
6. Upgrading of very large informal settlements in rapidly developing cities.
7. Co-design and collaboration in plan making and implementation including early engagement of local Indigenous communities.

As the world continues to urbanise, 'CAP 50 years on' will play a vital role in planning education. The value of the connections and a shared understanding will become even more important and a positive contribution to a better place for all.

References

Denoon-Stevens, S.P., Andres, L., Jones, P., Melgaço, L., Massey, R. and Nel, V. (2022), 'Theory Versus Practice in Planning Education: The View from South Africa', *Planning Practice & Research*, 37 (4), pp. 509–525, https://doi.org/10.1080/02697459.2020.1735158

Gurran, N., Norman, B. and Gleeson, B. (2008), *Planning Education Discussion Paper*, Kingston, ACT, Australia: Planning Institute of Australia.

IPCC. (2021), 'Summary for Policymakers', In Masson-Delmotte, V. et al. (eds.), *Climate Change 2021: The Physical Science Basis. Contribution of Working Group I to the Sixth Assessment Report of the Intergovernmental Panel on Climate Change*, Cambridge: Cambridge University Press.

IPCC. (2022), 'Summary for Policymakers', In Pörtner, H-O. et al. (eds.), *Climate Change 2022: Impacts, Adaptation, and Vulnerability. Contribution of Working Group II to the Sixth Assessment Report of the Intergovernmental Panel on Climate Change*, Cambridge: Cambridge University Press.

López-Carr, D. and Marter-Kenyon, J. (2015), 'Human Adaptation: Manage Climate-Induced Resettlement', *Nature*, 517, pp. 265–267, https://doi.org/10.1038/517265a

Menon, P., Needham, K. and Westbrook, T. (2022), 'New Zealand Water Ship Unloads in Tonga as Other Aid Trickles in', *Reuters*, 21 January, Available at www.reuters.com/world/world-rushes-aid-tsunami-hit-tonga-drinking-water-food-runs-short-2022-01-20/ (Accessed 21 July 2022).

Moore, T. (2020), 'Grantham Reborn: Meet the Little Queensland Town that Moved', *Brisbane Times*, 27 February, Available at www.brisbanetimes.com.au/national/queensland/grantham-reborn-meet-the-little-queensland-town-that-moved-20200227-p5450g.html (Accessed 9 March 2022).

Norman, B. (2022), *Urban Planning for Climate Change*, New York and London: Routledge.

Norman, B. (2018), *Sustainable Pathways for Our Cities and Regions: Planning within Planetary Boundaries*, London and New York: Routledge.

Norman, B., Newman, P. and Steffen W. (2021), 'Apocalypse Now: Australian Bushfires and the Future of Urban Settlements', *Nature Urban Sustainability*, 1 (2), Available at. www.nature.com/articles/s42949-020-00013-7 (Accessed 9 March 2022).

Princes Foundation. (2022), *Rapid Planning Tool*, Available at www.rapidplanningtoolkit.org/ (Accessed 14 May 2022).

RMIT Centre for Urban Research. (2022), *Healthy Liveable Cities Lab,* Available at https://cur.org.au/research-programs/healthy-liveable-cities-group/ (Accessed 4 August 2022).

RTPI. (2021), *Plan the world we need*. London: Royal Town Planning Institute, Available at www.rtpi.org.uk/new/our-campaigns/plan-the-world-we-need (Accessed 9 March 2022).

UCCRN. (2022), *Urban Climate Change Research Network*, Available at https://uccrn.ei.columbia.edu/ (Accessed 22 July 2022).

United Nations Department of Economic and Social Affairs, Population Division. (2022), *World Population Prospects 2022: Summary of Results*. UN DESA/POP/2022/TR/NO. 3, Available at www.un.org/development/desa/pd/ (Accessed 4 August 2022).

14

ENDPIECE

Perspectives on the past and future of planning in the Commonwealth

Cliff Hague, Clive Harridge, Bryce Julyan, Ruiz Nik and Ian Tant

Authors from five continents have contributed to this book, reflecting on experiences at either end of – and throughout – a 50-year time period. This is the first time that any serious attempt has been made to bring together a history of CAP. This is important because people move on and carry their knowledge with them: for small organisations run by volunteers this is both endemic and problematic. In normal times for normal people, recording what happened has less priority than making things happen. As new leaders turn on the taps with enthusiasm to let ideas flow, those stepping down take the plug with them and corporate memory drains away. So for CAP as an organisation facing the world in the 21st century, simply telling the story of five decades of action is not just indulgence in nostalgia or even a homage to the endeavours of those who have gone before; it is a necessary building block to inform and strengthen present and future action.

Similarly, the book has looked forwards as well as backwards. While celebration of CAP's 50th anniversary is a legitimate end in itself, we hope that through this combination the book contributes to knowledge and understanding of wider issues in planning, sustainable urban development and urban studies. While the book was being written the Commonwealth Heads of Government agreed a Declaration on Sustainable Urbanisation (The Commonwealth, 2022) that stated

> the long-term trajectory of urbanisation across Commonwealth members will have important consequences for national economies and that by 2050, an additional 2.5 billion people will be living in the world's towns and cities, almost 50 percent of them in the Commonwealth.

Hopefully history will show that this was a landmark that drove cooperation across the Commonwealth to deliver sustainable urbanisation.

This Endpiece addresses four themes:

- The role of the Commonwealth in relation to sustainable urbanisation.
- CAP and autobiographical writing as planning history.
- Agency and activism in planning and the relationship among international, national and local scales.
- Beyond the SDGs – knowledge, attitudes and skills for the future.

Colonialism, land and planning: the Commonwealth in relation to sustainable urbanisation

It is beyond dispute that the ancestry of the Commonwealth is in colonialism and a form of urbanisation that was not sustainable. The legacy of the British Empire remains in the networks and relationships we share in the modern Commonwealth. The imprint of imperialism remains and will resonate into the future of all Commonwealth countries. Any review of planning in the Commonwealth must address these facts.

Land directly connects planning to the colonial exercise. Sometimes by agreement, sometimes by force, the colonists implanted a British model of land tenure, with private ownership and property rights that were alien to most indigenous peoples. Land was often imbued with sacred beliefs and held in stewardship through tribal or family structures. Land that had been the basis of indigenous livelihoods was taken over and became a means for investment and the generation of wealth. It continues to be so.

Private ownership, subdivision, planning and development of the land was fundamental to facilitate the establishment of an economy through the extraction of wealth from the colony. To create a society for new settlers, missions, settlements and farms were necessary. Land was required for buildings – the administrative headquarters, the railways stations, churches, private schools – that imposed the presence, authority and mores of the colonisers. In the early days it was mainly the military engineers who did the planning (see Box 14.1), though as planning developed in Britain in the early 20th century professional planners became increasingly involved (see Photo 14.1).

BOX 14.1   EARLY COLONIAL PLANNING – SINGAPORE.

Perhaps the best known example of early colonialist planning was the Jackson/Raffles Plan for Singapore. Sir Thomas Stamford Raffles, born at sea off Jamaica in 1781, established a trading post for the British East India Company in Singapore in 1819, to compete with the Dutch colonisers in the region. When he returned three years later Raffles was dissatisfied with the haphazard growth of the colony and appointed Lieutenant Philip Jackson, the colony's engineer, to produce a lay-out plan according to Raffles' own vision. The basic grid produced is still part of the city's downtown structure, though – like many plans – the full ambition was not realised. As well as designating locations for administrative and commercial purposes, ethnic segregation was part of the plan, with separate zones for Europeans, Chinese, Indians and Arabs and Malays.

PHOTO 14.1 Lutyens and Baker's New Delhi. In 1911 the British decided to move the capital of India from Calcutta to Delhi, and British architects Lutyens and Baker (who also designed many buildings in South Africa, Kenya and what was then Southern Rhodesia) created a plan for monumental neo-classical buildings within a highly geometrical street pattern of circles, radial connectors and grand vistas. The grandeur remains, though shrouded in Delhi's toxic air pollution.

Source: Cliff Hague

Ethnic spatial segregation characterised much of the planning. As Kamazani and Mpeta (2018, p. 45) note 'In most towns and cities in Tanzania, for example, there are spaces that are termed uzunguni (lit. 'where white people live'). These are areas in which colonials and officers during the colonial period lived. These are rather spatially planned areas.'

PHOTO 14.2   A Colonial Garden City, Taiping, Perak, Malaysia. The Taiping Lake was the first public park built over an old mining area in 1884. It has been the catalyst to transforming the place from its mining past into a sustainable township that contributes positively to community well-being and enriches biodiversity through the greening of the town. Taiping has become one of the best places to retire in Malaysia. Planned during the colonial era as a Garden City, it is now a heritage town, with planning policies seeking conservation of historic buildings, and there has been much tree planting. Taiping is enjoyed by the local communities and was recognised as one of the top three sustainable destinations in the world by the German based Tourismus-Börse (ITB) in 2019.

Source: Ruiz Nik

In 1931 British planner Professor Stanley Adshead was commissioned to plan Lusaka, a new capital for Northern Rhodesia (now Zambia). He sought to apply Garden City principles to create a 'generous gracious city' with landscaping, open space and wide streets. The plan was based on racial segregation: there is a 'European Hospital' and a 'Native Hospital' on a smaller site at the end of a road leading from the 'Native Compound' and adjoining the 'Native Industrial Schools' (Home, 2014). The Garden City approach to lay out of areas was not uncommon (see Photo 14.2).

King (1977) has described how planning was exported to the colonies. Stevens (1955) noted how the English 1932 Town and Country Planning Act had become a template for planning legislation across the Empire, beginning with the Trinidad and Tobago Town and Country Planning Ordinance of 1938. The Gold Coast Town and Country Planning Ordinance, 1945 was the next, then came Nigeria (1945), Sierra Leone (1946), Nyasaland (1948) and Uganda (1948 and 1951). Fiji, Sarawak,

Mauritius, Aden and the Seychelles followed. Stevens noted (p. 123) 'the 1932 Act has left its mark in all corners of the world' but added 'unfortunately, in many of the territories this legislation has been enacted far in advance of capacity to provide either finance or personnel for its execution.'

He might have added that the 1932 Act had not worked well at home either. In particular, provisions for compensation to landowners and developers, together with limited enforcement powers, meant that the act presented few obstacles to development and left planning authorities in a weak negotiating position (Ward, 2004, p. 44). The landmark 1947 Planning Act was seen as necessary for that precise reason.

The idea of 'orderly development' as a planned alternative to 'haphazard development' was a concern that drove the 1932 Act. The influential professional manual *Principles and Practice of Town and Country Planning* (Keeble, 1964) first published in 1953 stated

> Town and Country Planning might be described as the art and science of ordering the use of land and the character and siting of buildings and communication routes so as to secure the maximum practicable degree of economy, convenience and beauty.
>
> *p. 9*

This mindset ill fits the reality of many Commonwealth cities over the past five decades (see Photo 14.3). Many planning systems fight a losing battle against street trading, a key source of livelihoods for many of the urban poor, many of whom display ingenuity in respect to their business premises (see Photos 14.4 and 14.5). Ironically, in post-industrial cities street trading is encouraged to enhance the urban cultural experience (see Photo 14.6).

Similarities in legal systems are often seen as a strength of the Commonwealth. For example, the Commonwealth Secretariat (2018) hailed it as a 'trading advantage.' However, it is clear that from the early days of CAP the planning legislation shared from an earlier era in the UK was a problem, and it continues to be so. However good the intentions may have been, the form of planning implanted in colonies in the 1940s and 1950s was inappropriate, flawed and doomed to fail. As the pace and scale of urbanisation increased, systems based on the UK's 1932 Act collapsed. As mentioned by Christine Platt in Chapter 6, CAP sought to address legislative reform, but the work was never completed.

Even more pertinent is that the Commonwealth Secretariat attaches a high priority to the rule of law and to supporting law makers in Commonwealth countries, yet during the lifetime of CAP it has never addressed planning legislation. This reflects the Secretariat's more general lacuna about the pan-Commonwealth significance of urbanisation. Legislative reform should be a priority for planning across the Commonwealth to create systems that are fit for purpose in terms of the climate emergency, public health and reducing inequalities, while respecting cultural and local differences.

PHOTO 14.3 The vibrancy of the street, Lagos, Nigeria. Pedestrians, traders, shoppers and vehicles jostle for space in a traditional street as more modern orderly development approaches.

Source: Cliff Hague

PHOTO 14.4 Mobile shop, Galle, Sri Lanka. Tuk Tuks are a ubiquitous form of urban public transport across the Indian sub-continent and can be adapted to accommodate a side business to help ends meet.

Source: Christine Platt

PHOTO 14.5 Street trading, Dodanduwa, Sri Lanka. On the main road through Dodanduwa, just north of Galle, an enterprising street trader taps into the international tourist market with his eye-catching display of fresh fish.

Source: Christine Platt

PHOTO 14.6   Farmers' Market, Fredericton, New Brunswick, Canada. Markets can add life to urban spaces. Markets like this sell local produce reducing food miles and supporting the local economy, as well as adding to the ambience of the city.

Source: Christine Platt

Colonialism erased indigenous rights and relations to land. Together with practices that followed through much of the twentieth century, it made indigenous people poor (particularly in terms of equitable access to education, health and housing) and vulnerable (e.g. to disease and social and environmental deprivation). In particular, colonialism largely devalued and undermined traditional knowledge, language and cultural values or practices. Land is central to the cultural and spiritual values of many; this is tied intrinsically to the plight of indigenous people and their future well-being, security and prosperity.

> First, traditional lands are the 'place' of the nation and are inseparable from the people, their culture, and their identity as a nation. Second, land and resources are the foundation upon which indigenous people intend to rebuild the economies of their nations and so improve the socio-economic circumstance of their people – individuals, families, communities and nations.
>
> *Anderson et al., 2005, p. 106*

The imposition of a land tenure system for settlers from Britain often conflicted with traditional forms of ownership or stewardship, particularly communal or tribal authority that indigenous nations had developed.

In Aotearoa-New Zealand, in 1840, representatives of Queen Victoria and Māori signed the Treaty of Waitangi. It set out the 'principles' for the partnership between Māori and the NZ Government (the Crown). As the late NZ historian Michael King (2003, pp. 156–157) stated, this document would become 'the most contentious and problematic in New Zealand's national life.' Land rights were a central concern: the Crown acquired the right to buy land, while the Māori were guaranteed *rangatiratanga* (authority over their own affairs) including their lands, forests, fisheries and other resources, which to them – but not to the settlers – included cultural and spiritual values that were intangible assets to the settlers. However, Māori land and waters were subsequently taken into the Crown's control, often unjustly and without consent or compensation.

Campaigns from the 1970s onwards have resulted in proactive steps towards achieving redress. Māori as *tangata whenua* (people of the land) and the various *iwi* (tribal affiliated groups or 'nations') as *mana whenua* (groups with claims over regions or areas) now have a special and defined role under both the Resource Management Act and Local Government Act, the legislative framework for the planning system. While still maturing, this has resulted in a much more culturally sensitive approach in planning practice, engagement and education. Crucially, this recognition of Māori rights and their role as *kaitiaki* (guardians and stewards) of their culture, values and the environment highlights the importance of planning to health and social and economic well-being.

Cultural perspectives and values become relevant concerns in planning. Practice of this more holistic interpretation of the scope of planning – extending beyond the physical or even environmental perspectives – is exemplified in Photo 14.7 and Box 14.2. Such an approach could be promoted through the Commonwealth and forms the basis for the future of the profession.

Similar change is happening in Canada, as shown in Chapter 8, where the Canadian Institute of Planners (CIP) uses the term 'reconciliation' to refer to the commitment to establish and maintain a mutually respectful relationship between indigenous and non-indigenous peoples (CIP, 2019, p. 2). CIP make clear that 'many goals of Canada's Indigenous communities (First Nation, Inuit, Métis and Urban Aboriginal) intersect with planning concerns.' Examples cited are 'preserving language and culture, building governance and planning systems, investing in community health and wellness, practicing sustainable resource management, establishing self-reliant economies, developing sustainable food and energy systems and improving community housing and infrastructure.' Such shifts signpost a direction in which planning in the Commonwealth needs to move: understanding and respecting indigenous cultures and aligning the scope and practice of planning accordingly would enhance the capacity of planning systems to deliver on sustainable urbanisation. The introduction of the Awards for

PHOTO 14.7   Development and Management of Sacred Landscapes, Maungawhau (Mt Eden), Tāmaki Makaurau (Auckland), Aotearoa-New Zealand. *Ngā Tūpuna Maunga o Tāmaki Makaurau* (Auckland's ancestral mountains) are very significant cultural, historical and geological landscapes. They are sacred to the Indigenous Mana Whenua as *taonga tuku iho* (treasures handed down the generations). However, as the photo shows, a considerable amount of development has been permitted. The Tūpuna Maunga Integrated Management Plan from 2016 ensures that future management will reflect Mana Whenua values. See also Box 14.2

Source: Tūpuna Maunga Authority and Boffa Miskell

BOX 14.2   EMBEDDING MAORI VALUES INTO PLANNING PRACTICE – THE TŪPUNA MAUNGA INTEGRATED MANAGEMENT PLAN.

Ngā Tūpuna Maunga o Tāmaki Makaurau (Auckland's ancestral mountains) are very significant cultural, historical and geological landscapes. They are sacred to the Indigenous *Mana Whenua* as *taonga tuku iho* (treasures handed down the generations). Local communities have an emotional connection with – and draw a sense of identity from – the Tūpuna Maunga.

The inaugural Tūpuna Maunga Integrated Management Plan from 2016 outlined a long-term vision and set out Values and Pathways to achieve integrated

> outcomes. A series of overarching strategies apply across all Tūpuna Maunga. These strategies will be reflected at the local level in individual Tūpuna Maunga Management Plans that will detail the ongoing care and management of each Tūpuna Maunga. Both the plan and the strategies provided the opportunity for *Mana Whenua* and the people of Auckland to bring together different world views and weave together the strands of the relationships, experiences and connections that all Aucklanders have with the Maunga. The strategies are underpinned by inclusion and acknowledgement by each party of the other's interests.
>
> Future provision of recreational activities and facilities on, around and between Tūpuna Maunga will reflect *Mana Whenua* values, celebrate important features and provide experiences which connect recreational users with the *Whenua*. The project was commended in CAP's Awards for Outstanding Planning Achievement, 2020.
>
> Source: Tūpuna Maunga Management Strategies submission for CAP Awards 2020.

Outstanding Planning Practice has enabled CAP to showcase work that is being done with indigenous peoples and share practices. However, it is also clear that governments have a crucial part to play in setting a legislative and funding framework.

Despite such progress, Commonwealth human settlements more generally face many challenges, as the chapters in the book show. The need to address the climate and biodiversity emergencies, build a circular economy and reduce inequalities stands in contrast to the way cities in the Commonwealth developed in the first two decades of the new millennium. Watson (2013) highlighted the yawning disparity between what she termed the 'urban fantasies' of international property development, with their 'glass-box towers, manicured lawns and water features on developers' and architects' websites', and the reality in African cities where the majority live 'in deep poverty and with minimal urban services' (p. 215).

Watson referenced Goldman (2011) on similar changes in India where large-scale displacements of poor people living and farming on the urban fringe had occurred to enable high value urban development; women in particular found it very difficult to prove ownership of the land or were tenants with no long-term rights in their plot. It would be nice to think that the NUA and the CHOGM Declaration in 2022 on sustainable urbanisation would change perceptions and practices or that the Covid pandemic might have alerted policy makers everywhere to our interdependent vulnerabilities, but all the signs are that change will be contested.

This makes it all the more important that the Commonwealth acts to support the NUA and similar calls to action. The *Call to Action on Sustainable Urbanisation across the Commonwealth* (Commonwealth Sustainable Cities, 2022) in which CAP was a key player was a welcome step in that direction. Rightly it highlighted the role of local government, Commonwealth organisations, NGOs and universities to deliver ways to build more sustainable urban spaces in Commonwealth countries. But it is vital that governments and the private sector make similar action and commitment.

A theme in previous chapters has been the disconnect between the Commonwealth as an inter-governmental body and the now chronic crises of urbanisation. One reason for this neglect may have been the persistence of a British-centric set of Commonwealth institutions. If such ties are loosened in the future, urbanisation may gain greater attention. Indeed, putting issues of place and the urban poor, active travel, clean air, blue and green infrastructure, biodiversity, indigenous rights and respect for the environment to the fore could galvanise and modernise the Commonwealth. CAP and its partners have an important role to play if this is to happen.

CAP and planning history

The book has provided a unique insight into the way that CAP developed and operated for its first 50 years. As such it is a contribution to the history of planning and even to the history of the Commonwealth. In the grand scheme of things, CAP's story is modest but still worth telling. It fills a gap in public and professional understanding of planning. For example, the section on Urban and Regional Planning in the Canadian Encyclopaedia (2022) makes no mention of CIP/ICU involvement in CAP or even of the significance of Habitat I in Vancouver in 1976. Even a publication more directly targeted at planners, the Tanzanian Planners' Handbook (Lifuliro et al., 2018), makes no mention of CAP and only passing reference to one study by the Commonwealth Secretariat in a document that runs to 563 pages and was compiled by 60 persons. In part this reflects the challenges that CAP as a small, volunteer-run organisation has faced in getting its messages through even to planners in its member organisations. However, it also comes about because planning is so much a practice enshrined in national or – in the case of larger countries – province-scale legislation and procedures.

Of course, each country is different and international transplants of 'best practice' are fraught with risks of inappropriate transfer. The export of the 1932 Act from Britain to its distant colonies proves just that. However, national/local rootedness also militates against innovation and adaptation. One message from the chapters written by past presidents is that there can be benefits in co-production of applied, policy-focused works, as seen in the case of CAP's work on food security or gender, for example. Furthermore, with so many small states in the Commonwealth, where the numbers of planning professionals can be well below a critical mass to generate new approaches, networking through CAP has been an important means of accessing ideas. This is most evident in the Pacific and in the Caribbean. Again the history of CAP shows how it has been able to facilitate regional networks in both regions, albeit that in the Pacific it has gone through phases when it fell into abeyance, though CAP strongly supported planners in Fiji in their efforts to establish a national association and welcomed it into CAP membership.

The advent of the internet dramatically changed the way that knowledge can be accessed and how an organisation like CAP was able to operate. However, as Bill Robertson's chapter reveals so clearly, in the 1980s CAP played a vital role in introducing planners, not least those from small countries, to emerging land information technologies. A history of digital transition in planning needs to recognise that work, which also highlights the obstacles that held back the use of GIS in mainstream planning practice.

There has not been much interest from academic planning historians in international planning organisations as institutions, though there is an interesting paper by Jacquand (2018) on the relation between the International Federation for Housing and Planning (IFHP) and the Congrès internationaux d'architecture moderne (CIAM) and other writings on IFHP in the interwar period (e.g. Riboldazzi, 2015, Wagner, 2016). Instead, much planning history, understandably, focuses on landmark plans, initiatives in particular cities or themes such as inter-war housing. This pattern is evident in the *Journal of Planning History*, for example, produced by the Society for American Regional and Planning History, which understandably tends to carry an American, rather than a Commonwealth, focus. Indeed, more generally, the English-language planning literature remains skewed by American heft.

The 'New Institutionalism,' however, has found a niche within work on planning theory (Sorensen, 2017). This approach defines 'institutions' in wider terms than just an organisation, extending to the 'rules of the game' (North, 1990) and political cultures and procedures. The fundamental point is that 'institutions matter' and that organisations such as CAP sit within – and are agents within – those broader structures.

Where international planning organisations have produced work on their own history, it has tended to be largely descriptive, again understandably, rather than benefitting from more critical institutionalist analysis. Thus van den Berg (2015) penned a short history of the first 50 years of the International Society of City and Regional Planners, while Allan (2013) documented the longer history of the IFHP at much greater length, with a wealth of original detail and graphics.

What emerges from this history of CAP, which distinguished it from other international planning organisations, is the importance of the Commonwealth, its history, structures, proclaimed values and opening up to civil society. While this may be obvious, three aspects need to be emphasised. First, the relationship with the Commonwealth Foundation has been vital over a long period. CAP has been most active and effective when it has been able to access core and project funding, and that funding has mainly come from the CF. Second, the relation to the Commonwealth as a whole has enabled CAP to operate within the boundaries of a set of inter-governmental relationships. Third and just as important, CAP has been able to thrive when it has shown that its own actions are outward-looking and aligned with those of the Commonwealth and the UN.

Apart from a brief period around 2008–2010, CAP has struggled to engage the Commonwealth Secretariat, where other sectors such as trade, human rights and law are strongly embedded and are reinforced by the funding provided to the CS by the

UK government. For example, UK government priorities for the Commonwealth set in 2015 support sustainable development, but this support is cast as building prosperity, and two of the four bullet points illustrating the concern are about trade and business practices. A further priority highlighted is 'Working with the Royal Household to support the role of the British Monarch as Head of the Commonwealth' (Foreign and Commonwealth Office, 2015). Towards the end of the first decade of the 21st century, the CS was engaging with CAP and beginning to recognise sustainable urbanisation as a significant concern. Then the UK House of Commons Foreign Affairs Committee (2012) produced a critical report on the Commonwealth, which stated that 'the work programme assigned to the Commonwealth Secretariat requires critical review with the objective of concentrating on priority matters that will bring the greatest benefit to the people of the Commonwealth' (p. 11). The CS then consulted with High Commissions on priorities, and sustainable urbanisation was dropped. A decade was lost until the Declaration from the Kigali CHOGM in 2022.

The UK's role as the major funder gives it particular influence, and it has not sought to use that influence to prioritise concerns with urbanisation. Had it done so, arguably CAP and planners across the Commonwealth could have achieved much more. A further barrier is that it is rare for somebody with a planning background to work in the CF or CS: Vijay Krishnarayan is the exception. This matters because people from a diplomatic background or arts and culture have rarely been exposed to the idea that spatial planning can be a driver of economic and social progress. In particular, if they are UK based, they are likely to have been imbued with the notion that planning is a local regulatory practice that holds back development and jobs. Nevertheless, as shown in previous chapters, CAP has managed to bring its concerns to the Commonwealth Peoples Forum and through that to CHOGMs.

CAP has been able to benefit from Commonwealth links in other ways. There has been cooperation with architects, engineers and surveyors through BEPIC, and it would be true to say that CAP helped point BEPIC to the Habitat Agenda. ComHabitat brought together CAP, the Commonwealth Human Ecology Council (CHEC) and Homeless International, under the aegis of the CF, and it made possible the work on the State of the Commonwealth's Cities (see Chapter 6). It fed into the ministerial and senior official level Commonwealth Consultative Group on Human Settlements, which was set up in 1999 by the then Commonwealth Secretary-General Don Mackinnon to help Commonwealth countries deliver the Habitat Agenda from Habitat II. In addition, the Commonwealth connection helped CAP to build a long running relationship with The Prince's Foundation, which has translated to projects on the ground using the Toolkit that was developed and is discussed in Chapter 7.

The previous chapters also show how CAP became credible in the eyes of UN-Habitat. Undoubtedly the 2006 WUF was a catalyst in this respect, but just as important is the way that CAP and others were able to build on that in the years that followed, and hopefully this will continue to be the case in the future. A key reason for this success is that CAP actively sought such a connection and was comfortable in embracing the perspectives and language of the UN. The fact that it was UN language gave legitimacy to CAP's position, while CAP and those it worked with were able to connect that language into the scope and practice of planning. Individual actors were vitally important in making that connection, particularly Christine Platt, for example in leading work on the International Guidelines on Urban and Territorial Planning (UN Habitat, 2015). However, the channels provided by UN-Habitat for civil society engagement were also critically important. The creation of the WUFs from 2002 opened a door, bringing NGOs into closer contact with governmental bodies, just as the Commonwealth Peoples Forum enabled transmission of ideas to the CHOGM. There are important messages here for what we might call 'policy co-production.' Hopefully the future will see much stronger partnerships in the Commonwealth connecting governments with professionals, researchers and grassroots expertise. As Christine Platt highlighted in her chapter, tapping the resources in civil society will enable the Commonwealth to achieve much more than if it relies overwhelmingly on governments.

Ironically but perhaps not surprisingly, CAP has found it more difficult to sustain active support (and even membership) amongst its member organisations, yet such support is crucial to its very existence, as CAP's crisis of the early 1990s showed. In part this reflects the point made earlier about the national blinkers on planners imposed by national legislation and procedures. International activities have often been seen as peripheral to mainstream members whose personal subscriptions are the lifeblood of those national professional bodies. There are also very practical obstacles, not least changes in personnel and also fluctuating exchange rates and bank charges that can easily result in a year or two of CAP membership dues being deferred. As we have seen, major members of CAP such as the ITPI or the Australians have at times dropped out, before returning to membership. Again, much depends on key individuals to sustain a good two-way flow of information.

More widely, some of the language and positions taken by CAP, while aligning closely with the UN, can be uncomfortable for more traditionally minded members who struggle to see why gender should be mainstreamed or why planning should be 'pro-poor.' What is legitimate language in UN meetings can simultaneously be perceived as 'unprofessional' to those who conceptualise planning as a neutral, technical expert-driven activity. Indeed, that has been – and for many remains – an orthodoxy. As Chapter 3 showed, in the early 1970s planning was a relatively new and small profession across much of the Commonwealth, struggling to assert its identity alongside architecture, engineering and surveying, while looking to those construction professions for a narrative of professionalism. More recently, the hostility of neo-liberal governments towards planning has meant that professional bodies have been averse to taking stances that could be deemed to be 'political.'

This tension between what countries sign up to in UN meetings and what they actually do is by no means unique to sustainable urbanisation or to professional planning associations. Hollow promises have dogged delivery of real action on climate change or poverty alleviation, for example. The undermining of the authority of the

UN has been evident from at least the 1990s, but that only makes it more important for those seeking sustainable urbanisation to support the UN, as CAP has done.

In the belief that 'institutions matter' and not least the UN, the idea of building a Global Planners' Network (GPN) was a key part of CAP's strategy for the 2006 WUF. The aims were to bring together professional planners from around the world into one strong, democratic voice for the role of planning in delivering sustainable urbanisation, bolstering planning within UN-Habitat, while also providing a direct channel for UN thinking on urbanisation and planning to reach thousands of practising planners. The GPN was indeed established, thanks to support mainly from the American Planning Association, the CIP/ICU and the RTPI and has operated since 2006. However, the form that GPN has taken is very different than what CAP sought. Instead of being truly global and operating on UN and Commonwealth principles that all members are equal, it has just a few members and none from the professional bodies in rapidly urbanising countries. As previous chapters have shown, CAP has remained involved and GPN has done some useful networking, but CAP's 2006 vision was to have a truly global body of professional planning organisations, the equivalent of the International Union of Architects or the International Federation of Surveyors. In the end, CAP was not able to persuade others to go in that direction. There were risks to them and concern about potential further demands on their resources that, if there was a wide membership, would be beyond their control.

Despite itself operating on the basis of 'one member, one vote,' the history of CAP shows that the RTPI has played a dominant role throughout. As Chapter 3 reported, it was the RTPI who took the initiative to propose the creation of a CAP. It provided the Secretariat from 1971 until 1988 and again from 2000 onwards. Three of the ten presidents have been UK-based. Some might interpret this as a perpetuation of a colonial set of relationships. However, the small scale and largely voluntary nature of CAP does constrain options. In particular, the willingness of RTPI in 2000 to allow CAP to use the services of Annette O'Donnell in the RTPI's Scotland office as CAP's part-time paid, professional administrator was a turning point, providing expertise and continuity that was essential as CAP's activities increased. In addition, as chapters by the past presidents show, face to face meetings with people in the London-based CF have been crucial throughout, building tacit understanding and trust.

In summary, viewing CAP's first 50 years through an institutional perspective contributes to planning history. Naturally, the context within which CAP operated changed substantially over that time in many ways – the expansion of the Commonwealth, its opening up to civil society, the emergence of sustainable urbanisation as a global issue, the arrival of the internet and then video conferencing, the ascendency of neo-liberalism, feminism and the changes within the planning profession itself, to name a few. CAP's history is specific to itself, yet also relevant to other planning organisations. It shows that the broader context and structures are always important in shaping action, setting rules and boundaries that can constrain, be tested or provide opportunities. Making connections – to concepts, language and then to possible partners – is a way to generate momentum. It is a form of adaptive innovation, taking, giving and producing something new. Targeted communication is part of this process.

Leadership also matters, and as discussed more fully later, the actions of individuals, particularly presidents and secretary-generals, have also shaped the paths that CAP has followed. Margaret Mead famously said 'Never doubt that a small group of thoughtful, committed citizens can change the world. Indeed, it is the only thing that ever has.' CAP operates among the global parameters, Commonwealth structures and its individual volunteers; it is a small, charitable organisation, with no significant financial assets but, vitally, a capacity to tap into a substantial, international set of professional resources. It is limited in what it can do directly to advance sustainable urbanisation but able, through building partnerships, to be a resonant leader, advocate and campaigner.

Is advocacy enough? The Commonwealth Housing Trust, for example, provides financial and material assistance for housing development in Commonwealth countries, arguably a more direct and practical approach to sustainable urbanisation. To raise this begs an age-old question, which was rehearsed in Brecht's poem *A Bed for the Night*: giving a homeless person a bed for the night won't change the world, but it will protect them from the wind and the snow, but keeping a few people out of the wind and the snow for a night won't change the world. Both approaches are needed.

Activism and agency

In constructing this history of CAP, the editors opted to rely heavily on personal accounts from past presidents and leaders of CAP networks. There was little alternative, since they were the people who knew most about the history. Autobiography amongst planners is rare and little used in academic research on planning. Readers can judge how successful or otherwise this approach was when combined with the longer, more critical chapters.

Beyond their reflections, there are questions about the motivations, nature and effectiveness of active volunteers. Simply put, why do people devote their precious time to unpaid service to a charity? What circumstances enable or block such volunteering, and how might this change in future? In CAP's case, scale is also important. Most activism in planning is at a local level, typically with non-planners resisting unwanted development. Even where planners are involved in supporting such action, e.g. through forms of planning aid or advocacy planning, the scale is usually local.

The scope for activism – and the form it might take – is also influenced by structures of governance and by cultures, which also affect the practices of public engagement in planning more widely. One way to approach the actions of those who have given their time to CAP is through the literature on volunteering. Empirical studies risk being unconsciously culturally rooted, so it is more helpful to step back and look at more theoretical writing. As Hustinx, Cnaan and Handy (2010) point out, such theories are found in several distinct social science disciplines, while the notion of what constitutes volunteering can also be elastic. Drawing on their work and that of Einolf and Chambré (2011), while avoiding a detour into an extensive literature, we can pose a set of questions about those who over the 50 years became involved in CAP.

First, what is the context that prompts people to get involved? It seems that at the international scale the trigger is proactive rather than reactive. It is clear from Part 2 that those who took on leadership roles did so out of a belief in the benefits that could be achieved through planning. Different actors perceived those benefits in different ways, e.g. gender equity, social justice, environmental sustainability, the potential application of new technologies etc. All professions conceive of themselves as conferring benefits to the wider society, but for planners there is a long tradition of commitment to public service and to social progress. No doubt this played a part. Perhaps more unusual was the belief also in international action and in the Commonwealth. As we have argued, the national/regional/local focus of planning systems, procedures and practice locks many planners into blinkers on the global nature of the challenge of sustainable urbanisation.

Active involvement in CAP has tended to follow similar engagement in a CAP member institute. This is not surprising since CAP is an umbrella organisation and member institutes are unlikely to nominate a representative who has no track record of national involvement. Similarly, this means that CAP attracts volunteers who are already inclined to give their services for free and who have some social capital. We might also recognise that some might see the titles and travel that CAP affords as ways to enhance their own careers while jetting round the world. Direct personal engagement in an international organisation necessarily has been limited to relatively small numbers of people. While it cannot be denied that some blurring occurs between the person and the post and that it confers some status to the individuals, the time and work demands of deep activism within CAP are not for the faint-hearted or indolent! See Box 14.3. Thus the context of involvement is also blended with individual characteristics.

BOX 14.3   LEADERSHIP AND SERVING A CAUSE.

In his autobiography, *Long Walk to Freedom*, Nelson Mandela wrote 'It is better to lead from behind and to put others in front, especially when you celebrate victory when nice things occur. You take the front line when there is danger.' Mandela wrote that a great leader 'stays behind the flock, letting the most nimble go out ahead, whereupon the others follow, not realizing all along that they are being directed from behind.'

Many people make the mistake of thinking that holding voluntary office is glamourous or gives a person power of some kind. There certainly are glamorous and exciting moments but the veneer of glamour is microns thin. There can also be opportunities to use office to make a difference but these come only on the back of long hours of dedication, hard work,

> listening, engaging and thinking. Credibility always has to be earned and power is never a consequence of simply holding office.
>
> There is a much greater purpose behind voluntary service, namely, servant leadership or leading from behind in furthering a cause in which you believe. The rewards which come from serving a cause, fighting for what you believe in and creating opportunities for others to make their contributions, far outweigh those which come from simply serving one's own interests. But this requires an understanding of when you need to stand up and be counted versus when to stand back to enable others to make their mark. Leading from behind means giving others the opportunity to move an organisation forward through free thinking and by making their own contributions.
>
> Christine Platt, CAP President 2006–2014
>
> Source: comment to the editors from Christine Platt.

The second factor that shapes involvement is individual circumstances. As noted earlier, in practice active involvement in CAP is likely to be open only to those who have already been active at a senior level in a professional planning body that is a member of CAP. Thus CAP is less 'open' than other international planning organisations such as ISOCARP, EAROPH or IFHP. In addition, it excludes organisations representing planners from non-Commonwealth countries (there is provision of participation as a 'friend' of CAP, though no voting rights are extended under this classification).

Arguably, individual circumstances have become more influential as CAP's profile and activity increased. Despite regionalised systems of vice presidents or executive membership, the reality is that the main burden of representing CAP, as well as overseeing its management, has rested with the presidents and secretary-generals. Quite simply, this means that those willing to take on such posts must be able to devote significant time – and blocks of time – to CAP. This prevents or curtails the ability of many to contribute, e.g. those with caring responsibilities or those whose employer is unsympathetic or single practitioner consultancies. In addition, the diversity within the CAP member bodies has also influenced decisions about the secretariat. Quite simply, it is difficult for a member organisation with few members to have the critical mass needed to carry out the range of tasks that are involved.

Between the 1970s and the early 2020s when the Covid pandemic struck, long haul travel became easier and relatively cheaper. Together with the internet, this enabled CAP to increase its activity, for example by working with member organisations to put on regional conferences. However, there is a clear disjuncture between long haul flights and a body committed to environmental sustainability. The dramatic increase in use of video conferencing and home working in response to the pandemic was embraced by CAP. The future is likely to see further developments like this, which should also remove some of the barriers that have constrained active involvement in CAP.

Finally, any critical assessment of activism through CAP must ask whether expectations were met and whether CAP made a difference. As we have seen, expectations changed over time, broadly speaking from consolidating and growing the status of planning as a distinct profession to shaping international agendas and influencing members' practices in the cause of sustainable urbanisation. Readers can make their own judgements, based on the evidence in this book or from other sources. The starting proposition would be that CAP managed to survive for 50 years, riding out at least one major crisis. It did this over a period when planning was weak, even flawed, across much of the Commonwealth. It became part – but a significant part – of a wider movement to focus on the need for governments at all levels to focus urgently on sustainable urbanisation. This succeeded in getting SDG 11 and the NUA, then the Kigali Declaration but not, at the time of writing, in radically reorienting the way that urban and rural areas across the Commonwealth are developing.

So yes, some success, some failures, and it is difficult to say with certainty what might have been different if CAP had not existed. What is clear is that through the NUA and the International Guidelines and the climate, biodiversity, food, poverty and urbanisation crises it is clear that effective and equitable planning is needed, and we also know what that type of planning should look like. The next 50 years have to be about putting this into practice, and professional planners individually and collectively carry a responsibility to do that, even if that means working beyond traditional structures and legislation.

Beyond the SDGs: knowledge, attitudes and skills for the future

The major challenges for CAP and its members lie ahead, not in the past. Cities and human settlements need to be de-carbonised, adapted to the impacts of climate change and natural hazards and made more equitable and inclusive. These interconnected outcomes do not depend on the efforts of planners alone, but if the idea of planning places is to have future credibility then planners must embrace them. This will often require changes in planning legislation, and if that change cannot be achieved then the use of planners' expertise through other channels.

In many respects, the required knowledge already exists. We know that carbon emissions are still driven by richer countries, and so action there to reduce car-dependent forms of urban development (e.g. densification, transit-oriented development and support for public transport and active travel) need to be pursued with vigour. The Covid pandemic triggered a switch to home working for many in office jobs, a pattern that should be supported into the future. Similarly, we know that carbon is embedded in buildings and other infrastructure, so there has to be a presumption against demolition and in favour of reuse and refurbishment in local scale plans, while recycling and repair hubs need to be identified at city and regional scale. This will require new understanding and methods of carbon accountancy.

We know how to design buildings and neighbourhoods so that there is passive cooling in the heat and warming in the cold. We have data and other know-how about locations vulnerable to disasters, and that it makes sense to plan and manage those areas so that people and businesses are not exposed to unnecessary risk. There is now awareness of the biodiversity emergency and the links between a good quality environment and human well-being. Any planner reading this could easily extend the list and customise it to her or his local situation.

We also know that cities remain beacons of hope for many people and can both help lift people out of poverty through the economic opportunities they offer but also concentrate poverty and embed social spatial segregation. Where we do need more knowledge is on how to ensure wealth is recycled locally and shared more equitably. On the consumption side, public open space freely accessible to all, affordable housing and transport, along with clean air and water – all very traditional planning concerns – contribute to social equity, but planners need better to understand how housing markets respond to upgrading and trigger displacement. On the production side, there needs to be better understanding of informal economies and increasingly of the kind of hybridity that connects traditional street traders with 21st-century digital technology.

What is required in respect to attitudes? Mention has already been made of the benefits of respect and engagement with the attitudes and values often found in indigenous cultures. Similarly, we have seen how the language of the UN can sit uneasily with some traditional assumptions of the profession. A 21st-century sense of professionalism needs to be forged. In the early years of CAP, an insecure profession sought to bolster its exclusivity and uniqueness in relation to longer established construction professions. The inter-connected nature of the challenges of urbanisation mean that we need a professional identity that allows for fuzzy edges. Sustainable urbanisation requires working together, not just across professional boundaries but also across the expert/local activist divide. There needs to be ladders into planning for those who cannot afford to study to Master level and education of those privileged to be able to access higher education so that they are exposed to the needs and aspirations of the diverse groups of people different to themselves.

Commitment and confidence are also important. To quote from Bob Marley's *Redemption Song*, 'None but ourselves can free our minds.' As we have seen, commitment is fundamental to activism and planners need to be active in the cause of sustainable urbanisation. Daunting challenges require commitment to make progress. Similarly, confidence is needed: for much of the first 50 years of CAP a neo-liberal hegemony left planners on the defensive, content only to claim that they 'facilitate development' as if all development was beneficial to social equity and the environment, when we know it is not.

In terms of skills, the digital gap, which CAP was seeking to address back in the 1980s as Chapter 4 showed, remains a concern. Already the technology exists to enable much more informed decision-making. Real-time data can provide insights into the dynamics of urbanisation, the interconnectedness of drivers of change and the impacts of planned interventions. There is great potential for opening access to views from communities and to analysing them and engaging, including in mediation. Virtual reality should be part and parcel of the toolkit of a future-oriented profession.

Scoping planning practice globally over the first two decades of the 21st century, three broad approaches can be recognised. There is the residue of colonial systems, in the case of the Commonwealth often bearing the imprint of the 1932 British Town and Country Planning Act. It is ill suited to rapid urbanisation and to low-income countries, not least in respect of the impracticality of enforcement. Second, there is the neo-liberal model of 'entrepreneurial planning' in which project-led development is facilitated in the name of urban competitiveness, with the unfulfilled promise that benefits will trickle down. This model originated in, and has been exported by, the USA. Linked to it is austerity urbanism, which has hollowed out the welfare role of states and realigned public action with private wealth creation, creating disparities within and between cities. The third model is that of China, which has been adopted across many Commonwealth countries in Asia and Africa. This involves spatial planning at a transcontinental scale with the Belt and Road project. Big infrastructure – highways, ports, airports, fast trains but also new towns – is planned and developed, usually on a Chinese template and using Chinese contractors and labour, in exchange for long term resource (e.g. oil and minerals) access. It has been extremely successful in delivering the planned urban transition of China, taking millions out of poverty. However, it also created significant pollution, as the Chinese authorities have recognised and are seeking to manage. It is a top-down system that still has a way to go in achieving environmental sustainability. There are also geo-political implications in this model.

The fact that there is no Commonwealth model to compete with these three is a tragedy. The diversity of the Commonwealth and its urbanisation challenges uniquely equips it to be in the vanguard of experiment and advocacy. It has failed to respond to that challenge, being late to grasp the importance of sustainable urbanisation and then weak in its resolve to give it priority when the UK threatened to withdraw funds unless the CS narrowed the focus of its actions. Yet the Kigali Declaration shows it may not – must not – be too late. With the SDGs and the NUA it points a way forward. Planners generally, CAP in particular, need to redouble their effort to implement then go beyond these. A key lesson from CAP's first 50 years is that the Commonwealth can tap into immense resources from civil society, and in so doing it also makes the Commonwealth relevant to all its citizens. 'There is a tide in the affairs of men, which taken at the flood, leads on to fortune. . . . On such a full sea are we now afloat. And we must take the current when it serves, or lose our ventures' (Shakespeare: *Julius Caesar*). For the Commonwealth and for its planners, that tide is the 2020s.

References

Allan, G. (2013), *A Hundred Years at the Global Spearhead: A Century of IFHP, 1913–2013,* Copenhagen: International Federation for Housing and Planning.
Anderson, R.B., Camp II, R.D., Dana, L.P., Honig, B., Nkonglo-Bakenda, J-M. and Peredo, A.M. (2005), 'Indigenous Land Rights in Canada: The Foundation for Development?' *International Journal of Entrepreneurship and Small Business,* 2 (2), pp. 104–133, https://ssrn.com/abstract=2495582 (Accessed 18 May 2022).
Canadian Encyclopaedia. (2022), *Urban and Regional Planning,* Available at www.thecanadianencyclopedia.ca/en/article/urban-and-regional-planning (Accessed 18 May 2022).
Canadian Institute of Planners/Institute Canadien des Urbanistes. (2019), *Policy on Planning Practice and Reconciliation,* Ottawa: CIP/ICU, Available at www.cip-icu.ca/Indigenous-Planning# (Accessed 18 May 2022).
Commonwealth Secretariat. (2018), *Harnessing the Commonwealth Trade Advantage,* Available at https://thecommonwealth.org/news/harnessing-commonwealth-trade-advantage (Accessed 17 May 2022).
Commonwealth Sustainable Cities. (2022), *Call to Action on Sustainable Urbanisation across the Commonwealth,* Available at https://commonwealthsustainablecities.org/calltoaction/ (Accessed 6 August 2022).
Einolf, C. and Chambre, S.M. (2011), 'Who Volunteers? Constructing a Hybrid Theory', *International Journal of Nonprofit and Voluntary Sector Marketing,* 16, pp. 298–310, https://doi/10.1002/nvsm.429
Foreign and Commonwealth Office. (2015), *Policy Paper: FCO Priorities for the Commonwealth,* Available at www.gov.uk/government/publications/fco-priorities-for-the-commonwealth/fco-priorities-for-the-commonwealth (Accessed 2 June 2022).
Goldman, M. (2011), 'Speculative Urbanism and the Making of the Next World City', *International Journal of Urban and Regional Research,* 35 (3), pp. 555–581, https://doi.org/10.1111/j.1468-2427.2010.01001.x
Home, R. (2014), *Lusaka: 'The New Capital of Northern Rhodesia' – Introduction by Robert Home,* Abingdon and New York: Routledge.
Hustinx, L., Cnaan, R.A. and Handy, F. (2010), 'Navigating Theories of Volunteering: A Hybrid Map for a Complex Phenomenon', *Journal for the Theory of Social Behaviour,* 40 (4), pp. 410–434, https://doi:10.1111/j.1468-5914.2010.00439.x
Jacquand, C. (2018), 'The Town Planning congresses at the Paris Exhibition of 1937. Ultimate encounters', *International Planning History Society Proceedings,* 18 (1), *Looking at the World History of Planning.* Available from https://journals.open.tudelft.nl/iphs/issue/view/Yokohama/Download%20PDF (Accessed 10 February 2023).
Kamazani, A. and Mpeta, D. (2018), 'Historical Perspectives on Development Planning in Tanzania', In C. Lifuliro, I. Zilihona, T. Mdendemi, A. Kamanzi, G. Kinyashi and T. van Dijk (eds), *Tanzania Planners' Handbook: A Guide to Development Planning,* Leiden: African Studies Centre, Leiden, pp. 43–50.
Keeble, L. (1964), *Principles and Practice of Town and Country Planning,* Third Edition, London: The Estates Gazette Ltd.
King, A. D. (1977), 'Exporting "Planning": The Colonial and Neo-Colonial Experience', *Urbanism Past & Present,* 5, pp. 12–22, Available at www.jstor.org/stable/44403550 (Accessed 2 June 2022).
King, M. (2003), *The Penguin History of New Zealand,* Auckland: Penguin Books.
Lifuliro C., Zilihona, I., Mdendemi, T., Kamazani, A., Kinyashi, G. and van Dijk, T. (eds) (2018), *Tanzania Planners' Handbook: A Guide to Development Planning,* Leiden: African Studies Centre, Leiden.

North, D. C. (1990), *Institutions, Institutional Change, and Economic Performance*, Cambridge and New York: Cambridge University Press.

Riboldazzi, R. (2015), 'The IFHTP Discourse on Urbanism in Colonial Africa between the Wars', In Silva, C.N. (ed.), *Urban Planning in Sub-Saharan Africa: Colonial and Post-Colonial Planning Culture*, Oxford: Routledge, pp. 41–52.

Sorensen, A. (2017), 'New Institutionalism and Planning Theory', In M. Gunder, A. Mandianipour, and V.Watson (eds.), *The Routledge Handbook of Planning Theory*, Oxford: Routledge, Available at www.routledgehandbooks.com/doi/10.4324/9781315696072.ch20 (Accessed 19 May 2022).

Stevens, P.H.M. (1955), 'Planning Legislation in the Colonies', *Town and Country Planning*, March, pp. 119–123.

The Commonwealth. (2022), CHOGM 2022 Communiqué, Leaders Statement and Declarations on Delivering a Common Future, Available at https://thecommonwealth.org/news/chogm-2022-communique-leaders-statement-and-declarations-delivering-common (Accessed 7 July 2022).

UK House of Commons Foreign Affairs Committee. (2012), *The Role and Future of the Commonwealth*, https://publications.parliament.uk/pa/cm201213/cmselect/cmfaff/114/11405.htm (Accessed 11 February 2023).

UN Habitat. (2015), International Guidelines on Urban and Territorial Planning, Available at https://unhabitat.org/international-guidelines-on-urban-and-territorial-planning (Accessed 8 July 2022).

Van den Berg, M. (2015), 50 Years ISOCARP, Past, Present, Future – Developments in Planning 1965–2015, Available at https://isocarp.org/50-years-isocarp-past-present-future-development-of-planning/ (Accessed 19 May 2022).

Wagner, P. (2016), 'Facilitating Planning Communication Across Borders: The International Federation for Housing and Town Planning in the Interwar Period', *Planning Perspectives*, 31 (2), pp. 299–311, https://doi.org/10.1080/02665433.2015.1102643.

Ward, S. (2004), *Planning and Urban Change*, Second Edition, London, Thousand Oaks and New Delhi: Sage.

Watson, V. (2013), 'African Urban Fantasies: Dreams or Nightmares?' *Environment & Urbanization*, 26 (1), pp. 215–231, https://doi.org/10.1177/0956247813513705.

APPENDIX 1

Chronology of key events in CAP's 50-year history

The following chronology is just a selection from the many key events which have taken place over CAP's 50-year history.

(Events marked in **bold** are important non-CAP events)

1970: Preliminary meeting to discuss establishment of CAP: London, UK.

1971: **First meeting of Commonwealth Heads of Government, Singapore. There were 32 countries in membership.**

Official founding of CAP: Accra, Ghana. Arthur Ling (UK) elected CAP's first President. Philip Rathbone (UK) appointed Secretary.

1972: **UN Conference on the Human Environment, Stockholm, Sweden.**

1973: CAP's Inaugural Conference, New Delhi, India.

1976: CAP Plenary Conference, Auckland, NZ. Andrew N. Ligale (Kenya) elected President.

UN Conference on Human Settlements, Habitat I, Vancouver, Canada.

1980: CAP Plenary Conference, Uxbridge, UK. George Franklin (UK) elected President.

1984: CAP Plenary Conference, St John's, Newfoundland, Canada. Dr Peter Pun (Hong Kong) elected President; George Franklin elected Secretary-General.

1987: **Publication of the Brundtland Report, 'Our Common Future.'**

1988: CAP Plenary meeting, Hong Kong. Bill Robertson (NZ) elected President; David Sherwood (Canada) elected Secretary-General.

1990: Launch of CAP's Land Information Technology Programme to promote use of GIS technologies.

Declaration from CHOGM in Harare, Zimbabwe, strengthened Commonwealth commitment to democracy, human rights and equality.

1991: CAP Plenary Conference, Trinidad and Tobago. Jacqueline daCosta (Jamaica) elected CAP President.

Survey of Planning Education in the Commonwealth undertaken by Dr Mohammed Qadeer, Queens University, Kingston, Canada.

1992: **UN Conference on Environment and Development, Rio de Janeiro, Brazil.**

1993: Ruth Pottopsingh (Jamaica) appointed CAP Secretary-General.

1996: CAP participated in **UN's Habitat II Conference, Istanbul, Turkey,** where the Habitat Agenda was adopted.

CAP's Plenary Meeting, Auckland, New Zealand. Bill Robertson (NZ) elected President for second time; Robert Schofield (NZ) appointed as Secretary-General.

1997: On the transfer of Hong Kong to China, the Hong Kong Institute of Planners left CAP.

1999: CAP conference in Durban, organised by South African Association of Chartered Town Planners, as a fringe event in the **Commonwealth Heads of Government Meeting.**

2000: **UN Millennium Development Goals 2000–2015 adopted**.

CAP Plenary Meeting and Conference, Belfast, UK. Cliff Hague (UK) elected President; John Anderson (UK) appointed as Secretary-General. Annette O'Donnell (UK) appointed as CAP's first Administrator.

CAP Women in Planning Network established, led by Olusola Olufemi (South Africa).

Former CAP President Jacqueline daCosta received UN Habitat Scroll of Honour award for her outstanding contribution in the field of human settlements.

2001: CAP Conference '2001 A Planning Odyssey' and Business Meeting, Gold Coast, Queensland, Australia.

2001: CAP web site established, www.commonwealth-planners.org.

2002: CAP Business Meeting and Conference, Manchester, UK.

CAP participated in the **World Summit on Sustainable Development, Johannesburg, South Africa.**

CAP supported the first 'Planning Africa' conference, organised in Durban by the South African Planning Institute, and was part of the working group that set up the African Planning Association.

CAP Americas event in Port of Spain, Trinidad and Tobago, developed a Regional Work-Plan.

2003: CAP East African Regional Workshop held in Nairobi, Kenya.

Chronology of key events in CAP's 50-year history **213**

CAP Pacific Regional Forum held in Brisbane, Australia.
CAP participated in **CHOGM, Abuja, Nigeria.**

2004: CAP Business Meeting and World Congress, Kuala Lumpur, Malaysia.

CAP participated in **UN Habitat's World Urban Forum 2004, Barcelona, Spain.**

2005: CAP provided support to Sri Lanka planners following Indian Ocean Tsunami.

CAP European Regional Meeting, Limassol, Cyprus.
CAP participated in **UN Beijing +10 meeting on Women's Rights and Gender Equality, New York, USA.**
CAP participated in **CHOGM, Valetta, Malta.**
CAP West Africa Region conference, Anuja, Nigeria.

2006: CAP participated in **World Planning Congress** and **UN Habitat's World Urban Forum 3, Vancouver, Canada.** CAP signed the Vancouver Declaration, creating the Global Planners Network and the Reinventing Planning paper (Farmer et al., 2006).

CAP Business meeting, Vancouver, Canada. Christine Platt (South Africa) elected President; Cliff Hague appointed Secretary-General.

2007 CAP participated in **CHOGM, Kampala, Uganda.**

Pacific Islands Planning Association launched with CAP support.
East African Planning Association launched with CAP support.
CAP participated in **UN Habitat Governing Council Meeting, Nairobi, Kenya.**

2008: CAP Business Meeting, Johannesburg, South Africa.

CAP participated in **World Urban Forum 4, Nanjing, China.**
CAP President Christine Platt and Secretary General Cliff Hague meet with the former Prince of Wales to discuss collaboration with The Prince's Foundation for the Built Environment.

2009: CAP participated in **CHOGM, Trinidad and Tobago** and the importance of Planning was recognised in a CHOGM Communiqué for the first time.

CAP signed Memorandum of Cooperation with The Prince's Foundation for the Built Environment.
CAP discussion paper 'Gender in Planning and Urban Development' (Malaza et al., 2009) published by the Commonwealth Secretariat.

2010: CAP participated in **World Urban Forum 5, Rio de Janeiro.**

CAP Business Meeting, Montreal. Clive Harridge (UK) appointed Secretary-General.
CAP received RTPI President's Award from RTPI President Ann Skippers.

ComHabitat published 'Urban Challenges: Scoping the State of the Commonwealth's Cities' (ComHabitat, 2010).

CAP discussion paper 'The state of the cities' (Hague and French, 2010) published by the Commonwealth Secretariat.

CAP Young Planners Network formed and held first Young Planners' Essay Competition.

Cliff Hague appointed as Honorary vice president.

2011: CAP participated in **CHOGM, Perth, Australia.**

CAP sent message of support to New Zealand Planning Institute following Christchurch earthquake disaster.

Caribbean Urban Forum launched with support from CAP.

2012: CAP Participated in **World Urban Forum 6 Naples, Italy.**

Commonwealth Heads of Government adopt the Charter of the Commonwealth, December 2012 setting out the 16 core values and principles of the Commonwealth. The Charter provides the context for all the work that CAP undertakes.

CAP Business Meeting, London, UK.

Caribbean Planning Association launched with support from CAP

2013: CAP participated in **CHOGM, Sri Lanka.**

CAP Participated in **WUF 7, Medellin, Colombia.**

2014: CAP Business Meeting, Singapore. Dyan Currie (Australia) elected President. Christine Platt appointed as Honorary vice president.

Viral Desai became leader of Young Planners Network.

Commonwealth Foundation published 'Perspectives on Planning for Agriculture and Food Security in the Commonwealth' (Caldwell and Lang, 2014).

2015: **UN Sustainable Development Goals 2016–2030 adopted.**

CAP participated in **CHOGM, Valetta, Malta.**

2016: CAP participated in **Habitat III, Quito, Ecuador. New Urban Agenda adopted by UN.**

CAP Business Meeting and Conference, Fiji: launch of Rapid Urbanisation Toolkit by video message from The former Prince of Wales.

Former CAP President Cliff Hague received OBE award in the Queen's Birthday Honours list.

CAP Secretary-General Clive Harridge met Her late Majesty Queen Elizabeth II at Buckingham Palace, London at the launch of The Queens's Commonwealth Canopy initiative.

2018: CAP participated in **WUF 9, Kuala Lumpur, Malaysia.**

CAP Participated in **CHOGM, London, UK.**
CAP launched Youth Manifesto with Commonwealth Association of Architects at CHOGM London.
CAP Business Meeting, Cape Town, South Africa: Trudi Elliot (UK) elected first Patron of CAP.
CAP helped launch **UN Habitat's 'Planners for Climate Action' initiative, COP 23, Bonn, Germany.**
Former CAP President Christine Platt (South Africa) awarded Lifetime Achievement Award by the South Africa Planning Institute.
CAP held inaugural Awards programme for Outstanding Planning Achievement in the Commonwealth.
Former CAP President Dyan Currie received Australia Medal Award.

2019: CAP published final report of Caribbean Disaster Recovery Project (Commonwealth Association of Planners, 2019).

CAP awarded major grant from the Prince of Wales's Charitable Fund for range of project work including Rapid Urbanisation Toolkit and Commonwealth Sustainable Cities Initiative.

2020: CAP Business Meeting held online due to COVID-19 Pandemic. Eleanor Mohammed (Canada) elected President. Dyan Currie appointed Honorary vice president.

Survey of Commonwealth Built Environment Professions published (Oborn and Walters, 2020).
CAP issued COVID-19 statement (Currie and Harridge, 2020).

2021: Kelley Moore (Canada) appointed CAP Secretary-General.

CAP participated in **COP26, Glasgow, UK**.
Clive Harridge appointed Honorary vice president.

2022: CAP participated in **CHOGM, Kigali, Rwanda, which agreed the Declaration on Sustainable Urbanisation (The Commonwealth, 2022).**

Togo and Gabon joined the Commonwealth, taking the membership up to 56 countries.
CAP participated in **WUF 11, Katowice, Poland.**

References

Caldwell, W. and Lang, K. (2014), *Perspectives on Planning for Agriculture and Food Security in the Commonwealth.* Available at. www.commonwealth-planners.org/publications-1 (Accessed 15 August 2022).

ComHabitat. (2010), *Urban Challenges: Scoping the State of the Commonwealth's Cities*. London: ComHabitat.

Commonwealth Association of Planners. (2019), *Vulnerability, Risk Management and Adaptation: Responding to Climate Change Challenges in the Commonwealth Caribbean*. Available at. www.commonwealth-planners.org/publications-1 (Accessed 15 August 2022).

Currie, D. and Harridge, C. (2020), *CAP COVID-19 Statement*. Available at. www.commonwealth-planners.org/covid-19-statement (Accessed 15 August 2022).

Farmer, P., Frojmovic, M., Hague, C., Harridge, C., Narang, S., Shishido, R., Siegel, D., Taylor, P., and Vogelij, J. (2006), *Reinventing planning: A New Governance Paradigm for Managing Human Settlements'*, Position Paper for the World Planners Congress, Vancouver 17–20 June. Available at. http://globalplannersnetwork.org/wp-content/uploads/2016/10/reinventingplanningenglish-1.pdf (Accessed 5 April 2022).

Hague, C. and French, W. (2010), *The State of the Cities – Why and How the Commonwealth Must Address the Challenge of Sustainable Urbanisation, Commonwealth Secretariat Discussion Paper 8*, London: Commonwealth Secretariat.

Malaza, N., Todes, A. and Williamson, A. with Hague, C. and the Women in Planning Network of the Commonwealth Association of Planners. (2009), *Gender in Planning and Urban Development, Commonwealth Secretariat Discussion Paper 7*. London: Commonwealth Secretariat.

Oborn, P. and Walters, J.G. (2020), *Planning for Climate Change and Rapid Urbanisation: Survey of the Built Environment Professions in the Commonwealth, Survey Results*. Available at https://commonwealthsustainablecities.org/survey/ (Accessed 2 August 2022).

The Commonwealth. (2022), CHOGM 2022 Communiqué, Leaders Statement and Declarations on Delivering a Common Future. Available at. https://thecommonwealth.org/news/chogm-2022-communique-leaders-statement-and-declarations-delivering-common (Accessed 15 August 2022).

APPENDIX 2

Biographies of editors, authors and contributors

The biographies of authors, contributors and editors are set out in alphabetical order of surname/family name.

Kristin Agnello – author

Kristin Agnello is an interdisciplinary scholar-practitioner based in Victoria, Canada and an active member of the Canadian Institute of Planners. She has served many roles including vice president (Canada) of CAP from 2017–2021, inaugural Chair of the Commonwealth Women in Planning Network from 2018–2021, Regional Coordinator (South Vancouver Island) of the British Columbia Council for International Cooperation from 2019–2020, TeachSDG Ambassador and Design Specialist with the UK Design Council (2021–present).

Kristin has advocated for women's equity in urban planning at two UN Commissions on the Status of Women and three World Design Summits. In 2018, Kristin was named one of Canada's Top 25 Women of Influence and, in 2022, was inducted into Canada's Women of Impact gallery by the Federal Department for Women and Gender Equality for her work towards advancing gender equality in the built environment.

Jua Cilliers – author

Jua Cilliers is Head of the School of Built Environment and Professor of Urban Planning at the University of Technology Sydney (Australia), as well as adjunct Professor at North-West University (South Africa). She holds professional registrations from both the South African Council for Planners and the Planning Institute of

Australia. Jua is Chair of the Women in Planning Network of the Commonwealth Association of Planners (*www.commonwealth-planners.org/cwip-network*) and Board Member of the International Society of City and Regional Planners (*https://isocarp.org/board-executive-committee/*).

In 2019 she was the recipient of the National South African Teaching Award for Teaching Excellence in South Africa. She was a finalist of the National Science and Technology Forum Awards and prize winner at the Woman in Science Awards. In 2021 she received the North-West University Award for Excellence in Community Engagement. Her research expertise pertains to the planning of sustainable cities, smart cities and strategic spatial planning.

Dyan Currie AM – author

Dyan Currie is Brisbane City Council's Chief Planner and the Brisbane 2032 Olympic and Paralympic Games Host City Office Lead. Dy is a highly experienced planning executive with national and international experience in planning and economic development. She is the immediate Past President of the Commonwealth Association of Planners, a member of the World Economic Forum Global Future Council on Cities of Tomorrow and Co-Chair of UN Habitat's Stakeholder Advisory Group. Dy was recognised in the Australia Day Honours list in 2020 for significant service to town planning and strategic urban development and appointed as a Member of the Order of Australia (AM).

A past National President of the Planning Institute of Australia, Dy is a life fellow of PIA, Honorary Lifetime Member of the Royal Town Planning Institute (UK) and also a fellow of the Urban Development Institute of Australia. Dy is also a board member for Place Leaders Asia Pacific.

Anne T. Gallagher AO – contributor

Dr Anne T. Gallagher AO is Director-General of the Commonwealth Foundation. In that role she works closely with Member States to advance the principles and ideals of the Commonwealth – most particularly the Commonwealth's commitment to vibrant and free civil societies.

A lawyer, practitioner, teacher and scholar, Anne's long international career has involved several decades of service at the United Nations. Her current and recent appointments include Chairperson of Girls Not Brides and Academic Adviser at Doughty St Chambers.

Anne's work for human rights, justice and equality has been widely recognised, earning her, among other honours, the Australian Freedom Award and the Peace

Woman of the Year award for the Women's International League for Peace and Freedom. In 2012, she was appointed Officer of the Order of Australia (AO) and named a '2012 Hero' by the US Secretary of State.

Cliff Hague OBE – editor and author

Cliff Hague, OBE, has been President of CAP and of RTPI. He is Emeritus Professor in Planning and Spatial Development at Heriot-Watt University and a fellow of the Academy of Social Sciences. He is Chair of the Cockburn Association (Edinburgh's Civic Trust) and a patron of PAS (Planning Aid Scotland). He has been Secretary General of CAP and Chair of Built Environment Forum Scotland, the intermediary body between the Scottish Government and the sector.

As a freelance consultant and researcher he has worked mainly in European Union regional co-operation projects and for the European Observatory Network for Territorial Cohesion and Development (ESPON). He led the International Advisory Board for UN-Habitat on Spatial Planning in Area C of the Israeli-occupied West Bank of the Palestinian Territory. He is an essayist in B. Hasselberger (ed.), (2017), *Encounters in Planning Thought: 16 essays by key thinkers in spatial planning*.

Clive Harridge – editor and author

Clive Harridge is a member of the Royal Town Planning Institute. He has a geography degree from Nottingham University, a postgraduate diploma in town planning and business management qualifications.

Clive has been involved with CAP as a volunteer since 2006. He was Secretary-General and Trustee between 2010 and 2021 and currently continues as Trustee and Honorary vice president.

Before 'retiring' in 2019 Clive was Director and Head of Planning, Transport and Design at the international consultancy Wood. In 2003 Clive was identified in the *Independent* on Sunday newspaper as one of Britain's Top Ten Chartered Town Planners.

Clive was President of the Royal Town Planning Institute in 2006 – the first ever President elected by membership ballot. Clive's Presidential theme was '*Get Real about Sustainable Development!*' and he championed good practice in all aspects of sustainability.

Clive became a Freeman of the City of London in 2007. In 2019 he was awarded Honorary Fellowship of the Ghana Institute of Planners.

Bryce Julyan – editor and author

Bryce Julyan is a Fellow of the New Zealand Planning Institute (NZPI) and Honorary Fellow of the Planning Institute of Australia. He holds a bachelor of town planning degree from the University of Auckland, New Zealand.

Since 2014 he has been a vice president on the CAP Executive Committee. In 2016, on behalf of NZPI, he convened the Sustainable Development Conference and CAP Business Meeting in Fiji. He has contributed to many CAP initiatives including a review of post-hurricane planning methodologies in the eastern Caribbean.

A senior technical director at Beca, a NZ-owned consultancy covering the Asia-Pacific region, he leads the Planning & Engagement practice. He is a Beca technical fellow, recognising his expertise in urban and strategic planning.

Bryce served on the NZPI Executive Council from 2008 and was elected as inaugural Chair of the Board in 2012, serving two terms before stepping down in 2018.

Vijay Krishnarayan – author

Vijay Krishnarayan has focussed his career on strengthening participation in processes that shape people's lives. Over the last 35 years, he has advanced this agenda with governments, not-for-profits and businesses in the United Kingdom, the Caribbean and the wider Commonwealth. He served two terms at the head of the Commonwealth's agency for civil society – the Commonwealth Foundation.

During a seven-year tenure from 2012–2019, he focussed the organisation on strengthening people's participation in governance. He established the Commonwealth Foundation as having a recognised role in bringing civic voices to Commonwealth political processes, including seven Commonwealth Heads of Government Meetings. He served as the Foundation's Deputy Director from 2006–2012.

Before joining the Commonwealth Foundation, he spent over a decade in the Caribbean, supporting the participatory and collaborative management of natural resources. He was based in Belize (1995–1997) and then joined the Caribbean Natural Resources Institute (CANARI) in Saint Lucia (1997–2000). The Institute is one of the region's sustainable development think tanks and he was appointed as its Managing Partner in 2000. In the early 1990s he worked as a planning aid worker in London's Brixton, supporting minority and less-heard voices engaging with the planning system.

Eleanor Mohammed – author

Eleanor Mohammed is President of the Commonwealth Association of Planners, Co-Chair of the UN-Habitat Professionals Forum and the Founder/Principal of

Strategic and Resilient Together. She is an executive leader with over 17 years of public, private and not-for-profit sector experience. As a passionate professional who regularly speaks and presents at international events on city building, Eleanor is a champion for the planning profession, climate action, equity and inclusion, healthy communities, technology adaptation and sustainability.

Eleanor has served as President the Canadian Institute of Planners and President of the Alberta Professional Planners Institute. She holds a masters with distinction in town and country planning from the University of the West of England, Bristol, UK and has an honours bachelor of arts from the University of Toronto with a specialisation in environmental management.

Kelley Moore – contributor

Kelley is passionate about planning and preparing communities for the future. Over her 25-year career, she has served in several progressive roles and has overseen award-winning, transformative initiatives. Her experience ranges from town, city, regional and international planning to public administration in the areas of policy, program development, infrastructure planning, service and project delivery. She currently serves as Assistant Deputy Minister with the government of Saskatchewan, Ministry of SaskBuilds and Procurement. In 2021, Kelley accepted a voluntary appointment as Secretary-General and Trustee for the Commonwealth Association of Planners.

Kelley has a master's degree in interdisciplinary studies (2013) and is an elected member of the University of Saskatchewan Senate. She is a proud registered professional planner and Fellow of Canadian Institute of Planners (CIP). She has received several distinguished awards over her career including the CIP President's Award and The Fraser-Gatrell Memorial Award for Distinguished Contribution to Planning.

Ruiz Nik – editor and author

Ruiz Nik is one of the council members of the Malaysian Institute of Planners (MIP). He was trained as an architect at Birmingham School of Architecture (RIBA Part 1 and 2) and continued with his masters in planning at Oxford Brookes University.

Ruiz has been the representative for MIP at CAP since 2018 and is currently leading the Heritage and Urban Design network at MIP. Advocating the awareness of Universal Design and planning for Autistic children has been one of Ruiz's key initiatives currently undertaken at MIP.

He is currently heading the second generation of Rekarancang, a Malaysian planning firm that has been established since 1977. Ruiz has been involved in managing planning research studies and development at a range of scales from rural planning for isolated communities such as in Tunoh, Bukit Mabong in Sarawak, Malaysia to strategic planning studies particularly in the importance of reforestation and security planning at national and regional level in Malaysia.

Barbara Norman – author

Professor Barbara Norman is Chair and Professor of Urban and Regional Planning, University of Canberra and Visiting Fellow at the Australian National University. Professor Norman has a combined professional and academic background as a former national president of the Planning Institute of Australia and a current leader in urban and regional research.

Recent international research includes *Sustainable Pathways for our Cities and Regions: planning within planetary boundaries* (Routledge, 2018); *Are autonomous cities our urban future? Comment in Nature Communications* (Nature Communications, 2018) and *Apocalypse Now: Australian Bushfires and the future of Urban Settlements* (Nature Urban Sustainability). Professor Norman's most recent book is *Urban Planning for Climate Change* (Routledge, 2022).

Christine Platt – author

A South African with a master's degree in town and regional planning, Christine is a Chartered Member of the RTPI, a Corporate Member of the South African Planning Institute and a Registered Planner with the South African Council of Planners. She has worked in academic research, local government and private practice.

Christine is Past President and Honorary vice president of the Commonwealth Association of Planners and Past-President of the South African Planning Institute 2002–2006. She has addressed and chaired many meetings of Commonwealth Ministers at CHOGM and CCGHS, facilitated Plenary Dialogue sessions of UN Habitat and served on many Expert Groups for the UN. She also served as Chairman of the UN Habitat Expert Group on Urban and Territorial Guidelines for Planning and was a member of the UN Habitat WUC Steering Committee, the UN ISDR Resilient Cities Campaign Advisory Board and the Advisory Panel for the UN Habitat World Cities Report. Christine was Chairman of the Ministerial Advisory Panel for the Minister of Human Settlements in South Africa and Vice Chairman of the Board of Directors of SA Housing Development Agency.

Peter Pun OBE, SBS **– contributor**

Dr Pun worked in the town planning field from 1964 until retirement in 1999. For some of this time he was a civil servant and Director of Planning in the Hong Kong government.

Dr Pun was Council Member and Chairman of the Hong Kong Branch of the RTPI and a founder member of the Hong Kong Institute of Planners of which he was President for several terms. He was a part-time/honorary lecturer/professor at universities in Hong Kong and he was on the Council of the Eastern Regional Organization for Planning and Housing for many years.

Dr Pun was President of the Commonwealth Association of Planners between 1984 and 1988. Dr Pun was awarded an OBE in 1993 and in 1999 he was awarded the Silver Bauhinia Star (SBS) by the Hong Kong Government for his outstanding work as a civil servant.

Bill Robertson – author

William (Bill) Alexander Robertson studied town planning under Professor Robert Kennedy and Gerhard Rosenberg at Auckland University where he is a Distinguished Alumnus.

His planning career was largely in the environmental and land use fields. He served as Chief Planner for the New Zealand National Parks Authority and Director of Planning for the New Zealand Department of Lands and Survey.

Bill was President of the NZ Planning Institute during the major environmental restructuring of Government Departments in NZ and the replacement of the Town and Country legislation with the Resource Management Legislation.

Bill finished his government career as Director General/Surveyor General of the NZ Department of Survey and Land Information. Bill has been a consultant to several World Bank Land Administration projects. He was Commissioner on the UN Iraq/Kuwait Boundary Demarcation Commission and UN Special Consultant to three International Boundary Commissions in West Africa.

Bill was President of CAP from 1988–1991 and 1996–2000.

The Rt Hon Patricia Scotland KC – contributor

The Rt Hon Patricia Scotland KC, who took office as Secretary-General of the Commonwealth in April 2016, serves the 56 governments and 2.5 billion people of the Commonwealth.

Born in Dominica, she moved to the UK at an early age and was brought up in a large close-knit Caribbean family where she was taught the importance of hard work, education, pride in her heritage and the obligation to give back to the region of her birth and to the society in which she was raised. This ethic has guided her throughout her dynamic career in law, public service and politics.

A lawyer by profession, she became the first black and youngest woman ever to be appointed Queen's Counsel. Appointed to the House of Lords as Baroness Scotland of Asthal in 1997, between 1999 and 2007 she served as a Minister in the Foreign and Commonwealth Office and the Home Office. In 2007 she became the first woman since the post was created in 1315 to be appointed Attorney General for England and Wales and was also Attorney General for Northern Ireland. She has been Alderman for Bishopsgate Ward in the City of London since 2015.

In 2022, Commonwealth Heads of Government asked her to serve a second term as Secretary-General.

Maimunah Mohd Sharif – contributor

Ms Maimunah Mohd Sharif (Malaysia) is Executive Director of the United Nations Human Settlements Programme (UN-Habitat), appointed at the level of Under-Secretary-General by the Secretary-General, following an election by the General Assembly on 22 December 2017. She succeeds Dr Joan Clos of Spain.

As Executive Director of UN-Habitat, Ms. Sharif has focused on reforming and rejuvenating the agency, mobilising for internal and external support for the organization's restructuring and new Strategic Plan 2020–2023. Key initiatives undertaken by Ms. Sharif as Executive Director of UN-Habitat include the adoption of the General Assembly Resolution 73/539 after 14 years of negotiation, which established a new governance structure with universal membership, governed by the UN-Habitat Assembly.

Prior to this appointment, Ms Sharif was Mayor of the city council of Penang Island, Malaysia. In 2011, she was the first woman to be appointed president of the Municipal Council of Seberang Perai. As mayor of a local authority, she led the Municipal Council of Seberang Perai to achieve its vision of a 'cleaner, greener, safer and healthier place to work, live, invest and play.' Ms Sharif began her career as a town planner at the Municipal Council of Penang Island in 1985. In 2003, she was promoted to Director of Planning and Development, a position she held until November 2009.

Born in Kuala Pilah, Negeri Sembilan, Malaysia, on 26 August 1961, Ms Sharif holds a bachelor of science with honours in town planning studies from the University of Wales Institute of Science and Technology, UK and a master's of science in planning studies from the Malaysia Science University.

Olafiyin Taiwo – author

Olafiyin Taiwo is a chartered town planner with experience working in public, private and non-profit sectors. She is Doctoral Researcher at University College

London and leads the Commonwealth Association of Planners Young Planners Network as the Convener. She is Co-chair for the UN-Habitat Planners for Climate Action (Education and Capacity Building) and a member of the Royal Town Planning Institute General Assembly and International Committee. Olafiyin is also the co-founder of the BAME Planners Network.

Olafiyin is committed to improving the quality of life and experiences of local communities in urban areas. She is the co-founder of Life Brooks International, a charity dedicated to bringing hope and transforming lives of children and young people in urban communities.

She was awarded the RTPI Special Presidential Award 2020/2021 for her contribution to promoting diversity and inclusion in the planning profession. She was also recently recognised as Woman of Influence 2021 in the *Planner* magazine.

Ian Tant – editor and author

Ian Tant is a chartered town planner with over 40 years' experience in the public, private and voluntary sectors. He has degrees in environmental sciences and town and country planning. Now semi-retired, Ian maintains strategic advisory roles and is currently the UK representative on the Commonwealth Association of Planners, to which he dedicates appreciable time.

Ian began his career in local government in the south of England before joining the planning and design consultancy, Barton Willmore (now part of Stantec), becoming a partner in 1990 and for ten years the senior partner. He has wide-ranging experience in development projects across the UK with a clear focus on delivery.

Since retiring from the firm in 2016, he has given time to the Royal Town Planning Institute and CAP. He was a board member of the RTPI from 2017 to 2021 and President of the institute in 2019.

APPENDIX 3

Sponsor details

CAP is extremely grateful for the support of our sponsors. Further details about our sponsors are set out here.

Beca **Beca** is one of Asia Pacific's largest, most innovative and progressive employee-owned professional services consultancies, offering market leading design, engineering, technical and advisory services.

Our planning practitioners, including master planning and urban planning specialists, work together with peers from other disciplines, alongside our clients and partners, on a wide range of city and community shaping projects.

'Creative people together transforming our world' is our vision. It reflects our culture, our aspirations and our purpose – to make every day better.

After a century of operation and our origins as a family-owned business, we have grown to employ more than 3,800 people in 23 offices around the world and have delivered projects in over 70 countries.

Our world is changing faster than ever, presenting new and unique challenges for regions, nations, cities and settlements. To achieve sustainable and equitable outcomes for all, we recognise that collaboration is vital – and it is through meaningful partnerships and engagement with our diverse communities that together we will create a fairer, better world.

Whether it's through delivering climate adaptation and resilience solutions to the Pacific, designing Green buildings in Singapore or planning for urban growth in Australia and New Zealand – we are passionate about the big picture and delivering the social, cultural, environmental and economic outcomes needed for a safer, better and more sustainable tomorrow.

Find out more about Beca, or get in touch at www.beca.com

Turley is a full-service planning and development consultancy.

Our planning expertise is complemented by business cases and funding, design, economics, EIA, expert witness, heritage, townscape and landscape, strategic communications and sustainability services. All services can be provided together or individually.

We help clients achieve good growth in all jurisdictions in the UK and Ireland from our locations in major cities and growth areas. Our teams are experts in their fields; they shape better places and achieve success for our clients.

We apply our knowledge to deliver sustainable places and buildings that meet local needs; mitigate and adapt to a changing climate; enhance well-being and promote social connectivity. We are sustainability and energy, social and governance (ESG) experts, supporting delivery consent, advice on existing property assets and corporate strategies.

We embed ESG at a corporate, portfolio and asset scales to achieve regulatory compliance, demonstrate climate leadership and future proof investments. We have contributed to the production of key national climate change and net zero carbon guidance from the Institute of Environmental Management and Assessment (IEMA) and UK Green Building Council.

As a carbon-neutral certified business, sustainable growth shapes all our consultancy advice, activity and ambition.

We bring deep thinking, smart strategy and expert delivery.

www.turley.co.uk

About Atkins

Atkins is a member of the SNC-Lavalin Group and one of the world's most respected design, engineering and project management consultancies, employing over 19,000 people across the UK, North America, Middle East, and Africa, Asia Pacific and Europe. We build long-term trusted partnerships to create a world where lives are enriched through the implementation of our ideas.

About SNC-Lavalin

Founded in 1911, SNC-Lavalin is a fully integrated professional services and project management company with offices around the world. SNC-Lavalin connects people, technology and data to help shape and deliver world-leading concepts and projects, while offering comprehensive innovative solutions across the asset lifecycle.

Our expertise is wide-ranging – consulting and advisory, intelligent networks and cybersecurity, design and engineering, procurement, project and construction management, operations and maintenance, decommissioning and sustaining capital – and delivered to clients in four strategic sectors: engineering, design and project management (EDPM), infrastructure, nuclear and resources, supported by capital. People. Drive. Results.

www.atkinsglobal.com

APPENDIX 4

Glossary

2030 Agenda   A United Nation Agenda for Sustainable Development adopted in 2015 that set 17 Sustainable Development Goals (SDGs) and 169 associated targets.

Agenda 21   A comprehensive plan of action agreed at the 1992 UN Environment Summit to be taken globally, nationally and locally by organisations of the United Nations System, Governments and Major Groups in every area in which human activity impacts on the environment.

Apartheid   A policy that upheld segregationist policies against non-white citizens of South Africa from 1948 until the early 1990s.

Austerity Urbanism   Austerity urbanism is a concept developed to explain forms of public policy and urban development that were fashioned after the 2008 financial crisis. Typically these include restricting and seeking to reduce public spending, especially at sub-national levels and privatisation of urban assets such as public spaces or buildings, along with de-regulation of planning and other forms of restriction on private development.

Beijing Declaration   A resolution adopted by the UN at the end of the Fourth World Conference on Women on 15 September 1995. The resolution adopted a set of principles concerning the equality of men and women.

Business Meeting   See Conference of Delegates.

Charter of the Commonwealth   Commitment of Commonwealth member states to the development of free and democratic societies and the promotion of peace and prosperity to improve the lives of all the people of the Commonwealth. The charter also acknowledges the role of civil society in supporting the goals and values of the Commonwealth.

Circular Economy   A production and consumption model which involves sharing, leasing, reusing, repairing, refurbishing and recycling existing materials and products to reduce exhaustion of resources.

Commonwealth The Commonwealth is a voluntary association of 56 independent and equal countries. It is home to 2.5 billion people and includes both advanced economies and developing countries. Thirty-two members are small states, including many island nations. Member governments have agreed to shared goals like development, democracy and peace. Although the origins go back to the British Empire, not all members of the modern Commonwealth are former British colonies.

Commonwealth Foundation An inter-governmental organisation established by Heads of Government, it is the Commonwealth agency for civil society.

Commonwealth Heads of Government Meeting The Commonwealth Heads of Government Meeting is a biennial summit meeting of leaders from all Commonwealth nations.

Commonwealth Secretariat The inter-governmental organisation that supports Commonwealth countries and co-ordinates Commonwealth activities.

Community Wealth Building Community wealth building is a people-centric approach to local economic development that redirects wealth back into the local economy to benefit the local community.

Committee of the Whole The meeting that is held in preparation and which sets the agenda, for the Commonwealth Heads of Government Meetings. It is this body to which submissions are made seeking involvement in the activities and debates at CHOGM.

Conference of Delegates Meetings of delegates from CAP member organisations to decide on actions and elect an executive. These are usually hosted together with a conference associated with one of CAP's member organisations and since the late 1990s have been held every two years.

Developing Countries Countries with a low level of industrial and/or economic development, which leads directly or indirectly to social, political, economic and environmental challenges that significantly impede quality of life.

Geographical Information Systems A system that creates, manages, analyses and maps all types of data. It is the basis of modern mapping and analysis of spatial data.

Human Settlements It refers to the totality of human community with all the social, material, organisational, spiritual and cultural elements that sustain it. It embraces not just cities but the full range of places where people live.

Integrated Development Plan An approach to strategic planning that through collaboration and citizen involvement seeks to co-ordinate different sectors and agencies across the entire municipality and connect the plan to budgets.

International Guidelines for Urban and Territorial Planning UN Habitat Guidelines published in 2015 that provide national governments, local authorities, civil society organisations and planning professionals with a global reference framework that promotes more compact, socially inclusive, better-integrated and connected cities and territories that foster sustainable urban development and are resilient to climate change.

Kigali Commitment The Built Environment Professionals in the Commonwealth Commitment to Collaborate in support of Sustainable Urbanisation across the Commonwealth. It was endorsed by 20 Commonwealth Built Environment organisations in 2022 with the intent to expand it in the future.

Land Information Technology The integration and collective name of geographical information system (GIS), geographical positioning system (GPS), remote sensing (RS) and other advanced technology in computer technology and normal methods of measurement and survey.

Low Elevation Coastal Zones A contiguous area near the coast and less than 10 m above sea-level.

Maritime Spatial Planning A strategic planning approach to manage the use of our seas and oceans, including the interface with land, coherently and to ensure that human activities take place in an efficient, safe and sustainable way.

Millennium Development Goals A group of eight development goals adopted by the United Nations in September 2000 to combat poverty, hunger, disease, illiteracy, environmental degradation and discrimination against women. They were superseded by the Sustainable Development Goals in 2015.

New institutionalism A social scientific approach that focuses on how institutional structures, rules and customs enable and constrain the actions of groups and individuals.

New Urban Agenda Adopted at the UN Conference on Housing and Sustainable Development (Habitat III Oct 2016) the New Urban Agenda represents a shared vision for a better and more sustainable future. If well planned and well managed, urbanisation can be a powerful tool for sustainable development for both developing and developed countries.

Paris Agreement Also known as Paris Accord or Paris Climate Accords, the Paris Agreement is a legally binding international treaty on climate change. It was adopted by 196 Parties at COP 21 in Paris, on 12 December 2015 and intended to limit global warming to well below 2 degrees Celsius and preferably to 1.5 degrees Celsius, compared to pre-industrial levels.

Physical Planning A design exercise that entails a survey and a land use plan as a framework to propose future physical development that includes infrastructure for a settlement or area, including infrastructure for public services, housing, transport, economic activities, recreation and environmental protection.

Slum A slum is a highly populated urban residential area consisting of densely packed housing units of weak construction quality and often associated with poverty.

Small Island Developing States A distinct group of 38 UN Member States and 20 Non-UN Members/Associate Members of United Nations regional commissions that face unique social, economic and environmental vulnerabilities.

Spatial Development Framework A framework or plan that seeks to guide the overall spatial distribution of land uses, infrastructure and connectivity over a municipal or wider area, without necessarily being specific in identifying precise sites or boundaries.

Sustainable Development Development that meets the needs of the present, without compromising the ability of future generations to meet their own needs. It contains two key concepts: overriding priority should be given to the essential needs of the poor, and there are limitations imposed by the state of technology and social organisation on the environment's ability to meet present and future needs.

Sustainable Development Goals Included in the 2030 Agenda for Sustainable Development (adopted by all United Nations Member States in 2015), the 17 Sustainable Development Goals (SDGs) are an urgent call for action by all countries – developed and developing – in a global partnership. They recognize that ending poverty and other deprivations must go hand-in-hand with strategies that improve health and education, reduce inequality and spur economic growth – all while tackling climate change and working to preserve our oceans and forests.

Sustainable Urbanisation The key concepts of sustainable development applied to the processes and forms of urban development including conservation of finite resources, prioritisation of the needs of poor and marginalised groups, respecting universal human rights and integrating environmental, social and economic actions to these ends.

Tactical Urbanism Low-cost, often temporary changes to the built environment in order to improve local neighbourhoods or community spaces, often identified as local solutions to local planning issues.

Washington consensus Refers to the convergence in the 1980s and 1990s between Washington based institutions such as the International Monetary Fund (IMF), World Bank and US Department of the Treasury around policies developed by the Reagan (US) and Thatcher (UK) administrations. These include privatisation, de-regulation, tax cuts and re-ordering public expenditure but also property rights at acceptable cost and were imposed as conditions on borrowing by poorer countries.

Windrush Generation People from Caribbean Commonwealth countries whose Commonwealth citizenship conferred rights of free movement to the UK and its colonies and who moved to Britain to overcome severe labour shortages in the wake of the Second World War. Those rights were withdrawn by the UK by legislation in 1971.

Windrush Scandal Began to surface in 2017 after it emerged that hundreds of Commonwealth citizens, many of whom were from the 'Windrush' generation had been wrongly detained, deported and denied legal rights in the UK.

Women's Design Service A mission that promotes the diverse communities of women who live in towns and cities that should enjoy a quality environment that is well designed, accessible, environmentally sustainable, affordable and safe.

World Urban Campaign An advocacy and partnership platform to raise awareness about positive urban change in order to achieve green, productive, safe, healthy, inclusive and well-planned cities. Its goal is to place the Urban Agenda at the highest level in development policies. It is coordinated by UN-Habitat and driven by a large number of committed partners from around the world.

INDEX

Page locators in **bold** indicate a table

Aboriginal and Torres Strait Islander 124
Acheampong, Ransford A. 37
Act of Parliament 11
activism 77, 138, 164, 188, 203, 206–207
Adshead, Stanley 190
advocacy: difficult 89; effective 19, 23, 99, 104; gender equality 94, 126, 134; international 112; pandemic 116; planning 203; roles 107
African Planning Association (APA) 82, 92
Agenda 21 34
Agnello, Kristin 23, 111, 129
agriculture 13, 34, 82, 152
Abu Dhabi 107, 113, 116
American Planning Association (APA) 113, 114, 156, 202
Amos, F.J.C. 37
anti-racism 25, 122, 124
apartheid 25–26, 43, 77–78, 149
Archer, Carol 83, 128
Archer, John 110
Association of Commonwealth Universities (ACU) 22, 107, 117
Atkins 10
austerity urbanism 153, 208
Australia: metropolitan growth 57; planning organizations 25, 36, 42, 55, 90, 133
Australian Agency for International Development (AUSAID) 83
autonomous 71, 154, 161
Ayebare, Pamela 128

Bahamas 55, 62
Bangladesh: flooding 26; poverty **32**; University of Engineering and Technology 128
Barbados: delegates/representatives 62, 69; planners 50–51, 90–91, 97, 126; planning challenges 54–55, **59**
Beca 9
Beijing Declaration 131
Bermuda 52, 55, 57
best practice 114, 198
biodiversity 19, 137, 145, 150, 152, 180, 197–198, 206–207
Black Lives Matter 27
Black, Indigenous and People of Colour 122, 124
blue-green network 146
Botswana 54–55, 141
Bourne, Luther 50
Brewster, Roger 81, 83
British: imperialism 25, 78; planning 146, 148, 188–190; regeneration 42, 65
British Colonial Office 148
British Commonwealth of Nations 25
British East India Company 188
British Empire 25, 188, 200
British Virgin Islands 112, 140

Brundtland Commission/Report 12, 35, 79
Brundtland, Gro Harlem 13, 34
Building Better Data 118
Built Environment Professionals in the Commonwealth (BEPIC) 75, 83, 95, 200
business meeting 12, 78, 81, 92, 104; *see also* Conference of Delegates, 105

Caldwell, Wayne 94, 102
Call for Action 5
Canada 23, 39, 41, **59**; delegates/representatives 61, 69, 83, 90, 94, 114; partnerships 117, 119, 121; planning 84, 91; workshops 71
Canadian Geographic System 71
Canadian Institute of Planners (CIP) 16, 105, 116, 132, 195
Canadian International Development Agency (CIDA) 68
CAP Newsletter 68, 80
car-dependency 13, 38, 82
Caribbean: advocacy 116; natural disasters 111–112, 140; partnerships 22; planners/planning 81, 83, 90–92; racism 28, 148
Central Area Sub-project 57–58
Centre for Urban Studies and Urban Planning 64
Chambré, Susan M. 203
Charitable Trust 9, 26
Charter of the Commonwealth 166
China 35, 63–64, 92, 146, 208
Choe, Alan F.C. 58
Cilliers, Jua 23, 130–131
circular economy 13, 151–152, 177, 183, 197
civil society: connecting 3, 14, 16, 85, 96, 117, 120; organisations 17, 28, 85, 98, 117, 129, 134, 166
Clarke, Phillip 110, 118
climate change: impacts 19, 28, 138, 145, 180, 185, 206; planning for 99, 183; threat 3, 21, 28, 83, 98, 107, 119
Cold War 26
Colombo 67, 97
colonialism 27, 36, 78, 122, 138, 188, 194
colonisation 15, 23, 122
colonisers 42, 188
Committee of the Whole 97
Commonwealth: core beliefs 25; formation of 25; funding 91, 97; members 26; observation day 108
Commonwealth Association of Architects (CAA) 22, 107, 117–118

Commonwealth Association of Planners (CAP): challenges of planning 11, 34, 54–57, 107; early priorities 16, 38, 53; establishment 50; foundation of 25, 77; gender imbalance 126; inaugural conference 60; membership growth 61–62, 67; mission 1–2, 5, 9, 11; partnerships 22, 78, 89–90, 94, 100, 104, 113–116, 121, 132; planning awards 109, 149; planning history 23, 137–138, 187, 198; urban planning education 177, 184
Commonwealth Association of Surveying and Land Economy (CASLE) 70–71, 118
Commonwealth Consultative Group on Human Settlements (CCGHS) 95, 200
Commonwealth Engineers Council (CEC) 118
Commonwealth Foundation (CF): establishment of 26; leadership 138, 159, 199; message from director 3; partnerships 94, 129; research grant 93, 111; vision 80–81
Commonwealth Fund for Technical Cooperation 26, 155
Commonwealth Group of Experts 26–27
Commonwealth Heads of Government Meeting (CHOGM) 1, 11, 25, 81, 111, 119, 169, 175
Commonwealth Human Ecology Council (CHEC) 75, 200
Commonwealth Local Government Forum (CLGF) 22, 90, 107, 117
Commonwealth People's Forum (CPF) 27, 81, 83, 91, 93, 95, 97, 111
Commonwealth Secretariat (CS): founding of 26; gender equality 92, 124, 128–129; partnerships 94, 166, 199–200; rule of law 191
Commonwealth Sustainable Cities Initiative (CSCI) 22, 106–107, 113, 117–119, 121, 173
Commonwealth Women in Planning Network (CWIP) 21; establishment 126; future plans 133–134; goals for gender equality 131–133; history 127–128; Strategic Plan 2008–2010 129
Commonwealth Youth Forum 27, 169, 175
communication: circulations 102; early forms 18, 68; international 36, 178; issues 56, 181; technology 12, 69, 184, 203
community: development 151; international 35–36; participation 37, 143, 149, 178,

183; professional 100; well-being 2, 127, 155, 164, 180, 185, 190, 195
computer technology 21, 69, 71, 80
Concept Plan 46, 57–58
Conference of Delegates 51–52, 104
Conference of Partners (COP) 15, 27
Congres internationaux d'architecture moderne 199
conservation 33–34, 151, 190
consumerism 12, 163
corridor, development/growth 43, 46, 58
COVID-19: economic recovery 5, 161; impacts 116, 142, 163, 180, 182, 197, 205–206; rapid urbanisation 107, 119, 145
Cross, Jeremy 107
culture: indigenous 124, 194–195, 200, 203, 207; urban 13, 26, 153, 170, 178
customary land 42
Cyprus 55, **59**, 62, 69

Dato' Seri Ong Ka Ting 84
de-regulation 34
Decade of Action 5
Declaration on Sustainable Urbanisation 1, 19, 187
Declarations on Reinventing Planning 7
deindustrialization 12
Denoon-Stevens, S.P. 179
density (low-high) 38, 40–41, 47, 58, 64
Desai, Viral 10, 111, 171
developing countries: climate change awareness 26, 32; commitment to 122; LIT programme 71; planning education 53, 57, 177
dialogue, continuing 84, 92, 117, 121
digitisation 70, 154
discrimination, systemic 123, 144
diverse: communities 172, 207; insights 15, 138, 152, 167; planning 77, 129
diversity 26, 43, 68, 122, 128, 175; *see also* equity, diversity and inclusion
drought 145; *see also* extreme weather

Earth Summit 34
East Timor 83
economic: development 2, 33–34, 37, 58, 82, 146, 163, 170; opportunities 58, 150, 207; outcome 171; well-being 195
Edinburgh 12, 26–27, 54, 75–77, 84
Einolf, Christopher 203
electric transportation 154, 180

emissions 75, 82, 206
energy: consumption 12; renewable 13, 29; services 144, 177, 180
environment: global risk 33; issues and concerns 36; natural 9–10; safe living 3
environmental: awareness 23, 163; crisis 32, 36; objectives 31, 34–35, 38–39, 54, 131, 169, 178, 184; pollution 12; protection 26, 180
equity 9
equity, diversity and inclusion 23, 122, 124, 144
extreme weather 19, 35, 82, 145

Fancourt Declaration 27
Farmer, Paul 147
Farmers' Market 194
Fiji: business meeting 108; conferences 22, 61, 67, 83, 90, 106; knowledge of planning 55, 118, 126, 198; natural disasters 140
Fiji Declaration 105, 108, 132
Fiji Planners Association (FiPA) 105–106
financial: crisis 15; difficulties 22, 73; support 68, 78, 98
flooding 26, 82, 146, 150, 178
Floyd, George 27
food: deserts 78; scarcity 147; security 3, 18–19, 94, 146, 152, 198
forced eviction 30, 44, 151
Forester, John 15
Franklin, George 68–69
Freestone, Robert 14
French, Will 95
Frojmovic, Michel 95
Fryer, David 69, 74

Gallagher, Anne T. 4, 218
Garden City principles 146, 190
gender-equality 19, 23, 26, 128, 131–132, 134, 146
gender-responsive planning 134, 139
Geographical Information System (GIS) 22, 69–71, 180, 199
geographical positioning system (GPS) 151
Germany 28, 121
Ghana: food shortage 152; National Physical Development Plan (1963–1970) 37; planning 38, 55, **59**, 118; political instability 37; poverty **32**; Sweet Potato project 153
Gill, Richard 15, 50–51, 91, 99

236 Index

Global Planners Network (GPN) 85, 100, 104–105, 202
Global Report on Human Settlements 7, 85, 99
global warming 145; *see also* climate change
Goldman, Michael 197
good governance 27, 127
green: bans 39; belts 43; infrastructure 13, 45, 154, 180, 184, 190, 198
greenhouse gas emissions 75
Groote, Peter 39
growth: economic 33, 58, 119; metropolitan 55, 57; population 54, 182; rapid 14, 39, 46; slums 29, 32

Habitat I 14, 33–34, 198
Habitat II 13, 22, 34, 79, 200
Habitat III 7, 22, 89, 97–98, 100, 105, 108, 116, 139; Quito 8, 22, 105, 108, 116
Habitat Professionals Forum (HPF) 23, 98, 116
Hague, Cliff 17, 21–22, 52, 75–76, 79, 84, 86, 88, 95, 97, 137
Hall, Peter 14
haphazard development 12, 188, 191
Harare Declaration 26
Harridge, Clive 2, 17, 21, 95, 100–101, 106, 109–110, 160
Haselsberger, Beatrix 15
Hong Kong: CAP conference 68–69, 71; planners 16, 50; planning process 56, **59**, 62–64; technology development 17
Hong Kong Institute of Planners (HKIP) 16, 63
housing: affordable 38–39, 46, 130, 207; poor/informal 13, 21–23, 30, 57; public 58
Houston, Susan 94
human rights 26, 28, 123–125, 145, 199
human settlements: development 19, 33, 177; planning 28, 132; safe 14, 46; sustainable 12, 22, 34–35, 79
hurricane: damage 112, 140; Gilbert 26; Hattie 146; Irma 140; Katrina 35; Maria 140

Imperial Conference, fifth 25
India: delegates/representatives 61–63; migration 145; natural disasters 181; New Delhi conference 60–61; planners 74, 94, 143, 189; poverty **32**, 150, 197; public protests 165; urbanisation 178, 192

Indigenous people: colonisation 23, 42, 194; early engagement 185; reconciliation 144, 195; rights of 28, 43, 123, 188, 196–198
Industrial World Cities 12
inequality 13, 26–27, 134, 153, 155; *see also* equity; gender
initiatives: global 14, 18; planning 19, 39, 68, 71, 74, 94, 122; policy 104
Integrated Development Plan (IDP) 43, 149
Intergovernmental Panel on Climate Change (IPCC) 27, 145–146
International Guidelines on Urban and Territorial Planning (IGUTP) 7, 85, 89, 127, 132, 139, 147, 201
International Monetary Fund (IMF) 34
internet 18, 52, 80, 85, 199, 202, 205
Ireland 9, 50, 76
Irish Free State 25
Istanbul Declaration and Habitat Agenda 22, 79, 80, 200

Jackson, Philip 188–189
Jamaica 26, 52, **59**, 73, 83, 90–92, 188
Johnson, Louise 42

Kamazani, Adalbertus 189
Kenya: delegates/representatives 61–62, 69, 97; food shortages 152; planning challenges 56, **59**; poverty 29–30, **32**, 57
Kigali Declaration 23, 32, 116, 121–122, 146, 155, 206, 208
King George V 25
King, Anthony D. 190
Kiribati 67, 83
Kirk, Ancil 112
Krishnarayan, Vijay 19–20, 138, 160, 164, 200
Krumholz, Norman 15
Kudu, Donald 68–69

labour market 129, 145, 208
Land Information Technology (LIT) 17, 69–71, 73
land tenure 42, 188, 195
land use: complex 149; map 147; planning 34, 38, 174, 182, 223; transport 58, 144, 182
Leaders of the Group of 7 (G7) 23, 35, 121–122, 137
Ligale, Andrew 53
Ling, Arthur 51, 53, 61–62

London 2, 17; heart of Commonwealth 25–27; meeting site 15, 25, 37, 50–51, 53, 64, 71, 80, 94, 96, 100, 107
low elevation coastal zones 146, 178–179

Mackinnon, Don 200
Malawi 50, 56
Malaysia: delegates/representatives 61, 69, 83; planning 56, **59**; rapid planning 118; urban growth 29, 39, 45, 190
Malaysia Institute of Planners (MIP) 105, 113
Malta 1, 18, 56, **59**, 111, 126
Mandela, Nelson 204
Māori people 195
maritime spatial planning 45
market: confidence 40; global 152; housing 207; labour 129, 145, 208; principles 75
Mauritius 56, **59**, 92, 191
Mead, Margaret 203
megacities 28–29
Mentek, Mohammad 7
migration 4, 29, 36, 43–44, 54, 92, 145, 147
Millennium Development Goals (MDGs) 14, 27, 35, 44, 96
minority 26–27, 220
Mohammed, Asad 112
Mohammed, Eleanor 23, 113–114, 120
Mohd Sharif, Maimunah 6–7, 8, 105, 120
Moore, Kelley 23, 120
Mpeta, Daniel 189
Mumbai 28–29, 31, 145

Narang, Shipra 84
natural disasters 4, 19, 131, 139–140, 181
Nauru 14, 67
Nel, Andries 130
Nelson, Brendan 106
neo-liberalism 12, 201–202, 207–208
New Institutionalism 199
New Urban Agenda (NUA) 5, 7–8, 14, 17, 35, development of 88–89, 104–105, 114, 127, 139; re-inventing planning 83, 85
New Zealand (NZ): delegates 61–62, 69; development 83, 90; partnerships 195–196; planning 22, 42, 51, 54, 56, **59**, 182; women in planning 93–94
New Zealand Planning Institute (NZPI) 18, 67, 90, 105, 112, 132
Newfoundland 25

Nigeria: delegates 59, 61, 94; reverse migration 145; Town Planners Registration Council 11, **59**, 93; urbanisation action plan 83, 90, 119; women in planning 126
Non-Government Organisations (NGOs) 26–27, 166, 198, 201
Norman, Barbara 20, 138
North America 14, 40, 64, 71
Nottingham 54

O'Donnell, Annette 78, 85, 100–101, 106, 202
OBE (Order of the British Empire) award 85–86, 102
Oborn, Peter 107
Operation Murambatsvina/ Restore Order 44
Outstanding Planning Practice 152, 197
Overseas Development Administration (ODA) 78, 80, 83, 85

Pacific Island Planning Association (PIPA) 68–69, 90
Pakistan: Lahore Master Plan 39; poverty 29, **32**; urban planning 63, 78, 118–119
Papua New Guinea 42–43, 67, 83
Paris Agreement 131
participation: active 181; civic 161, 165–166; planning 83; public 34, 56
physical planning 34, 37, 39, 53–54, 56–57
Physical Planning Act 42
place-making 45
Planners for Climate Action (P4CA) 19, 111, 116
planning: associations 7, 54, 58, 79, 83, 178, 182, 201; lack of training 70, 184; lack of understanding 57, 172; pro-poor 80, 82; role of 8, 21–23, 33, 35–36, 138, 172, 202; suburban 38; survey 37–38, 54–56, 60, 94, 97, 107; systems 13, 34, 43, 142–143, 149, 155, 195, 204; urban 63, 95, 99, 127, 139, 145, 177, 180, 182–183
planning education: effective 20; establishments 52, 58, **59–60**, 68; gaps 143, 148, 172; gender responsive 134; nature of 177, 184; provision 37, 40; survey of 97
Planning Institute of Australia (PIA) 15, 36, 90, 104, 124, 181; *see also* Royal Australian Planning Institute

Platt, Christine 19, 22, 82, 85–86, 91, 95, 101, 130, 137, 191, 201, 205
political: challenges 138, 175, 182, 208; climate 40; leaders 91, 146, 154; position 131
pollution: air 180, 182, 189; environmental 12–13, 32, 208
poverty: deep/deepening 92, 149, 197; global 13, 21–23; reduction 27, 35, 37, 44, 58; urban 36, 178
Preliminary Island Plan 58
Preston-Jones, Alice 107, 175
privatisation 34
professional: conduct 52; network 105; organisations 16, 28, 37, 51, 68; planners 11, 20, 33, 50, 53, 80, 97, 116, 122, 132, 148, 202
progress: report 71, 79, 121, 127; significant 32, 50, 64, 71, 94; social 200, 204
property rights 188
public health 45, 182, 191
public services 12, 145, 149, 155
Pun, Peter 16, 21, 61, 63–64, 69
Putrajaya, Malaysia 45
Pyati, V. 43

Queen Elizabeth 16–17, 26, 108
Queen Victoria 195

racism 27–28, 123; *see also* anti–racism; discrimination
Raffles, Thomas Stamford 188–189
rapid urbanisation: challenges 4, 10, 17, 89, 96, 119, 168, 177; climate change 104, 107, 119, 121; poverty 145–146; toolkit 18
Rapid Urbanisation Toolkit 22
Rathbone, Philip 53
Red Cross 181
Reeves, Dory 94, 128
regenerate 13
regeneration 40–42, 149
region: Commonwealth 92, 145, 147; far-flung 68; Pacific 90, 128, 178; rural 142, 152
regional: delegates 61, 63, 68; development 27, 33, 153; leadership 89; linkages 90; meetings 61–62, 205
remote sensing (RS) 70
Reynald, Joanna Arthurton 112
Rhodesia 50, 189–190
Robertson, Bill 22, 50, 69, 72, 78
Royal Australian Planning Institute (RAPI) 36, **59**, 70, 74, 81–83

Royal Institute of British Architects (RIBA) 159
Royal Town Planning Institute (RTPI) 11–12, 19, 37, **59–60**, 71–77, 105, 124, 132, 159
rules of the game 199
Rwanda 11, 107, 117
Rwanda Urban Planning Institute (RUPI) 120
Rwandan Ministry of Infrastructure 107, 119

sacred land 42, 188, 196
Sager, Tore 15
Salford Quays 41–42
Samoa 67, 83, 94
sanitation 12, 82, 129–130, 144
Sawyer, John Stanley 163
Scotland 40
Scotland, Patricia 2
segregation 43, 147, 189–190, 207
setbacks 32, 83
settlement: human (*see* human settlement); informal 29–30, 39, 54, 150–151, 178, 185
settlers 38, 43, 188, 195
Shishido, Ron 84
Sierra Leone 52, 54, 56, 110, 118, 170, 190
Sinclair, Ian 102
Singapore 25, 39; Concept Plan 46, 57–58; delegates/representatives 61–63, 69; planning 50, **60**, 188
Singapore Housing and Development Board 47
Slack, Lucy 107
slavery 27, 36
slums 29, 32, **32**, 44, 92, 129
small Commonwealth countries 10, 53
small island developing states (SIDS): small island states 26, 28, 68, 82–83, 90, 98, 145
smart city 151, 154
SNC Lavalin Group 10
social concerns 35
social justice 23, 33, 127, 166, 204
social progress 200, 204
Society for American Regional and Planning History 199
Solomon Islands 28, 67, 69
South Africa (SA) 23, 25; apartheid 43, 77; food shortages 94; Integrated Development Plans (IDPs) 43, 149; planning 43, 51, 77; poverty **32**; progress,

signs of 26; urban clusters 142, 147; women in planning 80, 126–128, 130, 132
South African Association of Chartered Town Planners 75
South African Cities Network 155
South African Council for Planners (SACPLAN) 11
South African Planning Institute (SAPI) 11, 82, 100–101
South East Asia 44, 52, 61, 63–64, 68
South West Pacific Region (SWPR) 67
spatial development framework 43
Sri Lanka: delegates/representatives 61, 94; natural disasters 179, 181; planning 60, 63, 68; urbanisation 192–193
Stevens, P.H.M. 190–191
Stockholm 32–33
Sustainable Development Goals (SDGs): 2030 Agenda 5, 13, 19, 116, 122, 131; adoption 88, 105; advancing 127, 131; challenges 105; collaboration 5, 13, 22–23, 36
sustainable human settlements 12, 22, 34–35, 79, 97, 125
sustainable urbanisation: accelerated delivery 147, 155, 187; cause of 9, 20, 121, 147, 202, 206–207; colonialism 188, 195; dynamic concept 13–14, 18, 45; future of 137; gender issues 126, 130; global partnerships 104; issues and challenges 2, 84, 138–139; Kigali Declaration 116; path to 25; planning 11–12, 139, 184; re-inventing planning 77, 147; youth involvement 168, 173
Swaziland 54, 57
Sydney, Australia 39, 70, 154

tactical urbanism 45, 155
Taiwan 63–64
Taiwo, Olafiyin 20, 111, 120, 138, 169, 175
Taylor, Paul 84
The Prince's Foundation 22–23, 184
Third World Cities 12
Todes, Alison 93, 129
Tonga 67, 83, 181
Town and Country Planning Act, 1932 190–191, 208
town planner 11–12, 51, 68
Town Planning Institute (TPI) 50, 60; *see also* Royal Town Planning Institute
trading advantage 191
trading post 188

traditional lands 194
transport: planning 34, 130; public 13, 44, 47, 129, 192, 206
Treaty of Waitangi 195
Trinidad and Tobago: delegates/representation 69, 94, 118; planning 78, 90–91; watershed study 164; workshop 71
Trinidad and Tobago Institute of Architects 159
Trinidad and Tobago Institute of Planners 81
Trinidad and Tobago Society of Planners (TTSP) 159
Trinidad and Tobago Town and Country Planning Ordinance 190
Tūpuna Maunga 196–197
Turley 9
Turner, John F.C. 66
Tuvalu 29, 67, 83

Uganda: planning 90, 190; poverty 32; women planners 80, 83
United Kingdom (UK) 25; delegates/representatives 61, 97; initiatives 116; planning authorities 57, 119, 182; Town Planning Institute (TPI) 50, 60
United Nations: Centre for Rural Development (UNCRD) 71; Climate Change Conference of the Parties (COP15, 21, 23, 26, 27) 19, 27, 107, 119, 146; Conference on Environment and Development 34; Declaration on the Rights of Indigenous Peoples (UNDRIP) 123, 144
United Nations (UN) 14
United Nations Commission on Human Settlements (UNCHS) 34, 75, 79
United Nations Habitat: Governing Council (GC) 89, 97; Habitat Professionals Forum (HPF) 116; headline issues 89; Human Settlements Programme 5, 7, 34, 85, 99; international guidelines 7, 36, 51, 85, 89, 201, 206; partnerships 19, 23, 98, 104
University of Hong Kong 63–64
urban: development 13–14, 35, 43, 56–57, 85, 100, 141, 144, 206; growth 10, 18, 29, 36, 97, 118, 129, 144–148, 178; planning 63–64, 95, 127, 129, 148, 177, 180, 182; transition 15, 29, 208
Urban Economy Forum (UEF) 117

urbanisation: informal 30, 39; planning and 27, 202, 206; rapid 9–10, 39, 106, 119, 121, 168, 170; *see also* sustainable urbanisation
US Department of Treasury *see* Washington Consensus

van den Berg, Max 199
Vancouver Declaration 33, 85
Vanuatu 67, 83
volunteer: effectiveness 203–204; limitations 138, 181; organizations 14, 23, 73, 77, 114, 187, 198
vulnerability 27, 130, 139, 145, 173–174, 197

Walters, Joseph 107
Washington Consensus 34
water: clean 12, 178, 181; fetching 139, 131; lack of/inadequate 82, 144; management 45, 89; resilience 119, 121; saltwater 146; WaterAid 121; waterfront 41
Watson, Vanessa 149, 197
Whitzman, Carolyn 93

Windrush scandal 28
Women in Planning Network *see* Commonwealth Women in Planning Network
Women's Design Service 126
World Bank 29, 34, 39, 66, 152
World Planning Congress 85, 139
World Population Review 29
World Urban Campaign (WUC) 19, 98, 105, 116–117, 121
World Urban Forum (WUF) 14, 19, 22, 83, 112, 116, 128–129, 139
Wright, Alex 107

Yeh, Anthony 69, 71
Yon, Alicia 81, 127–129
young: people 168, 170, 173–174; planners 17, 170, 172–174, 178; professionals 40, 173
Young Planners Network 10, 97, 111, 121, 133, 171, 178

Zambia 57, 61, 81, 118, 126, 128, 190
Zimbabwe 27, 44, 69

Ingram Content Group UK Ltd.
Milton Keynes UK
UKHW022006020723
424454UK00008B/39